SEMEIA 31

Reader Response Approaches to Biblical and Secular Texts

Editor of This Issue:
Robert Detweiler

© 1985

by the Society of Biblical Literature

SEMEIA 31

Copyright © 1985 by the Society of Biblical Literature

All rights reserved. No part of this work may be reproduced or transmitted in any form or by any means, electronic or mechanical, including photocopying and recording, or by means of any information storage or retrieval system, except as may be expressly permitted by the 1976 Copyright Act or in writing from the publisher. Requests for permission should be addressed in writing to the Rights and Permissions Office, Society of Biblical Literature, 825 Houston Mill Road, Atlanta, GA 30329, USA.

ISSN 0095-571X
ISBN 1-58983-181-0

Printed in the United States of America
on acid-free paper

CONTENTS

Contributors to This Issue iv

Preface 1

I. INTRODUCTION

Who Is "the Reader" in Reader Response Criticism?
   Robert M. Fowler 5

II. READING BIBLICAL TEXTS

The Bible as Literature: Reading Like the Rabbis
   Kenneth Dauber 27

The Joseph Story: A Narrative Which "Consumes" Its Content
   Hugh C. White 49

Double and Triple Stories, the Implied Reader,
     and Redundancy in Matthew
   Janice Capel Anderson 71

Prolegomenon to Reading Matthew's Eschatological Discourse:
     Redundancy and the Education of the Reader in Matthew
   Fred W. Burnett 91

History and Text: The Reader in Context
     in Matthew's Parables Discourse
   Gary A. Phillips 111

III. READING SECULAR TEXTS

Henry Vaughn: The Reader in Canticle-land
   Georgia B. Christopher 141

The Story of Reading and/in Pope's *Essay on Man* and the *Moral Essays*
   G. Douglas Atkins 155

"But the Draught of a Draught": Reading the Wonder of Ishmael's
     Telling
   David Scott Arnold 171

Brecht and the Bible: A Countersacramental Reading
   Petermichael von Bawey 195

IV. CONCLUSION

What Is a Sacred Text?
   Robert Detweiler 213

CONTRIBUTORS TO THIS ISSUE

Janice Capel Anderson
   517 East B Street
   Moscow, ID 83843

David Scott Arnold
   Department of Religion
   University of North Carolina
   Chapel Hill, NC 27514

G. Douglas Atkins
   Department of English
   University of Kansas
   Lawrence, KS 66045

Fred W. Burnett
   Department of Religious Studies
   Anderson College
   Anderson, IN 46011

Georgia B. Christopher
   Department of English
   Emory University
   Atlanta, GA 30322

Kenneth Dauber
   Department of English
   State University of New York
   Buffalo, NY 14260

Robert Detweiler
   Graduate Institute
    of the Liberal Arts
   Emory University
   Atlanta, GA 30322

Robert M. Fowler
   Department of Religion
   Baldwin-Wallace College
   Berea, OH 44017

Gary A. Phillips
   Department of Religious Studies
   College of the Holy Cross
   Worcester, MA 01610

Petermichael von Bawey
   American College in Paris
   17, Rue Larrey
   75005 Paris, France

Hugh C. White
   Department of Religion
   Rutgers University
   Camden, NJ 08102

PREFACE

Since reader response criticism began with, and has been mainly practiced by, scholars of non-biblical texts, I have designed this issue of *Semeia* to include attention to the secular backgrounds of this kind of criticism. A number of our essays employing variations on reader response criticism for the interpretation of biblical texts are balanced by a number of others that address, via similar approaches, "secular" texts, affording the opportunity for comparison. The issue begins and ends with more theoretical essays that show the place of reader response criticism in the larger hermeneutical enterprise. All of the essays together remind that reader response criticism is by no means a unified interpretive method but rather an aggregate of approaches that interact with each other.

Robert Detweiler

I
INTRODUCTION

WHO IS "THE READER" IN READER RESPONSE CRITICISM?

Robert M. Fowler
Baldwin-Wallace College

ABSTRACT

In spite of the fact that reader response critics talk a great deal about "the reader," there remains a great deal of equivocation as to who "the reader" of reader response criticism is. The goal of this paper is to clarify some of these latent equivocations. The first section of the paper discusses the distinction between the "reader," who "serves" the text, and the "critic," who acts as its "judge and master." The second section discusses the real reader, the implied reader, and the narratee, along with their authorial counterparts: the real author, the implied author, and the narrator. The third section discusses the rhetorical stance of the "ideal reader" that a critic must invariably adopt when addressing the guild. And the fourth section discusses one of the most important contributions reader response criticism is making to literary criticism, the rediscovery that reading is a rich and dynamic temporal experience and not the perception of a static spatial form.

The Reader and the Critic

To begin, we need first to make a major distinction between the reader and the critic. Often a literary critic (or a biblical critic) will talk about being a reader of a text as if he or she were a reader only. But he or she is clearly more than that, for being a critic means being part of a guild, or an "interpretive community," as Stanley Fish (1980) likes to say. Such a guild has a history, it has a language, and it has rules and rituals for entrance into its ranks, and for subsequent advancement, demotion, or excommunication. In speaking as a critic one speaks to be heard chiefly by fellow critics, and thus the entire critical tradition of that particular interpretive community is evoked implicitly. To be sure, reader response criticism generally tends, more than other brands of literary criticism, to grant value to *all* reading, whether expert or naive. But it is still reader response *criticism*, and that is where equivocation begins to creep in. Reader response critics do tend to value all reading, but insofar as they are critics working within the guild, the implicit critical presuppositions of the guild guide their work. They are not just readers; they are expert, critical readers. But the difference between being a critical reader and being simply a reader needs to be spelled out carefully.

One attempt to do just this is an article by George Steiner, entitled "'Critic'/'Reader.'" This is a rich and subtle essay, the intention of which is to pose a fictional, heuristic antithesis of "critic" versus "reader." He is careful to note at the beginning and end of his essay that this polarity is indeed fictional; "in the ordinary run of things, 'criticism' and 'reading' interpenetrate and overlap" (451). Yet, to understand the overlap we need to understand the nature of the opposing poles, even if they never exist in a pure state.

Because Steiner repeats and develops his critic/reader antithesis in almost the fashion of a fugue, it is difficult to summarize adequately the variety of insights found in his essay. Nevertheless, the foundational motif of his fugue seems to be that "the critic is judge and master of the text," while "the reader is servant to the text" (449). More specifically, we can observe two ways in which the "judge and master" of the text contrasts with the "servant" of the text. The first of these is the observation that the critic steps back from the text to strike a magisterial pose of critical, objectifying distance, while the reader tries to eliminate the distance between himself and the text. Since the critic stands over against the text, criticism is by nature "adversative," "competitive," even "parasitic," in its relationship with the text (433, 436, 437, 441). The reader, on the other hand, does not reify the text as an object, but finds in it a "real presence" and often a locus of "inspiration" or "revelation." In "dynamic passivity," a reader is read *by* the text (438–39); distance collapses as the reader seeks "to enter into the text and to be entered into by the text" (443).

A second way of formulating the antithesis is to say that a critic makes judgments about the text and declares them, while a reader does neither. Since it does not objectify the text, reading does not lend itself to discourse about itself. As Steiner says: "It is easy to say something about criticism worth looking at and/or disagreeing with. It is difficult to say anything useful about 'reading' in the sense in which this paper seeks to articulate the term. Criticism is discursive and breeds discourse. 'Reading' yields no primary impulse towards self-communication. The 'reader' who discourses is, in a certain manner, in breach of privilege. . . . Reading is done rather than spoken about . . ." (439). Criticism is the product of rational choice, and "the critic must declare; this is his public and legislative ordination." On the other hand, "the reader will often hold his illumination mute" (448). After all, to the reader the text is "'a real presence' irreducible to analytic summation and resistant to judgment in the sense in which the critic can and must judge" (440).

The legislative duty of criticism has as a central task the evaluation and ranking of texts; part of the critic's job is to tell us what we should and should not be reading. Steiner calls the set of texts prescribed by the critic the critic's "syllabus." The reader, too, has his selection of favored texts, which Steiner chooses to call the reader's "canon." The crucial difference is that the critic chooses his "syllabus" by an act of will, but the "canon" chooses the reader; a canon is unsought and unwilled. "Canon," in Steiner's usage, refers to those texts and text fragments that capture our imaginations without our seeking it and often without our being fully aware of it. "The canonic text enters into the reader, it takes its place within him by a process of penetration, of luminous insinuation whose occasion may have been entirely mundane and accidental—decisive encounters so often are—but not, or not primarily, willed" (446). "The occurrence is banal to anyone whose mind and body—both are involved—have been seized upon by a melody, by a tune, by a verbal cadence which he did not choose by act of will, which has entered into him unawares" (446). "The critic prescribes a syllabus; the reader is answerable to and internalizes a canon" (445). "A syllabus is taught; a canon is lived" (447).

A large part of the equivocation in reader response criticism regarding "the reader" can be explained by reference to Steiner's critic/reader antithesis. It is helpful to recognize that reader response critics can be positioned somewhere along a continuum running from the pure (but probably non-existent) "critic" to the pure (but probably non-existent) "reader" (cf. Mailloux, 1982:22).

Toward one end of the spectrum we have some reader response critics very much upholding the literary critical tradition, although in a roundabout way, since they are trying to shift the critical focus to something largely ignored by recent generations of critics: the reader and the reading experience. Their affirmation of the critical tradition is particularly noticeable when one common strategy is adopted. Often a reader response critic will attempt to elucidate the history of the criticism of a particular text by trying to find what has happened in the reading experience that has given rise to convergent or (more often) divergent critical assessments of the text. In other words, he or she will presume to use the text to explain the history of its reading. The goal here is to explicate, as much as possible, not the text per se, but all previous readings of the text, thereby comprehending, encompassing, and rising above a host of critical colleagues. As a critical strategy this is a powerful move, because it puts the reader response critic in a position of not only standing over against the text, but also standing over against one's critical peers, in a most decisive manner.

We could call the critic pole of the critic/reader continuum the "objectifying" pole. What is objectified by the reader-oriented critic, however, is not the traditional text object, but the experience of reading within a tradition of criticism. This could also be called the "sociological" or "ideological" pole, for we objectify our reading experience according to the critical presuppositions (or ideology) we share with our fellows in the guild.

The reader pole, on the other hand, is the pole of "subjectifying": this is the pole of the "individual" and the "psychological." A reader response critic positioned here will be less concerned to contribute to a critical tradition, and more concerned to contribute to a person (*not* a "critic") finding him/herself to be the subject of his or her reading experience. We frequently find here an unashamed acceptance of the non-expert reader, and a challenge to the implicit authoritarianism of the critical community. Such "subjective" or "psychological" critics as David Bleich (1975; 1978) and Norman Holland (1975; 1982), for example, eagerly welcome their students as fellow readers with full reading privileges, a democratization of the classroom that their colleagues in the guild may look upon as foolish or even heretical. Most empirical study of reading (the psychology of perception, developmental psychology, etc.) also tends to slide to this end of the continuum (see Mailloux, 1982:206).

Thus does Steiner give us one valuable measuring stick for sizing up "the reader." Applying this measuring stick, when reader response critics talk about "the reader," some are thinking primarily of Steiner's "critic," others are thinking primarily of Steiner's "reader," while most are probably somewhere in between. For me, and for most biblical scholars, I imagine, Steiner's antithesis is all too familiar. For us, Steiner's essay may even represent a pointed statement of knowledge we would just as soon repress, for most of us were readers of the Bible before we were critics of it, and we now struggle, in most cases, to reconcile the rational insights of criticism with the ecstasy of reading. Moreover, it would not be difficult to re-write Steiner's essay using the Bible as the paradigm in Western culture of a text that receives both the devotion of readers and the scrutiny of critics. And our experience with the Bible confirms Steiner's claim that reading is logically prior to criticism. Whether seen historically or ontogenetically, reading the Bible (or being read by it) precedes biblical criticism; the Bible was and is canon, in Steiner's sense of the word, long before critics placed it on their syllabus.

With a passion that I would suppose is missing in most other kinds of literature courses, a battle between critic and reader is fought in almost every college classroom where the Bible is read critically. In the first class meeting of an introductory course, the English professor is unlikely to be presented with a hard-core element of Shakespeare devotees, in the manner in which his biblical scholar colleague is likely to be faced with at least a few students who can cite chapter and verse of holy scripture. It is at once exhilarating and painful to have to fight such battles, but it confirms for me that at least the literature I study as a critic continues to matter to readers. If it should not matter to readers, why should it matter at all to critics?

I shall quickly abandon my battle imagery above, if it leads us to think that one side is destined to victory and the other to defeat. The struggle is indeed passionate and painful, but in those circumstances where one side seems for the moment actually to vanquish the other, the results are tragic. It sounds trite, but I find that a balance of readerly passion and critical distance is desirable. An imbalance on either side is unhealthy, and can be pathological. Steiner ably rebukes a current "hypertrophy" (437) of criticism, and biblical critics would do well to take his remarks to heart. But biblical critics also have a story to tell, and our story includes many incidents of biblical criticism opposed and hounded mercilessly by zealous readers. I would not tar all readers of the Bible with the same brush, but the fact remains that just as there can be a pathology, a hypertrophy, of criticism, there can be a pathology, a blind zeal, of reading. But inasmuch as most of us escape pathology, most of us live in the middle somewhere. Indeed, most biblical scholars of my acquaintance have experienced an oscillation between Steiner's two poles; most of us have moved from being readers to being critics, and then, for the lucky ones, back to a post-critical readership (Ricoeur: 351).

The personal pilgrimages of numerous biblical scholars would, I think, largely confirm Steiner's observations about critics and readers, but we would have some insights to add to his. Many of us found *in criticism* our "revelation" or our "ecstasy," because for the first time, with the obtaining of critical distance, we could *see* the features of the text that had hitherto read us, and we were enchanted and liberated by what we saw. Without criticism, we saw in retrospect, it had been impossible to see and to know the text that had read us, not even to know if it was the text we thought it was. He or she who "serves the text" with utter devotion cannot objectify and thereby know what text is in fact being served. In the case of the Bible, many are read by and serve 'versions' of the Bible that a critic in good conscience can only label per-versions. But only with critical distance can one see perversions; perversion is a concept of criticism. To add to Steiner's antithetical comparisons, the reader says of the text "It thou shalt not judge"; the critic says of the text "If it is so worthy of respect, it will emerge from judgment triumphant and with added glory." To the critic, the reader appears to serve texts he does not know and cannot understand. To the reader, the critic appears to master and judge even those texts to which he is inferior. Must there not be a middle ground?

I see myself striving to be both a reader and a critic of the Bible: a *critical reader*, if you will. And unless I specify otherwise, the "reader" who will be mentioned frequently hereafter will be just such a critical reader. To be a critical reader means for me: (1) to affirm the enduring power of the Bible in my culture and in my own life; (2) and yet to remain open enough to ask any question and to risk any judgment, even if it should mean repudiating (1). Nothing less than both of these points, together, will do for me. Even more specifically, however, I am pleased to confess that: I was a "reader" of the Bible before I was a "critic" of it; I found becoming a critic to be liberating and satisfying, and therefore I judge criticism to be of inestimable value and a high calling; but I also recognize the prior claim of the text and the preeminence of reading over criticism, and so, accordingly, I seek and occasionally am apprehended by moments in which the text wields its indubitable power. The critic's ego says this just could be the cherished "post-critical naivete"; the reader's proper humility before the text says it is not for a reader to judge such things.

The Real Reader, The Implied Reader, and The Narratee

Keeping in mind that our initial question was "Who is 'the reader'. . . ?," at this point we split our question into the following questions: (1) Who is "the reader?" (2) How does "the reader" relate to "the author" by means of the text? And, (3) Just who is "the author?" The terminology I have adopted in addressing these questions is borrowed from Seymour Chatman's *Story and Discourse* (146–151; cf. Wayne Booth, 1983; Prince, 1973; 1982; Rabinowitz). Chatman distinguishes between real author, implied author, narrator, narratee, implied reader, and real reader. One needs such distinctions in order to explore with care "the interrelation of the several parties to the narrative transaction" (Chatman: 147).

The *real author* and *real reader* are easy enough to grasp. They are the living, flesh-and-blood persons who actually produce the text and read it./1/ But in the act of reading we encounter, not a flesh-and-blood author, but the author's second self adopted for purposes of telling this tale, and similarly we as readers are not wholly ourselves as we read, but the reader the text invites us to be. The terms *implied author* and *implied reader*, therefore, have gained wide currency in recognition of the fact that a text implies a role or a persona for both the author and reader./2/ As Wayne Booth says, "the author creates, in short, an image of himself and another image of his reader; he makes his reader, as he makes his second self, and the most successful reading is one in which the created selves, author and reader, can find complete agreement" (1983:138). Finally, *narrator* and *narratee* are terms referring to the persons who are supposedly telling and listening to the story./3/ Every story may be supposed to have a storyteller and a listener, but as it happens some stories have only oblique, covert evidence of either a narrator or a narratee, while others may go so far as to have a narrator or a narratee overtly portrayed as a character in the narrative (as in *Thousand and One Nights*, where Scheherazade is the narrator and the sultan the narratee). Narrator and narratee are especially useful terms when it is clear that the implied author has distanced himself from his unreliable narrator or that the implied reader is expected to distance himself from a gullible narratee.

A number of critics, as I have noted, have proposed their own versions of these basic concepts. Their refinements often complicate matters, however, by drawing in some of the considerations about "the reader" that are better considered separately./4/ The terminology offered above is minimal and serviceable, without unnecessarily mixing in important but tangential reading concerns. It makes possible the careful consideration of a number of interesting phenomena in the narrative transaction, in spite of bearing within it the inevitable ambiguities and gaps of any critical vocabulary. I would like to address myself now both to the usefulness of this terminology and to its problems.

The critic/reader distinction introduced earlier, although not explicitly represented in this terminology, is implicitly present. It may be present, for example, in the way Chatman diagrams the functions of his various critical entities (151, 267). On a horizontal line, he positions from left to right: real author, implied author, narrator, narratee, implied reader, and real reader (151). Arrows pointing toward the right tie together each successive pair of entities. The middle four terms are within a box labelled "narrative text," and within the box the arrows linking successive pairs are solid. In the heart of the box, narrator and narratee are in parentheses, to signify that they are optional features of a narrative (but the arrow connecting them is still solid). Lying outside the box of the narrative, however, are the real author and the real reader, and the arrows going from the real author to the box and from the box to the real reader are made of broken lines. Exile from the box, plus the broken arrows, together suggest that real authors and real readers have a tenuous relationship to the reading of a text. This is implied also in Chatman's explanation of his diagram: "The box indicates that only the implied author and implied reader are immanent to a narrative, the narrator and narratee are optional (parentheses). The real author and real reader are outside the narrative as such, though, of course, indispensable to it in an ultimate practical sense" (151).

This is the language of a critic of literature—or better, a theorist of criticism—and not that of a reader. Indeed, real authors and real readers are outside the box of the critical concern, which is the realm of the critical apprehension of the literary text. Real authors, I suppose, are left to literary historians, while real readers are left to psychologists.

Bringing Steiner's language together with Chatman's, we would have to say that the "critic" will tend to focus on the text and on the critical entities immanent to it, while the "reader" will tend to take the reading experience to be an encounter with the discourse of a real author directed to him/herself as a real reader. That is, a critic will tend to live within Chatman's box, while a reader will not even recognize the existence of the box, thereby collapsing all of these careful critical distinctions into simply the author and the reader. Thus, Chatman's box does not divide neatly the realm of Steiner's "critic" from the realm of Steiner's "reader"; Steiner's language is not congruent with Chatman's language. However, if we may suppose for the moment that Chatman's "real reader" is in fact very close to being Steiner's "reader," then we may find in Chatman's language an insight that supplements the insights offered to us by Steiner. This is the recognition of just how much real authors and real readers have in common. Real authors often profess to write for real readers, and specifically disavow writing for critics. Similarly, the real reader believes in real authors; he *knows* he is encountering the real presence of a real author (and not just an implied one) when reading a narrative, while the critic knows no such thing. Thus Chatman's terminology helps to reveal an ally for Steiner's reader in the person of the real author (they are both willing exiles from the realm of criticism), while the terms inside his box specify helpfully some prominent concerns of the critical realm.

Working within Chatman's box for the moment, we can look at some of the concrete ways this terminology facilitates the critical discussion of reading. By distinguishing between the narratee and implied reader, for one thing, we indicate that there are often two major role models provided in the text for anyone reading it. The implied reader is the reader we must be willing to become, at least momentarily, in order to experience the narrative in the fullest measure (see Booth, 1983:79–81, 138–39, and passim; 1979:242 and passim; and Suleiman). The implied reader may relate to the narratee, in turn, in any number of ways, ranging from a close and intimate association to an ironic distancing, if the narratee appears to the implied reader to be gullible or otherwise deficient. In other words, a second benefit of Chatman's terminology is that it provides the vocabulary necessary to explore the myriad variations of distance that can exist between implied reader and narratee, between implied author and narrator, and, moreover, between any of these four entities and the characters in the story. Actually, the possibilities are reduced considerably by the fact that the implied author and implied reader, and, too, the narrator and narratee, are so closely linked. One might say that these pairs even represent mirror images. For example, the cluster of values and judgments that is the implied author is manifested in the implicit rendering of the text's reader—and vice versa. Similarly, the diction of the narrator is reflected like a sonar wave off of the outline of the posited narratee and returns to the sender to be emited again—each reflects the presence of the other (see Prince, 1982:7-25). This, then, is a third benefit of our adopted vocabulary: it recognizes and provides a rudimentary way to talk about the dialogical process that is built into the text and demanded by the reading experience.

Granted the usefulness of Chatman's terminology, he glosses over one problem spot that requires attention: the nature of the implied reader (and *mutatis mutandis* the implied author). He places both of these entities within the box labelled "narrative text," claiming them to be "immanent" to the text. A clean break is therefore made between the reader in the text and the reader outside of the text, a division that is problematic, to say the least. In fact, one of the recurring debates among reader-oriented critics concerns the relationship between the text and the reader. Stated in its most extreme form, the question here is: *does the text control the reader or does the reader control the text*? For example, Wayne Booth and Wolfgang Iser both talk about someone very much like Chatman's implied reader, but it is clear they mean something rather different when they talk about this entity. Booth's version of the implied reader, although it invites and requires the cohesion of a real reader, is ultimately *in* the text, and is the creation of an author (see Booth, 1983:138, 422-23). Iser's (1974) implied reader, however, is constructed by a real reader out of the material provided by the text, particularly its spots of "indeterminacy": "blanks," "gaps," etc. (Iser, 1978). Iser is careful to say that his implied reader is neither in the text, nor outside it, but is the unique product of the "interaction" of a text and a reader.

There are other points of view on the text vs. reader debate. Curiously outdoing even Wayne Booth in respect for the rhetorical power of the text, and outdoing even Wolfgang Iser in respect for the independence and creative activity of the reader, are the 'early' and 'later' positions of Stanley Fish. In his early reader-oriented criticism, typified by *Self-Consuming Artifacts* (see also Fish, 1970 = Fish, 1972:383-427 = Fish, 1980:21-67), Fish engages in brilliant word by word analyses of the way texts manipulate the developing response of the reader; no one could make a stronger case for thoroughgoing textual control over the reading experience. Fish even goes so far as to argue that all readers are textually directed in just the way he is describing. They just have not realized it because they have not paid attention to the ways texts have controlled them. In more recent work (1980), Fish still affirms the immense value of this kind of analysis in practical criticism; however, he admits now that it is not the only way to conceptualize reading. In fact, he has now swung over to the position that the text cannot really control reading in any objective sense, for the text is invented in the process of being read—the text and all its features are only defined and therefore brought into existence by the reader's interpretive strategies. So, having said earlier, essentially, that the text controls the reader, Fish now says that it is the reader who objectifies the text and its characteristics in the first place, and thus controls it. From this latter position, Fish's earlier position may be explained as a convenient and powerful critical fiction, adopted by the critic because of its potential for persuading a critical audience that already grants to texts an 'objectivity' and an 'authority' to control the reader. But now he wants to make clear that objectivity and authority are always, first, the reader's to grant.

Does this new position of Fish's now grant too much authority to the reader? In response to this question, Fish slides into the next station of his critical pilgrimage. The reader is not 'too powerful,' he says, and the critical enterprise is not doomed to subjectivism or solipsism, because the reader and his reading experience are defined and controlled by the critical community of which he is a part. The critical presuppositions employed by the reader to objectify and analyze the text are derived from the "interpretive community" in which the reading takes place. Readers may control texts, but that does not lead to anarchy, because interpretive communities control readers.

Fish has therefore bracketed Booth and Iser in his critical career, attributing at one point more control to the text than Booth, and then more control to the reader than Iser, and then locating the source of *all* control in the preexistent presuppositions of one's interpretive community. If Fish did not do what he does so brilliantly, one could dismiss him for a damnable protean slipperiness. But in sliding from one critical extreme to the next, he has helpfully highlighted, if idiosyncratically, what must be simultaneous foci for reader-oriented criticism. The issue is not about a two-sided relationship between text and reader, nor about the overarching preeminence of interpretive communities, but a matter of *text* and *reader* meeting *in the context of the critical community.* Granted that: (1) the community defines what the text is and tells the reader how to go about reading; at the same time, (2) the text (as defined by the community) molds its reader and constrains the critical gaze of the community; and at the same time, (3) the reader (as instructed by the community) construes the text and contributes to the evolution of the critical community. That is, granted the undeniable importance of the interpretive community, within that social setting the text will always have an objectivity and the reader a subjectivity that are also undeniable. Moreover, it is always possible that the objectified text will wield such power, or the subjectified reader exert such genius, that the interpretive community will be re-made after their images.

All of this is to say that the implied reader is the locus of a great deal of equivocation in current criticism, but only because reading itself is a mysterious merger of text, reader, and context. Yet for all its ambiguity, the term implied reader is still useful. When I use it, I shall use it to refer primarily to the reader implied *in the text*, but I shall take care to observe that different *critical readers* will grasp that reader in the text differently, due largely to differences in *the contexts of reading*, which are constrained by the critical presuppositions prevailing at the time and place of reading. With judicious use, the rest of Chatman's terminology is also helpful.

The Ideal Reader

Besides the terminology discussed in the previous section, there is another common family of terms clustering about the notion of the "ideal reader." One hears, not only of the ideal reader, but also of the informed reader, the optimal reader, the superreader, the competent reader, the educated reader, and so on. What critics are grasping for amidst this assortment is an idealized reader intimately related to the implied reader, as I shall indicate below. But "ideal reader" adds greater intensity to "implied reader"; it reveals the critical impulse, not just to apprehend the reader implied in the text, but to apprehend the readers implied in many texts, so as to encompass and supersede them all.

A succinct description of the ideal reader is offered by Jonathan Culler: "The question is not what actual readers happen to do but what an ideal reader must know implicitly in order to read and interpret works in ways which we consider acceptable" (123–24). The ideal reader possesses not only "linguistic competence" but also "literary competence": an intimate acquaintance with Steiner's "syllabus" and a full grasp of the accepted critical means of working on it. The ideal reader is Steiner's "critic," par excellence. This is very close to Stanley Fish's version of the ideal reader, whom he prefers to label the "informed reader":

> Who is *the* reader? Obviously, my reader is a construct, an ideal or idealized reader, somewhat like Wardhaugh's "mature reader" or Milton's "fit" reader, or to use a term of my own, *the* reader is the *informed* reader. The informed reader is someone who (1) is a competent speaker of the language out of which the text is built up; (2) is in full possession of "the semantic knowledge that a mature . . . listener brings to his task of comprehension," including the knowledge (that is, the experience, both as a producer and comprehender) of lexical sets, collocation probabilities, idioms, professional and other dialects, and so on; and (3) has *literary* competence. That is, he is sufficiently experienced as a

reader to have internalized the properties of literary discourses, including everything from the most local of devices (figures of speech, and so on) to whole genres. . . .

The reader of whose responses I speak, then, is this informed reader, neither an abstraction nor an actual living reader, but a hybrid—a real reader (me) who does everything within his power to make himself informed. (1980:48–49)

Wolfgang Iser discusses several versions of the "ideal reader," and expresses dissatisfaction with all of them, finding them all too nebulous and lacking in theoretical rigor (1978:27–38). In their place he offers his version of the implied reader, "a textual structure anticipating the presence of a recipient without necessarily defining him" (1978:34). Iser has perhaps sensed correctly that the implied reader is at the core of all the talk about idealized readers, but he loses the use of a significant heuristic device by limiting himself to the reader implied by any one text, which is what his implied reader is.

Steven Mailloux, for example, has seen that the ideal reader is in a sense the implied reader writ large:

The "ideal reader" is merely an abstracted version of the "implied reader." He is not a reader of a specific text but one implied by all literary texts; or put another way, he is a hypothetical reader with the general ability to comprehend literature. . . . We have, then, a specific text's *implied reader*, which is really only a textual interpretation (or part of one) using a reader vocabulary. And we have an *ideal reader* who is also an interpretive construct, one that is abstracted from many specific instances of textual interpretation, one that defines the conditions of literary response. (1982:203)

Mailloux's point is well taken, but it needs to be pushed further. The ideal reader is not simply a hypothetical enhancement of the implied reader. The "ideal reader" is a fictive role created and assumed by a critic as he or she presumes to address the critical community. It is, in other words, a pose adopted *by the critic* for rhetorical purposes. The fiction being acted out in the work of criticism is precisely the critical pretension to supersedure: to supersede the text, one's critical community and its history of reading, and even one's own self. One may not actually be the critic par excellence, but when playing the game of criticism you cannot pretend to be anything less and still hope to win over your critical audience.

This is hardly a revelation; numerous critics have admitted all of this candidly. But we can push still further to observe that the role of the ideal reader can be played in two major ways. First, there is the role of the individual ideal reader per se. This is where I adopt the stance—implicitly, perhaps, or explicitly, if I have nerve—of the supremely informed and skilled individual reader-critic, possessing impeccable linguistic and literary competence. We might call this the Ideal Reader I. It is also possible, and very common, to construct a kind of composite ideal reader out of the accumulated critical experience of one's critical community. In practice, this second, composite form of the ideal reader—Ideal Reader II, let us say—often goes hand in hand with the first. Rhetorically, they can uphold each other—I establish my credentials as a critic by demonstrating my personal knowledge of the syllabus and mastery of the critical tools, which is at the same time a celebration of the history and current vitality of the entire guild. The Ideal Reader I and the Ideal Reader II represent the opposing poles of another of those continua ranging from the individual to the social, but in this case the continuum is narrow in its range, since we are dealing with a dialectical relationship between subjective and objective poles within a very specialized social group: critics in particular literary critical tradition.

Stephen Booth, in the preface to one of the most highly regarded pieces of practical criticism done by reader-oriented critics, lays bare, in just a few lines, his use of both versions of the ideal reader: ". . . the responses I attribute to my hypothetical reader of the sonnets cannot ultimately be more universal or other than my own. I have attempted to demonstrate that the responses I describe are probable in a reader accustomed to Elizabethan idiom. I have also quoted at length from the responses of the critics and editors who have preceded me in the study of the sonnets; their comments, glosses, and emendations provide the best available evidence that the responses I describe are not idiosyncratic" (Stephen Booth: x).

The most pyrotechnic use of the Ideal Reader, I and II, however, surely must be found in the practical criticism of Stanley Fish. We have already seen Fish's definition of the informed reader. Tucked into that definition is an admission that the informed reader is really Stanley Fish: it is "a real reader (me) who does everything within his power to make himself informed." After putting himself in the picture modestly, at first only within parentheses, Fish proceeds to say that of course he can claim to be an informed reader, and, moreover, so can anyone else in the guild: "Each of us, if we are sufficiently responsible and self-conscious, can, in the course of employing [Fish's critical] method, become the informed reader and therefore be a more reliable reporter of his [reading] experience" (1980:49). It is, in other words, a rhetorical stance generally available to members in good standing of the critical guild. And in Fish's criticism (*Self-Consuming Artifacts*, for example), he makes use of this rhetorical stance masterfully.

Perhaps even more impressive is Fish's powerful use of the Ideal Reader II, the composite ideal reader. A frequent strategy in Fish's criticism is to examine an interpretive crux that has produced a diversity of critical assessments, and then to seek a supposed common reading experience that lies at the base of the disagreement. Fish asks, What reading experience have critics shared unconsciously that allows them to agree enough to disagree about this passage? He surveys "the critical history of a work in order to find disputes that rested upon a base of agreement of which the disputants were unaware" (1980:147). Fish elaborates thus:

> Typically, I will pay less attention to the interpretations critics propose than to the problems or controversies that provoke them, on the reasoning that while the interpretations vary, the problems and controversies do not and therefore point to something that all readers share. If, for example, there is a continuing debate over whether Marlow should or should not have lied at the end of *Heart of Darkness*, I will interpret the debate as evidence of the difficulty readers experience when the novel asks them to render judgment. And similarly, if there is an argument over who is the hero of *Paradise Lost*, I will take the argument as an indication that, in the course of reading the poem, the identity of its hero is continually put into question. There will always be two levels, a surface level on which there seem to be nothing but disagreements, and a deeper level on which those same disagreements are seen as constituting the shared content whose existence they had seemed to deny. In short, critical controversies become disguised reports of what readers uniformly do, and I perform the service of revealing to the participants what it is they were really telling us. (1980:177–78)

Rather than trying to reconcile differences and thus form his composite ideal reader at the "surface level," he forms his composite ideal reader from a base of unconscious agreement at a "deeper level." Wherever possible, Fish grounds the critical community on a hitherto unacknowledged but commonly shared foundation, thereby encompassing and surpassing the history of criticism. By descending to the "deeper level," he is able to transcend the critical disagreement altogether—"I perform the service of revealing to the participants what it is they were really telling us." This is skillful, rhetorical use of the metaphor of "levels." By supposedly descending to the "deeper level," he is actually putting himself in a position elevated above the debate. His skillful construction of an abstracted, composite, ideal reader is an indirect way of establishing his own credentials as, in his words, an informed reader. The thing that distinguishes Fish is that he uses the rhetorical strategy of the "ideal reader" so openly and so boldly.

Reading as a Temporal Experience

Were we to stop at this point, we would be left with still rather static abstractions of who "the reader" is. What we are missing is a model of the reading experience itself. At this point reader response critics are making a significant contribution to criticism by recalling to the critical consciousness the richness and dynamism of the temporal experience of reading.

One distinguishing characteristic of reader response criticism is the emphasis placed on the fact that a reading experience takes place through time; it is fundamentally a temporal experience. This is a radical shift in perspective, because we have not been taught to monitor our reading experience as it occurs. Rather, we have been taught to read to the end of a text and then step back and comment on the final outcome of the reading. We view the whole of the text from the perspective of the end of the reading experience. The path we have had to follow to get to the end of reading is regarded merely as prelude to the end product. Only at the conclusion of reading do we dare ask ourselves: "What is *the* meaning of the story? What is *the* point of the story? What content did I get out of it?"

Most reader response critics resolutely resist the inclination to concentrate on the end product of reading, what we have tended to call the point, the meaning, or the content of the story. The entire reading experience is to be valued—not just the end product of reading. Reading a text is a rich and dynamic experience; but focusing on the end product of reading lends itself to perceiving a text as a static, spatial form, like a painting or sculpture or piece of architecture. Also, the sheer physicality of writing has tricked us into thinking of texts as objects existing in space rather than as experiences existing in time. As Stanley Fish puts it: "Literature is a kinetic art, but the physical form it assumes prevents us from seeing its essential nature, even though we so experience it. The availability of a book to the hand, its presence on a shelf, its listing in a library catalogue—all of these encourage us to think of it as a stationary object. Somehow when we put a book down, we forget that while we were reading, *it* was moving (pages turning, lines receding into the past) and forget too that *we* were moving with it" (1980:43).

Fish also provides one of the clearest statements of the critical attitude needed in order to attend to the entire reading experience:

> The concept is simply the rigorous and disinterested asking of the question, what does this word, phrase, sentence, paragraph, chapter, novel, play, poem, *do*? And the execution involves an analysis of the developing responses of the reader in relation to the words as they succeed one another in time. . . .
>
> The basis of the method is a consideration of the *temporal* flow of the reading experience, and it is assumed that the reader responds in terms of that flow and not to the whole utterance. That is, in an utterance of any length, there is a point at which the reader has taken in only the first word, and then the second,

and then the third, and so on, and the report of what happens to the reader is always a report of what has happened *to that point*.... (1980:26, 27)

Wolfgang Iser has described helpfully not just the linear, temporal encounter with the words one is reading, but the psychological phenomena of anticipation and retrospection that are also involved. While we read, we are actively involved in reviewing what has preceded and speculating about what lies ahead. Iser goes so far as to liken the reading experience to a recreation of the author's original act of creating the text. Iser says: "We look forward, we look back, we decide, we change our decisions, we form expectations, we are shocked by their nonfulfillment, we question, we muse, we accept, we reject; this is the dynamic process of recreation" (1972:293).

This represents a dramatic shift in literary criticism away from the formalism of the New Critics, which objectifies the text and devalues the reading experience. Walter Ong helps us to put this recent development into the broadest historical perspective. Ong, in numerous discussions of the shift from orality to the technology of writing, has described with great insight how the physicality of writing, and especially print, lends itself to be taken as static spatial form (1982:135–38). Indeed, once the strict uniformity of printed language becomes deeply interiorized in the consciousness of the reader, it is well-nigh impossible to avoid the metaphor of language as a container or conduit, existing in space, which holds meaning within. According to this metaphor, the job of the reader or critic is to tap and drain off the contents—the meaning—of the container. Moreover, the metaphor promotes the idea that the container or text is a single entity, and that the contents or meaning is a single entity, and that therefore, in theory, we should all agree on what the meaning of the text is. This metaphor has a hard time accommodating the experience we have all had of disagreeing sharply over what a text says. Of course, a severe shortcoming of the metaphor is that it minimizes the active role of the reader in determining what the text is and what its meaning is. In short, it obscures the dialogical nature of true communication, which is inescapable even when the communication is taking place by means of a written text and therefore seems to be completely one-sided.

Reader response critics are rejecting the container metaphor altogether. The implications of this move are quite profound, yet we have scarcely begun to explore them. In arguing for a temporal model of reading, rather than a spatial one, we are actually returning to an understanding of language that has affinities with the language of oral culture. The written word is spatial; it constitutes a literate/visual mode of consciousness. The spoken word, however, is temporal; it constitutes an oral/aural mode of consciousness. Since the world of orality lingers and is still so prominent in the biblical texts (see Kelber), the temporal model of reading employed by reader response critics is well-suited to the study of biblical narrative.

Therefore, who is "the reader" of reader response criticism? It is I, as critical reader. And it is I, as a supposed ideal reader, although I shall strike that pose by formulating and putting forth a composite ideal reader created out of the best that has been thought and said by my critical community. But that ideal reader, individual or composite, can only be an abstraction from the countless readers implied by countless texts. And each manifestation of "the reader"—critical, ideal, implied—is to be conceptualized as reading through time, in a dynamic, temporal experience. Or to put it as simply as possible, the reader has an individual persona (mine), a communal persona (the abstracted total experience of my critical community), and a textual persona (the reader implied in the text). And all of these personas are seen at their best through time.

NOTES

/1/ Booth speaks of "the flesh-and-blood author, who tells many stories, before and after a given tale," and "the flesh-and-blood re-creator of many stories" (1983:428). Rabinowitz, who only deals with the audience side of the narrative act in his article, uses the term "actual audience" (126). Once beyond the narrator/narratee pair, Prince, like Rabinowitz, concentrates more on the audience side of the narrative than the authorial side; and Prince, like Chatman, uses the expression "real reader" (Tompkins: 9).

/2/ Booth is currently using the terms "the implied author of this tale" and "the postulated reader" (1983:429). Rabinowitz speaks (only on the audience side again) of the "authorial audience" (126). In a similar vein Prince uses the term "virtual reader" (Tompkins: 9).

/3/ Chatman credits Prince for the coinage of "narratee," the counterpart of the "narrator." Booth speaks of "the teller of this tale" and "the credulous listener" (1983:430). Rabinowitz uses the expression "narrative audience" (127).

/4/ For example, both Rabinowitz and Prince also want to talk about "ideal readers": for Rabinowitz, the "ideal narrative audience" (134), and for Prince, the "ideal reader" (Tompkins: 9). I want to reserve discussion of such ideal readers until later.

WORKS CONSULTED

Bleich, David
    1975   *Readings and Feelings: An Introduction to Subjective Criticism*. Urbana, IL: National Council of Teachers of English.
    1978   *Subjective Criticism*. Baltimore and London: Johns Hopkins University.

Booth, Stephen
    1969   *An Essay on Shakespeare's Sonnets*. New Haven and London: Yale University.

Booth, Wayne
    1979   *Critical Understanding: The Powers and Limits of Pluralism*. Chicago and London: University of Chicago.
    1983   *The Rhetoric of Fiction*. 2d ed. Chicago and London: University of Chicago.

Chatman, Seymour
    1978   *Story and Discourse: Narrative Structure in Fiction and Film*. Ithaca and London: Cornell University.

Culler, Jonathan
    1975   *Structuralist Poetics: Structuralism, Linguistics, and the Study of Literature*. Ithaca: Cornell University.

Fish, Stanley
    1970   "Literature in the Reader: Affective Stylistics." *New Literary History* 2: 123–62.
    1972   *Self-Consuming Artifacts: The Experience of Seventeenth-Century Literature*. Berkeley, Los Angeles, and London: University of California.
    1980   *Is There a Text in This Class? The Authority of Interpretive Communities*. Cambridge, MA and London: Harvard University.

Holland, Norman N.
    1975   *5 Readers Reading*. New Haven: Yale University.
    1982   *Laughing: A Psychology of Humor*. Ithaca and London: Cornell University.

Iser, Wolfgang
    1972   "The Reading Process: A Phenomenological Approach." *New Literary History* 3: 279–99.
    1974   *The Implied Reader: Patterns of Communication in Prose Fiction from Bunyan to Beckett*. Baltimore and London: Johns Hopkins University.
    1978   *The Act of Reading: A Theory of Aesthetic Response*. Baltimore and London: Johns Hopkins University.

Kelber, Werner H.
1983   *The Oral and the Written Gospel: The Hermeneutics of Speaking and Writing in the Synoptic Tradition, Mark, Paul, and Q.* Philadelphia: Fortress.

Mailloux, Steven
1982   *Interpretive Conventions: The Reader in the Study of American Fiction.* Ithaca and London: Cornell University.

Ong, Walter J.
1982   *Orality and Literacy: The Technologizing of the Word.* London and New York: Methuen.

Prince, Gerald
1973   "Introduction à l'étude du narrataire." *Poétique* 14: 178–96. [Now translated and abbreviated as "Introduction to the Study of the Narratee," in Tompkins: 7–25].
1982   *Narratology: The Form and Function of Narrative.* Berlin, New York, Amsterdam: Mouton.

Rabinowitz, Peter
1977   "Truth in Fiction: A Reexamination of Audiences." *Critical Inquiry* 4: 121–41.

Ricoeur, Paul
1967   *The Symbolism of Evil.* Translated by Emerson Buchanan. Boston: Beacon.

Steiner, George
1979   "'Critic'/'Reader.'" *New Literary History* 10: 423–52.

Suleiman, Susan
1976   "Ideological Dissent from Works of Fiction: Toward a Rhetoric of the *roman à thèse.*" *Neophilologus* 60: 162–77.

Tompkins, Jane P., ed.
1980   *Reader-Response Criticism: From Formalism to Post-Structuralism.* Baltimore and London: John Hopkins University.

II
READING BIBLICAL TEXTS

THE BIBLE AS LITERATURE:
READING LIKE THE RABBIS

Kenneth Dauber
State University of New York/Buffalo

ABSTRACT

The Jewish Bible is properly literature insofar as it resists traditional philosophy's grand project of knowing Being. There is no concept of Being in the Bible. From God's command to Abraham to journey to Canaan, through Israel's acceptance of the Torah, to the dialogue between God and Job, what it renders is not the revelation of an existence but the establishment of a certain relation. Accordingly, the Bible is not a text to be interpreted; rather, as the Rabbis understood it, interpretation is the text itself. No subject reader engages no object to be read. "Relationality," prior to both, defines subject and object according to itself.

Using Rabbinic practice as a model, various relational modes or statements are developed for potential use in studying secular literature. Relational statements for classicism and modernism are proposed. Period, genre, and theme are denied any status as constituting texts and are considered, instead, as discursive formations produced in criticism's existentialization of relationality. The skepticism known as deconstruction is attacked. For, seen as criticism's bad conscience for its existentialization, it may be left behind when relationality comes into its own.

I

I take as my text the beginning of the Hebrew Bible, or rather, the place where the Hebrew Bible might have begun, as the Rabbis tell us (Rashi, Gen. 1:1),/1/ after the God of all peoples has finished establishing all the world and enters into a particular dialogue with the first Hebrew about one corner of it:

> Now the Lord said to Abram, Get thee out of thy country, and from thy kindred, and from thy father's house, to the land that I will show thee. (Gen. 12:1)

This is a simple passage, but remarkably so. For the broad scope of all that has come before, the magnitude of the creation, the fall, the flood, mark this event off as of a different order. The narrowness of focus, here, the intensity, the limitation suddenly imposed on the scope of this Bible that began so universally, so philosophically, is not prepared for. It is not that we find God's intimacy with Abraham, the dialogue of the promise, a little demeaning. That God will talk to man, and more, that he will sometimes give him fairly explicit directions, has already been well established. We have seen this before, and we do not protest that the conversation between God and Abraham somehow violates the nature of the Bible's world, is a scandal or, perhaps, a miracle. Indeed, in a manner, through a series of "begats" from Adam to Abraham, we even have a sort of pre-history to the dialogue. We know, in a general sort of way, how God came to this condescension, what, that is, he has been doing since the Creation and, very particularly, what Abraham has been doing, who he is, his genealogy, his wife, and even, most interestingly, that he had been journeying with his father on the way towards the land of Canaan before God's command to him to journey. And yet, none of these things can quite explain why all that has come before should be reduced to this, why the story of the world should become the story of Israel. How God should have chosen this Abraham to talk to and how it was that Abraham could have understood him, known what faith was expected, what level of belief required, are finally inexplicable.

Compare, for example, the story of the flood, material from the universal beginning of the Bible. In a traditional reading, we might be tempted to say that it provides a context for the Hebrew beginning:

> And the Lord saw that the wickedness of man was great in the earth, and that all the impulse of the thoughts of his heart was only evil continually. And the Lord repented that he had made man on the earth, and it grieved him at his heart. And the Lord said, I will destroy man whom I have created from the face of the earth; both man, and beast, and creeping things, and the birds of the air; for I repent that I have made them. But Noah found favor in the eyes of the Lord.
> These are the generations of Noah: Noah was a just man and perfect in his generations, and Noah walked with God. (Gen. 6:5-9)

The story of the flood is an exemplum of certain universal principles, a result, or better, an allegory, of the operation of justice. It is because God was angry at the wickedness of the poeple that he turned away from them, and it is because Noah was good that God turned to him. Problems, of course, remain, traditional problems, such as how God could have let things get so bad or how he could have destroyed his own creation. But these are problems leading us not away from God and the nature of his universe, but into them. They are practical problems, part of the landscape of God's universe, whose geography the story thus invites us to map. Action, in the flood narrative, however complex or difficult, is yet predicated on certain essential qualities of the world and the actors in it and is exhibited as an unfolding of these qualities.

The actions of the actors in the Abraham story, on the other hand, are of a different order. They seem to exhibit nothing but themselves in their own singularity. Occurring in the world, they say nothing very readily about the world. They have no part in predication, cancelling even the notion of actors, replacing it with a stunning "relationality," as we might call it, a mutual disposition denying its dependence even on the subjects who dispose themselves. The existence of God and Abraham prior to their dialogue, the priority of their very existence *to* their dialogue, is held off. The story of Abraham creates for itself an unbridgeable gap, a vacuum, quite literally unthinkable, that is unphilosophical, though, philosophers all, we have continued to think it, abhorring the vacuum, filling it with explanation.

In the theological mode, for example—Christianity's version of philosophy—we say that God chose whom he wished to choose. Or, as the Rabbis proposed in the more historical mode of aggadah, Abraham had already proved himself a God-believer when he destroyed his father's idols. And yet, theology, naming the unnamable, making precisely the unexampled an example once more, rather reveals the limits of itself as a discipline, the closure of itself as a system against anything unsystematic, than explains the remarkable dialogue of God and Abraham. And, as the Rabbis recognized in their refusal to canonize it, aggadah is only aggadah and must, in fact, go on forever, merely displacing one vacuum with another.

Rather, all recourse to such matters as the nature, habits, Being of God or man, even to those matters the Bible would seem to go out of its way to raise, must finally be abandoned. The genealogy and the movement of Abraham toward the land he is then told to go to account for nothing. They are themselves to be accounted only as they appear again in the telling. It is a telling resisting all context. In the midst of a larger tale, it yet asserts itself as its own first principle. Such a telling, as we have said, cannot exemplify anything but itself. Its movement, what now becomes the Bible, does not unfold some prior state, but, coming from nowhere, merely develops. For lack of a better term, and in honor of its traditional war with philosophy, we may call this kind of telling literature. Literature is pure relationship, is the discourse of relationality. The story of Abraham would thus suggest that the current practice of considering the Bible as literature is not a sign of the failure of the Bible to command our faith as it once did. On the contrary, it is but a restitution of the Bible to its status before it fell into the hands of philosophy, into the hands of that transcendental contextualization known as logocentrism, and which, though it is being vigorously challenged in regard to secular texts, was yet wrong from the sacred genesis, as well. Indeed, to consider the Bible as literature will be to shed light on much of contemporary critical controversy, offering, as I believe, a way outside not only of logocentrism, but of that deconstruction which is its inevitable reflux.

II

Let us consider in detail the Bible as literature, the Bible as the discourse of relationality, and further justify our definition by citing the Rabbis, who go so far as to embody relationality in a text. The Rabbis recount how the Torah came to be given, glossing a famous passage in which the Jews, accepting the law, proclaim "we will do, and we will listen" (Ex. 24:7)./2/ Why this curious inversion? How is it possible to do what one has not yet even heard? At first God wished to give the law to the children of Esau. What does it say, they asked? Not to kill. And the children of Esau, claiming Esau's blessing, "by the sword shall you live," refused. Then God went to the children of Lot. What does it say? Not to be unchaste. And the children of Lot, remembering that they sprang from unchastity, refused. Then God went to the Ishmaelites. What does it say? Not to steal. And the Ishmaelites, cleaving to Ishmael and the "hand [that] will be against every man," refused, as well. But when God then went to the Jews, they accepted immediately, demonstrating their faith by not even waiting to consider what they were accepting, giving themselves from the start.

Now this story would appear to give relationality an origin. But, like the origin of Abraham and God's dialogue, so is the origin of the Jews' acceptance of the Torah recounted only to be abandoned. That is, we may reasonably suppose a foundation for the story in a certain moral or spiritual calculus. The gentiles are not good enough to receive the Torah. The Jews are. And yet, as the story ends, the concerns of goodness are pushed aside, for we get, instead, a story of the Torah as preceding its morality, preceding the very goodness which is its content, and whose materialization of relationality becomes the story's new subject. A reversal occurs, an emptying out of origins from relationality, like that of Abraham's journey to Canaan prior to his dialogue with God. Founding relationality is nothing, for relationality founds all. Solidified in a text—though this is a problem to which we shall need to return—relationality blocks out all behind it that it does not create anew, and thus attempts to contextualize the text, indeed attempts to decontextualize no less than to contextualize, must be wholly abandoned.

Here, again, we must be careful not to push off too much on God as solving all problems. After all, the whole point of the Rabbinic tale,

Israel's prime merit, is God's dependence on Israel to make himself manifest. The Torah reveals not God but Israel's acceptance of God. Contextualization, even so absolute a context as divinity, is in its own turn textualized, so that to insist on revelation is to leave ourselves endlessly circulating, pushed from text to context to text, in the classic deconstructive cycle. On the other hand, however, we must guard equally against that species of decontextualization that would subjectivize the text, elaborating Israel's merit into the ground of an endless freedom to make of the text whatever it wants. For it is only in accepting the Torah that Israel's freedom appears. No less than the God who ostensibly overdetermines the text does the Israel who makes the text indeterminate recirculate within it. We might better say the Bible is no more indeterminate than determined. We can relate to it, but we cannot know it. We cannot establish what—or even that—it "is."

Who are the children of Israel the Torah describes? The children of Israel *of* the Torah, by nature or culture nothing, but what the Torah, by their acceptance of it, has made them, nature and culture both. Even more strongly, who is God? The God of Israel, who has given the Torah but to be given in it. God, no more than his people or his Torah, "is," and indeed, there is no way of saying "is" in the Hebrew Bible. We move from "was," which may be said, to "will be," which is said with the addition of a single letter to the form for "was," passing over "is" entirely, excluding it from the language, and turning "was" and "will be" into activities rather than terms of presence. Who shall I say sent me, Moses therefore asks God, strictly speaking a better question than who are you. And God's answer, though it has been philosophically mistranslated as "I am that I am," is, quite literally, "I will be what I will be" (Ex. 3:14) (cf. Buber). Interaction, the relationality of manifesting, replaces the entity manifested. Textuality, we might say, displaces the logos. For language, not the expression of Being, not Being re-presenting itself, is no deconstructed trace of a Being always already absent, either. To read the Bible is neither to understand nor to misunderstand, but to constitute the text read. It is neither, passively, to receive nor, fantastically, to imagine, but really, responsibly or irresponsibly, to underwrite. The Bible "is" not, is not to be known, but to be accepted or rejected. Thus the Bible makes relationality prior to knowledge, and the Bible is literature because, denying anything outside of relationality, denying, that is, the very category of things which, existing unrelationally, may or may not be known, it replaces the traditional concerns of philosophy with the concerns of a textuality still insisting on itself even as the philosophic tradition winds down.

A new problematic opens up, a new set of questions in which the goal of criticism is something new. For in the beginning was not the Word at all. Nor was our fall into thought a fall from the Word. Rather, thinking itself is reinterpreted by the Bible as literature. While philosophy divides the thinker from the concept thought, in the Bible what is divided is a volition from a resistance. And if philosophical thinking would re-unite what it has divided in the grand self-thought of infinite Being or God, literary thinking would reconceive division without recourse to unity. Disclosure is replaced by definition, divinity in its infinite self-awareness by relationality in the finitude of engagement. Instead of interpretation we get what used to be called commentary. For a criticism that stands outside the text and tries to get behind it, we substitute a critical relation, as it were *in* the text, determining the text's operation.

III

Now it will be recognized, I believe, that criticism is already in the process of shifting in the direction I am describing. The freeing of the text from the being of the author, the insistence on the constitutive role of the reader, indeed the confusion of author and reader, are all features of current critical theories. And yet, such theories labor under two difficulties, their sense of themselves as modern and their ultimate domination by the notion of Being and Knowing, which is the root cause of their sense of modernity.

Consider, for example, the case of Harold Bloom. Bloom has argued the deep connection between reading and writing that makes all writers readers and all "strong" poets as much critics of earlier poets as makers of original verse (1973)./3/ Poetry, for Bloom, is precisely a relation, neither the reader's nor the writer's but that which goes on between them. And yet, what does go on between them is a curious struggle. Knowing he comes after, the poet must fight to overcome the one who came before, wresting from him a purer truth, breaking and reforming him in the light of a new vision yet defined as older. Literature for Bloom is a struggle of the moderns with the ancients for priority in respect of Being, so that even when he cites ancient sources as his own predecessors, as he does in *Kabbalah and Criticism*, they are revisionist ancients, themselves worried with coming after and struggling for a priority which, early as they may be, they can never achieve. Relationality is replaced by what Bloom calls belatedness, the sense of a truth already unreachable and half-way on the road to deconstruction. No deconstructionist himself, indeed a partisan of poetry as a never-ending process, neither a construct nor deconstructible, his commitment to the dialectic of priority is an enlistment under the sign of Being and so works to defeat the very literature he would preserve.

Similarly, we may charge most subjectivist criticism of the sort represented by Stanley Fish (1970; 1976). This is reader-response criticism of a radical sort, having gone so far as to reject the contextualization of some historically knowable readership to which conservative reader-response critics, such as Wolfgang Iser (1978), would yet hold on. And yet, it is criticism not radical enough, for in constructing reading *as* response, in reducing responsive*ness*, as we might call it, to the secondariness of "response *to*," it binds itself to Being as surely—and as sure to be undermined—as Bloom. Such criticism begins, too, in relationality, in "readers reading," as Norman Holland has phrased it. The infinite presence of the true text is banished in favor of the finitude of an individual's relatedness to the text. But because what the reader is related to yet "is"—what he is—before the relation and after it, a kind of contextualization persists. Undermined as objective by the reader's projection of himself onto it, the text's infinitude is preserved negatively in the form of reading forever indeterminate. Infinite absence replaces infinite presence. Relationality is invoked only to be absorbed into non-Being, destroying textuality as relational after all./4/

It is no wonder that deconstruction reigns in the critical world, today. It is the final gasp of the problematic of Being and Knowing. Bound, as Derrida tells us explicitly over and over again, to the very ideas it would destroy, it is at once avant garde and ancient, telos and origin of the idea of Being, the fullest exfoliation taking us back to the utmost concentration of Being, now, finally, playing itself out. If we would continue to read, accordingly, we must get around not only the illusion of a stable text, but the deconstruction of stability, as well. We must turn to a criticism, in fact, admittedly old, not avant garde, and whose newness is but the result of our having abandoned it for so long. We must turn to a criticism that, because from the start it was not an interpretation of Being, may never play itself out, though it may, of course, always be abandoned once more. And here, we may pick up at that abandonment in order to re-engage the issue.

IV

We have already seen that, for a criticism of relationality, in the beginning was not the Word. The Johanine misprision of Genesis, indeed, is well known and may be taken as the *locus classicus* of the Hellenization of Hebraic culture, the moment at which the Old Testament becomes new, in our terms the moment in which relationality is subdued by philosophy. I want, however, to dwell particularly on the consequences for literary criticism of this misprision, citing Frank Kermode, whose recent book on the New Testament broods admirably over the issue.

Kermode confronts the central problem of parable in the New Testament and, in particular, in Mark, Jesus' exasperation with his disciples for failing to understand him and yet his simultaneous insistence on speaking in figures that may not, at least immediately, be understood:

> And when he was alone, they that were about him with the twelve asked of him the parable. And he said unto them, Unto you it is given to know the mystery of the kingdom of God: but unto them that are without, all these things are done in parables: that seeing they may see, and not perceive; and hearing they may hear, and not understand; lest at any time they should be converted, and their sins should be forgiven them. And he said unto them, know ye not this parable? and how then will ye know all parables? (4:10–13)

The passage poses a serious ethical problem in seeming to represent Jesus as unfair and, even, vindictive. But, as Kermode notes, the ethics of the matter is rather subordinate to metaphysics. For a division is assumed in the state of humanity between those on the outside and those on the inside which parable, although it would bridge, yet simultaneously requires. Interpretation, that is, for that is what parable solicits, is the way from the outside to the inside, is an activity indeed generated by the notion of an outside and inside, with which it cannot, therefore, dispense. As Kermode puts it, secrecy must always exist if reading is to exist, and, as we might add, a certain mystification is thus announced as the condition of Helleno-Christian exegesis, which, sooner or later, cannot but be demystified as the Helleno-Christian tradition fulfills itself./5/

Now I believe it might be shown that the very idea of the logos was invented to suppress that inevitability. The idea of the infinite Word, of a Word in which human words, however inadequate, yet ultimately were contained, was an attempt to defend interpretation in the very condition of its inadequacy by making it the proof of mystery. Thus the heresy of Gnosticism, which was a threat critically as much as ethically, a devotion to the mystery that denied the usual terms of interpretation, severing the limitation which is experience from any possibility of intimating infinity. More to our purpose here, however, we may note that the Rabbis, committed to textuality rather than to the logos, to "we will do, and we will listen," thus did not divide mystery from interpretation in the first place. Even within the normative Christianity of the logos, since the end of every interpretation is Jesus Christ, the goal of every finite reading the infinite, mystery is ultimately more important than interpretation. But the end of Rabbinic interpretation is not God, but a finitude taken to be God's relation in experience. The end never existed in advance. Rabbinic interpretation is never an abstraction from the text of a principle that lies behind it, but, via comparison of various passages, an operation on the text which constitutes the text in all its literality./6/ As normative Judaism has always maintained, the oral law was given at

Sinai along with the written law, Rabbinic commentary, however new, with the books of Moses themselves. Rabbinic commentary is criticism of a literature it defines as outside logocentricity and its deconstruction, and so we must ourselves criticize. Defining our texts, too, as like the Rabbis' text, we must make reading as relational our new project.

V

We return, then, to the Bible as literature. For although we have dwelt on certain particulars of the Hebrew Bible which may seem specific to it, yet I would insist that it remains a type of literature in general. "We will do, and we will listen," after all, is but a radical statement of relationality that may be modified in a variety of forms. And, indeed, I believe that behind every group of texts, constituting it as a group—an epoch of literary discourse, let us say—lies some such modification that it is the business of a criticism of relationality to explore. Accordingly, in an admittedly sketchy manner, half prospectively and half heuristically, let me suggest some of the kinds of activity I believe such a criticism must perform.

First, a definition of the overarching relational statement, the specific relational framework or field, as we may call it, constituting a specific literature. Such a statement should be hedged against any avoidable existentializing tendency. Properly, the field is no existent to be described, Being to be Known, or even Being mediated as context—a language, for example, or culture. Thus it would escape description altogether, a situation devoutly to be wished. In practice, however, relational fields will accommodate cultural and linguistic description in varying degrees and ways. Relationality insists on itself in the face of existentialization. It is continued even into a culture engaged in breaking off relations. Accordingly, accommodation makes description the way back to relationality, and an analysis of accommodation in its varying character must be one of a relational criticism's chief undertakings. Traditional cultural and linguistic information would be used, but relocated. Its place would be reversed, positioned not behind the text but the critic. The critic's cultural bias, his ability to reach the work through the constraints of his time and his place or, on the other hand, his finding it inaccessible, would be precisely the situation he would have to describe.

The diversity in culture and language among Jews, even in ancient times, may be taken as a starting point. These, properly speaking, have an identity as Jews as they are "the people of the book" rather than people with certain kinds of customs, and their language is "the holy language," which, as it happens, is, but need not necessarily have been, the language of the Hebrews. As the Bible itself makes clear, a whole range of cultural insititutions are Jewish only "as it happens." The system of courts, the delivery of justice as it has extended itself into Jewish life in the present day, is introduced after the model of a Midianite. The order of the Levites, an order functioning today as well, is yet the consequence of an historical happenstance conjoined to a largely unvalued tribal organization. Such institutions, and others that might be multiplied, constitute no structure, no system one can call Biblical./7/ But their survival as a cultural residue within the Bible points to the Bible's relational strength. I would say that the characteristic of Biblical relationality is its ability to accommodate cultures without destroying them. For to relate in the Bible is to relate so nearly absolutely that culture or language, taken up in the relation, is yet in very little danger of objectifying itself *as* the relation. It cannot turn relationality into a field for cultural or linguistic knowledge, and so can be accommodated unproblematically. In the case of relationality less absolute, accommodation is necessarily less magnanimous, and we may pause at one or two examples.

"Sing goddess," says Homer, what we may take as the relational statement framing the literature of the West. Here relationality has been severely compromised. For the god whom Homer addresses, only half-way arises in the address; half-way she exists as god to be addressed, a muse or demi-god, if not fully known, yet not quite beyond knowledge. This god is saturated by culture. It is Greek that she speaks, "the wrath of Achilles" that is her song, the song, indeed, of Homer the Greek, his culture hypostatized, become Being overtly figured—or, more precisely suited to the figure, demi-Being—object of a knowing ostensibly universal, if finally of the culture alone. To actualize this muse, to sing this song, constitute this text, one must feel the wrath of Achilles as one's own. One must become his fellow, must be in his time and his place, forsaking all others. Or, let us say, one must become aware of one's proper time and place *as* other. Intraculturally this is the epic or heroic quality of the *Iliad*, the sense that our age cannot measure up to Achilles' age, which, no doubt, even the first Greek readers of Homer felt./8/ Extra-culturally it is the Western power to make of non-Western peoples others, its even greater power to assimilate what is not Western into the West. The *Iliad's* portrait of Hector will be recalled, the tender father and loving husband, a Trojan hero because he is prince of peace, transformed in this Greek song into prince of war, before he is crushed utterly. Western literature, we may say, is characterized not so much by its ability to accommodate various cultures as by its consumption of them. It is an imperialistic relationality, differentiating which would constitute an important part of relational studies.

Here, as a more immediate example, we may take "This may be read or not as any one pleases," from Benjamin Franklin's *Autobiography* (44), a representatively modern case. It is representative especially in its democratic character, its apparent non-imposition, in fact, of anything on anybody. Nothing compels. Everyone would seem to be free. The reader's liberty to choose is insisted upon. There is neither a god, here, something that "is" to be known even half way, nor yet an insistence that relations take place. And yet, the corrosiveness of "This may be read or not, as anyone pleases" should not be missed. To read this book, to choose, indeed, not to read it, is to choose only *as* an individual. It is to give up one's culture, to deny one has a time and a place. This is the modernity of the modern, an essential a-nationality, not even inter-nationality, a sense of reading that is of the moment, eternally cut off from what has brought the reader to the moment. Relationality in the modern period neither accommodates nor compromises with culture; it obliterates it. But more, such an obliteration, beyond the loss or gain, as we may feel, involved in it, thus establishes the individual independent of any context, any field of self-projection in which he may know himself and on which he might, therefore, claim to stand. To compare the situation with an aggadah that, at first glance, seems similarly about obliteration but which, in fact, is complementary to our aggadah on "We will do, and we will listen": God, it is told, held Mount Sinai over the Jews' heads, ready to drop it on them if they did not accept his Torah (Ginzberg: III, 92). Outside of biblical relationality there is no biblical people whom the Bible establishes or destroys. The Jews, if they did not read, would cease to be Jews and, accordingly, would cease to be the Bible's concern. But outside of reading or not as one pleases is the reader established as standing, at once, nowhere. We move beyond imperialism, beyond freedom, almost to nihilism. A more precise definition of such almosts, however, carries us to a second activity of a relational criticism, the business of periodizing within a relational field.

The problem here would be to describe stages within the field that are not linked as phases. That is, we must be careful not to see our stages as an increasing or decreasing or dialectical disclosure of the field's founding relation existentialized as a truth. These must not be stages of some idea separate from us and given over to our description of it, but a part of our description, which thus establishes it in the critical present. We must continue to refuse to differentiate a relationality within the text from a relationality without it. We must maintain our periods as but extensions of the founding relation from the first readers to ourselves. Here, most especially, relational criticism must acknowledge that it is a constitutive criticism. For only thus can it, like the founding relation it periodizes, resist indeterminacy or subjectivity, in the sense that we usually mean by subjectivity, freedom from being judged. The relational critic, beginning and ending his notion of a literary epoch according to his perhaps partial relation to it, yet himself participates in a history of relations. Continuous with the relational field he seeks to define, his, as it were, relation to relationality is precisely *what* he seeks to define. To periodize remains to act, rather than to know. It is neither right nor wrong, subjective nor objective, but responsible or irresponsible, by virtue of the power, the structure of authority it perpetuates even when it seeks to delimit that structure. Thus, neither true nor false, it may yet be judged against other powers, other structures which other acts of reading may perpetuate or delimit as alternatives.

To return to our starting point, the Hebrew Bible begins with Abraham's dialogue with God precluding the question who is God, and ends, as it might be shown, with God's answering Job—who, in effect, asks the precluded question—don't ask. The epoch of the Bible as literature, that is, runs from not asking spontaneously and immediately to not asking by virtue of will and a great deal of effort. No matter how many interpretations of the Bible may be proposed within this relational range, however, as long as they are proposed by a criticism which does operate within it, the epoch remains firm. Thus we may contrast Rabbinic and Christian exegesis. The Rabbis, whose interpretations are difficult and often impossible to reconcile, yet place themselves within the epoch of the Bible as literature by their commitment to the Bible, and accordingly, again as we find in normative Judaism, they are said to be equally true however much they contradict. On the other hand, the criticisms of the "Old" Testament by writers of the "New," even when not in substantial disagreement with those of the Rabbis, constitute an end of the epoch because of a radical change they effect in relationality, indeed because of their refusal to "relate" to the Bible altogether. Unsatisfied with "don't ask," unsatisfied with textuality as final, they bypassed the Bible for an inquiry into immediate or, at least, mediated presence. They denied the text for God, denied the God of the Bible for the God behind the Bible, he who used the Bible merely as an instrument of self-presentation. Contradictory interpretations could no longer be equally true, for outside of relationality there is only one Truth. Critics were separated from the text, no longer constituting it, but always, Kermode-wise, on the outside of it trying to get inside, humble servitors or foolish misinterpreters. The Bible ceased to be literature. It was, in fact, canonized, and biblical criticism, replacing textuality with texts—logoi, we might say, incarnated—became the model for the kind of criticism as priestly service that only now we are leaving in its own turn./9/

Once again, it is not my purpose to elaborate at length an adaptation to secular texts. But again, too, we might suggest prospectively the relationality inaugurated by Homer and closed with his canonization in Vergil. This is a periodization arbitrary enough—the canonization having already been accomplished, after all, by others before Vergil and the closure to be opened by still others after him. But if it is, thus, as much our relation to Vergil as Vergil's relation to Homer that actually establishes the period, the confusion is what a relational criticism solicits. Only thus may we insist on our responsibility for the consequences of our reading—in the case at hand, our perpetuation of a certain relational imperialism, though, as well, our effort to break free. In such a Vergil operating in such a Homeric field, therefore, what we might describe as a suspension across a dialectic of acceptance and resistance is especially evident. Homer is canonized from the inside, rather than, as with Christian canonization of the Old Testament, from the outside. But the relationality in Homer is raised to a certain self-limiting consciousness. "Muse cause me to remember," asks the *Aeneid*. This is Vergil becoming Homer, the Roman becoming Greek, but yet not quite believing it, or rather, wanting to remain Roman all the same. The singer no longer sings what his muse sings. He requests her aid in singing himself. Vergil would be Homer, but only as Vergil. He is Homer with a guilty conscience. He writes an imperialism, as it were, in bad faith, imperialism become propaganda. Unlike the Rabbi writing Torah in interpreting it, the rhetor no longer composes the *Iliad* in performing it. He becomes an author, his performance a separate book. He is thrust into the period of the moderns, where authors and books exist most clearly separated from each other, but where they exist, therefore, in denial of periodization, which, relating book to book, would destroy the very modernity it generated. That imperialism beyond imperialism which we described is especially evident here. For to relate to a work as modern is, in effect, to attempt to abandon relations. It is not only to let the work be alone, but to let the work let every other work be alone as well. It is no wonder that in the experience of modernity traditional conceptions of influence, development, history have come under such intense pressure./10/ As radically present, modernity precludes any real temporality. And, indeed, it precludes any real spatiality, as well. Here, however, we pass to a third activity of a criticism of relationality, a more direct attempt to describe spatiality. In traditional criticism, criticism under the sign of Being and Knowing, this is generally relegated to genre or form studies, but as relational critics we must give it a more reflexive turn, questioning the very institution of form.

In short, it would seem that form emerges in the sinking of relationality into Being, in a growing passivity of the reader that externalizes relationality. Form, apparently expressing Being, directing us to questions of adequation—of physical to spiritual, outside to inside, in general of representation to presence—converts our treating *with* a work to treatment *of* a work. The reader's constitutive power is denied him. He is himself constituted prior to his reading, in relation but in a secondary sense, and to a text constituted in much the same prior way. As we have indicated earlier, in a certain sense even the Rabbis thus externalize. Or, let us say, they "source" relationality, materialize the transparent relation of Abraham and God in a text that must forever after be treated as a relational model. Relationality takes a shape. It is engraved in stone, bound. What can be done but trace its form? And yet, it must also be said, relationality bound remains a far cry from the logos incarnated. We might thus read the "binding" of Isaac and Abraham's insistence on his own hand in the work. His repeated response, "Here I am," so far from Kierkegaard's fear and trembling, is a refusal of just such passivity as the knowledge—or ignorance—of God would grant. So the Rabbis insist on their own hands after all. "There is no before and no after in the Torah," as the traditional dictum goes: what is bound exists only to be unbound. As the Rabbis held, though they read the Torah, so did Abraham (Rashi: Gen. 26:5). If the Torah represents Abraham, it is Abraham's reading of himself that is represented. Relationality materialized is relationalized once more. Reading and representation alternate, and the process does not end. Canonized, the Bible is opened in the oral law. Codified in the Talmud, the oral law is opened in so-called "responsa." The alternation is often linearized, seen as a running down. But it is seen, simultaneously, as a perfecting. Written law, oral law, responsa—all are maintained, more than figuratively, to be Torah.

Perhaps the situation is no more clearly evident than in the Bible's indifference to form of the more conventional kind, its openness to what we would distinguish as history, poetry, fiction, and so on, all of which it cheerfully includes as Bible. This is a magnanimity with respect to genre comparable to the magnanimity we described in connection with culture. For genre, like culture, marking the reader's distance from relationality, is a mark the Bible would retrace. To modify our previous statement, if genre is the sign of passivity, yet the reader may appropriate it for relationality by reading the sign as a warning against distancing himself any further. Genre is relationality externalized, as we have said. Yet its very density, if attended to, will prevent such a transcendent externalization as would place relationality beyond recovery.

Crucial, here, is the Bible's refusal of any hierarchicalization of its forms, its ordering of its writings—Torah (Law), Nevi'im (Prophets), Ketuvim (Writings [proper])—according to a scale of authority, of relational closeness, as we should call it, in which form is an indifferent consideration. For such acceptance of formal variety of the kind we find in classical institutionalizations of literature, of variety that is dependent on hierarchy, only legitimates externalization. Such a hierarchy is the subordination of readers to forms which do not warn of further distancing but conduct deeper into it. The reader reads forms he takes as constituted prior to his reading, and a sort of prioritizing of one form to another continues that can end only in the logos. Form dissolves in the idea of form in general. Relationality, arrested in form, threatens completely to disappear. Once again, a sliding scale is in evidence. Even the classic, for all the hierarchical regularity it propounds in theory, in practice produces forms only more or less prior, and again, too, a description of such mores and lesses would be a relational criticism's task.

Thus we find in Homer a certain openness apparently less than that of the Bible only. Poetry and history are not distinguished. Subjective and objective discourses have not separated out. Inventing and reporting, creating and imitating are one. As we have already noted, Homer's reading of the Trojan War is his writing of it. Nor is his performance of this version of the work constrained by previous versions, for all performances of the *Iliad* are the *Iliad* itself. And yet, this having been said, a clear constraint, a boundedness beyond Homer's power to unbind meets him at the horizon of performance, in the *Iliad's* fixed and unchangeable outline within which performance must take place. Performance becomes a kind of improvization within the rhythm of histeron proteron, of the beginning meeting the ending (Whitman: 249–84). Homer is confined by a series of concentric figures he may never quite be conscious of, but which constrain him all the same. Being, let us say, has not yet been thought. Historically before philosophy, Homer does not as yet make Knowing his goal. No representation more or less adequate to presence appears before him to impose itself as a necessity on his song. Yet not being conscious of necessity does not cancel necessity's operation. Not-knowing is not equivalent to relationality, for something *to* be known—a language, a culture, an age—all *un*knowingly exists as a kind of boundary to relationality, an existential context beyond which relationality cannot, after all, go. The existence of such an unknown boundary is, in fact, what we call mythology, a proposition we cannot explore here. Suffice it to say its sign is the classic's demi-god, knowledge in the character of inspiration, limitation not as yet recognized, externality conceived of as internal but which sooner or later—as it were all consciously—will out.

Accordingly, in Vergil, we get—more than not yet knowing—a not quite successful attempt to forget. Vergil would dissolve his cultural horizon in Homer's. He would bury the necessity he knows in the work of one who as yet could not know. Vergil, as we have said, is Homer with a guilty conscience, and the difference shows in his work's status as no longer reading but *a* reading. It is, in other words, no longer a performance but overtly an imitation, a copy of one independent work in another work separate from it. Of course, it remains true, this separate work still would assert the authority of what it copies. The claims of the *Aeneid* are for a virtual equality with the *Iliad*. Vergil, as we have said, at the edge of the classic period, has not yet stepped outside it. Operating still within Homer's relational field, he construes Homer not yet as a form fixed beyond the possibility of at least some unfixing. As we take a further step, however, formalization becomes total. Writing and reading are now wholly distinct. The reader is completely subordinated.

Imitation becomes paraphrase, and it produces works separate and notably unequal—monographs, dissertations, academic studies. This is the situation of criticism today in respect of all texts it takes as classic. Or, where critical ambition is great, the critic elevates paraphrase to allegory. He gives up, that is, the Vergilian attempt to forget, and dreams, since he has fallen into the passivity of knowing, of at least becoming divinely passive, of knowing everything. Hermeneutics is born. The work no longer conducts back to relationality. It conducts in the other direction. It is logosized, given the character of an incarnation. The reader's subordination becomes his access to power and cannot, therefore, be given up. Hierarchy is theologized. And, indeed, even—as is more and more the case currently—where the formerly classic is read, instead, deconstructively, as modern, hierarchicalization remains the order of the day.

This rings, perhaps, a little oddly and requires some justification. Surely modernity tends, as it would seem, to a radical leveling. Writers and readers, texts and pre-texts run together. And yet, this leveling is an illusion, the result of priority so insistent that the work, so far from running into other works, is conceptualized as prior to itself. In modernity, I should say, all mediation is elided. That is, the modern independence of texts that we have noted is not a freedom from form but an identity with it. Form condenses. It is no longer, as it was in Homer, held at some far horizon. Relationality is formalized not somewhere else, but here and now, and the here and now become more and more immediate as the modernity of the work intensifies. In such a situation forgetting is impossible. Every particular is completely formed in its very particularity. The work fragments into an infinite number of works, presenting not a form to be known only finally, but a form to be known at every instant. Such knowing is not essentially different from allegorical knowing. It is as fully theological in ambition, its tendency as totalizing. The total, however, is no longer deferrable. It is no longer everything after all, but the current thing, which, in the totality of the instant, is all that there is. It is a thing increasingly small, ultimately no-thing. If writing thus becomes, as it does, difficult to separate from reading, this is not because relationality has recreated them as equal. Rather, denying altogether the relationality out of whose externalization they are born, both writing and reading cannot long endure. That passivity we spoke of that comes of the sinking of relationality sinks further into entropy. Even paraphrase disappears. Here, however, we must take up an issue in which performance, paraphrase, allegorization, indeed interpretation in any sense are collected. It is an issue we have been skirting throughout of what there might be *to* interpret in a text conceived of relationally. What content could such a text allow that interpretation would be called for? Accordingly, as we have been attempting to recuperate such activities as period and genre studies for a relational criticism that seeks, ultimately, to move beyond them, let us explore the possibility of recuperating content as well.

Now such a possibility is, I believe, a function precisely of the question of knowing and forgetting. That is, it depends upon the degree to which relationality requires what we have called "not-knowing" to sustain it, or, rather, on whether it is strong enough to take on knowing openly. We are, for example, struck by the boldness of the Bible in, as mentioned previously, describing Abraham's movement toward Canaan prior to the command to go to Canaan. In its first instance, relationality thus meets content, meets even itself as a content, and so interpretation is permitted to go on in the Bible, but within relational limits. To jump to the largest matter directly, the idea of monotheism: in the face of a content of such magnitude, surely knowing would seem to be our primary response. Must not interpretation take over, the infinitude of what is to be known resulting in interpretation infinitely expansible? And yet, even monotheism is relational, for its existence as a content is but the product of relationality accommodating a nationality that, for all its power, remains incidental to it. As historical critics tell us, the Bible seems to make two contradictory assertions, that there is only one God, and that every nation has its god./11/ Here is national competition siring multiple interpretation, but out of a relationality beyond multiplicity. An absolute at the center of some context like nation will be interpreted in a variety of—even competing—ways. But the only true absolute in the Bible is relationality itself, and relationality, no content, is past interpreting.

I would say that content, as it appears in the Bible, is always thus limited. It is never the cause of things, but the result. It is not what form and period, for example, lead into as expressing it, but like form and period, and perhaps even after them, a consequence of the externalization of relationality that we must never allow to assume the guise of what is internal. Like form and period, that is, content "places" relationality. It is a placing, however, masquerading as the end of place, as what period and genre conceal and which would best be revealed in their disappearance. Relationality contentualized, accordingly, must be kept in place most specifically. Are not the Jews a providential or, if you will, an imperialistic nation, for are they not commanded to take the land of others and to destroy the others entirely? Yes, but only a particular land and only the particular peoples of that land. The content "imperialism," in the Bible, is the content of a part which is neither part of a whole, as it is in the classic text, nor yet the whole itself, as in modernity. It can neither be extended to some universal or, here, even national value, nor can it be denied as incompatible with other values that, equally wholes, would occupy the same ground. Similarly, is not the world divided between God and man, light and dark, good and evil, clean and unclean, Jew and gentile? Yes, but these divisions may not be arrayed in a line. They are not, on the one hand, the dialectical poles of some unitary truth, nor, on the other, are they a competition of opposing truths suggesting the impossibility of truth. Divisions such as these, rather, are—and from the start—divided from each other as well. They are "different," let us say, not divided. That is, they are different not provisionally, not as varying manifestations of some ultimate—achieved or disputed—similarity, but permanently, by virtue of their limitation in a relationality precluding the dialectic of similar and different. If they can be said to be united at all, it is only in the arch-relational, the quite unphilosophical, principle of difference pure, and whose specific meaning is specific to the particular differentiation at issue. Content is neither everywhere nor nowhere, but somewhere and only there. Or better, it is articulable as, more or less, an isolable function. And the isolation is directly proportional to the force of the founding relational statement as it compromises itself in a particular period within a particular relational epoch. Here we may vary our procedure somewhat by citing not separate examples of separate epochs, but the same examples read in varying ways. Thus we may make quite tangible a point we have been arguing generally throughout, that it is not the text as independently constituted that determines our relation to it, but our relation that determines the text.

To take a well-known Biblical proposition, "Love thy neighbor as thyself." Now classically considered, we regard this as a principle, a truth, as it were behind the Bible, which the Bible merely states. To paraphrase, the proposition means, approximately, be good to your fellow man. More theologically—allegorically and beyond—it means, in Christian terms, a mystery or, in that corrosive theology of modernity, a mystification eminently demystifiable. The elements cancel each other out, for in loving thy neighbor as thyself neither self nor neighbor may stand. The sentence may mean somehing like Christian self-abnegation, a giving over of self or joining of self with other in some eternal oneness ultimately grounded in the enfolding oneness of God, or it may be a flat contradiction creating God as absent by its vertiginous shift of center from self to non-self in an endless cycle. But as relational, as a statement within "we will do, and we will listen," the proposition is rather a command. Its fulfillment, requiring assent, permits neither a union of selves nor even the failure of their union, but a dispositon of selves toward each other creating each other, allowing each other to exist but as a function of disposition. Union would abolish relationality. But relationality, founding even statements seemingly propounding union, delimits interpretation, defines it as opening not on truth but on itself as an activity, an operation of the attempt to fulfill the commandment, a stance preceeding even the ones who stand and that may not be abolished.

In much the same way, consider, for example, "Be fruitful and multiply." This has, again classically, been interpreted as an account of the origin of procreation. It is a figuration of how we came to be what we are, the description of our world's beginning, of nature as God—that is, nature as commanding culture—and, therefore, of culture's ultimately natural foundation. In the modern view we would, perhaps, challenge the simplicity of such an interpretation, raising the difficulties inherent in the very idea of origination. Thus we would note that we are told to do what, in effect, we would do anyway, the opposite case of the command to love thy neighbor as thyself, to do what cannot be done. In a Lévi-Straussian way, culture's claim of what belongs, properly, to nature would appear as scandalous and self-cancelling. And yet, whether we see them as foundations or, in the deconstructive term, as an abŷme, is not the difficulty that we have construed nature and culture as, in effect, united already? Rather, in "Be fruitful and multiply" neither nature nor culture may be dissolved. As the classic reading holds, nature remains, differentiated as culture, and, as deconstruction adds, culture as nature as well. Differentiation, however, no mere happening, no manifestation of some latent and essentially passive unity, is a creation, as it were ex nihilo. It is the activity of constituting the world as differentiated in the first place, of giving it the very terms by which it may be said, in fact, to be constituted (cf. Budick). Here is a world of infinite responsibility. In Emmanuel Levinas' slogan, "Be fruitful and multiply" establishes ethics as metaphysically prior to ontology. In our less technical language, it is a paradigmatic example of relationality's triumph, in the Bible, over philosophy. And indeed, might we not thus explain even the various cultic practices of the Bible as an elaboration of that triumph? For cult is but the "ethics" of man's relation to God—that is, a confrontation with Being as a radical absolute, yet restricting absoluteness to the particularity of what, in its arbitrariness, is practice differentiated almost too specifically. Here, however, we must close, for a more thorough investigation of these and other differentiations must await a fuller investigation of the relational statement in which they are involved. Such an investigation, for a variety of relational fields, must be the work of the future.

NOTES

/1/ Recorded in the name of Rabbi Ishmael. Rabbi Ishmael's own, more halakhically inclined choice for a beginning is the first commandment to Israel as a nation, Ex. 12:2. But the story of the creation, as he tells us, was intended for the gentiles.

/2/ This is the primary meaning. The secondary meaning of the Hebrew word for listen, as in English, is "obey," and is the meaning given in the Revised Standard edition, the Jewish Publication Society of America edition, and most other editions. The gloss is widely known. It is rendered most fully in Ginzberg (III:80–81).

/3/ Note, however, in light of our argument, Bloom's own more recent attempt to defend himself against the deconstructive strain implicit in his earlier work by giving the poet the power to install his precursor (1976: chap. 1).

/4/ The exchange between Fish (1981) and Iser (1981) on the issue is especially instructive. Fish's "deconstruction" of Iser is to my mind unanswerable, and Iser does not answer it, defending himself, instead, by pointing to the widespread acceptance he has won, even among formalists, as affirming the reasonableness of his position. And yet, if such a defense deserves anything like the scorn Fish gives it, it is difficult to make sense of Fish's own resort elsewhere to "interpretive communities" (1980). Fish is no more happy with deconstruction than Bloom. But he has not found any convincing way out of it either.

/5/ See, however, Atkins for a construction of contemporary exegesis as engaging some of the problems I am indicating while remaining within at least the Christian tradition.

/6/ The thirteen principles of interpretation of Rabbi Ishmael are a well-known example (*Sifra*, Introduction). Cf. Handelman (chap. 3).

/7/ The institution of the courts is described in Ex. 18:13–27. The historical happenstance is the worship of the golden calf, punishment for which Moses' tribesmen, the Levites, agreed to mete out. Evidently, their ritual work had been intended for the first-born sons of all Israel, irrespective of tribe. See Ex. 32:26–28 and Num. 3:44–51; 4.

/8/ But perhaps not the first Greek *hearers* of Homer. Cf. our discussion of Vergil. This is, arguably, the difference between Bakhtin's sense of the pastness of epic compared to his great Marxist predecessor Lukács' sense of its presentness. Or better, if we take the seductiveness of Homer's epic to lie in its representation of a certain past as more than present, indeed as presence itself, we may say that Bakhtin insists on a written Homer in protest against what Lukács, still in his pre-Marxist phase, reads too nostalgically as oral.

/9/ Canonization was, of course, the work of the Rabbis, too. Its force, however, is quite different. See our discussion later.

/10/ And not only in deconstruction, but in the post-World War I years and that older generation of "modernists" represented by T. S. Eliot's "Tradition and the Individual Talent."

/11/ The presumably late Deuteronomic author is credited with full-fledged monotheism. Cf., in Deuteronomy itself, however, the difficulty of interpreting the traditional statement of Jewish monotheism, "Hear O Israel, the Lord our God, the Lord is One" (6:4), where "one," in the opinion of many scholars, is better translated as "alone."

WORKS CONSULTED

Atkins, G. Douglas
    1980   "Dehellenizing Literary Criticism." *College English* 41: 769–79.

Bahktin, Mikhail
    1981   *The Dialogic Imagination: Four Essays.* Ed. Michael Holquist. Austin: University of Texas.

Bloom, Harold
    1973   *The Anxiety of Influence.* New York: Oxford University.
    1975   *Kabbalah and Criticism.* New York: Seabury Press.
    1976   *Poetry and Repression.* New Haven: Yale University.

Buber, Martin
    1982   *On the Bible.* New York: Schocken.

Budick, Sanford
    forthcoming   *The Dividing Muse: Images of Sacred Disjunction in Milton's Poetry.* New Haven: Yale University.

Derrida, Jacques
    1976   *Of Grammatology.* Trans. Gayatri Chakravorty Spivak. Baltimore: Johns Hopkins University.

Eliot, T. S.
    1921   *The Sacred Wood: Essays on Poetry and Criticism.* New York: Knopf.

Fish, Stanley
    1970   "Literature in the Reader: Affective Stylistics." *NLH* 2: 123–62.
    1980   *Is there a Text in this Class: The Authority of Interpretive Communities.* Cambridge, MA: Harvard University.
    1981   "Why No One's Afraid of Wolfgang Iser." *Diacritics* 11: 2–13.

Franklin, Benjamin
    1964   *The Autobiography of Benjamin Franklin.* Ed. Leonard Labaree. New Haven: Yale University.

Ginzberg, Louis
    1909–36   *The Legends of the Jews.* 7 vols. Trans. Paul Radiv. Philadelphia: Jewish Publication Society of America.

Handelman, Susan
    1982   *The Slayers of Moses: The Emergence of Rabbinic Interpretation in Modern Literary Theory.* Albany, NY: State University of New York.

Holland, Norman
    1975   *Five Readers Reading.* New Haven: Yale University.

Iser, Wolfgang
   1978   *The Act of Reading: A Theory of Aesthetic Response.* London: Routledge & Kegan Paul.
   1981   "Talk like Whales: A Reply to Stanley Fish." *Diacritics* 11: 82–87.

Kermode, Frank
   1979   *The Genesis of Secrecy: On the Interpretation of Narrative.* Cambridge, MA: Harvard University.

Levinas, Emmanuel
   1969   *Totality and Infinity: An Essay on Exteriority.* Trans. Alphonso Lingis. Pittsburgh: Duquesne University.

Lukács, Georg
   1971   *The Theory of the Novel: An Historico-Philosophical Essay on the Forms of Great Epic Literature.* Trans. Anna Bostock. London: Marlin.

Rashi
   1929–34   *Pentateuch with Rashi's Commentary.* 5 vols. Ed. A. M. Silbermann. London: Shapiro, Vallentine and Co.

Sifra
   1961   Jerusalem: Tehiya Press (Hebrew).

Whitman, Cedric H.
   1958   *Homer and the Heroic Tradition.* Cambridge, MA: Harvard University.

THE JOSEPH STORY: A NARRATIVE WHICH "CONSUMES" ITS CONTENT

Hugh C. White
Camden College
Rutgers University

ABSTRACT

This essay points to a fundamental tension in narratives arising from the semantic relation of the direct discourse of the characters to the indirect discourse of the narrative framework. This tension is shown to be rooted in the two axes of the sign, the communicative and the referential (Coseriu). The narrator can vary the degree of semantic dominance given to each of these modes of discourse. An analysis of portions of the Joseph story from this perspective shows that the semantic world of the direct discourse of the characters ultimately 'consumes' (Fish) or subordinates the referential system of meaning developed in the indirect discourse of the narrative framework, preventing the story from attaining closure.

The question of the role played by context in the semantic processes of language has been a critical problem in linguistics since at least the time of Ferdinand de Saussure. This problem, for him, was posed in terms of the relationship between the systematic dimension of language (*la langue*) and what has subsequently been called the performative dimension of language (*la parole*), i.e., language as a closed differential system vs. language as an occurence in acts of speech. In this view, to focus upon language as an occurrence required the study of many non-linguistic factors such as organs of speech, cultural patterns and customs, etc., thereby preventing a clear perception of language in its own right. He thus began his study of language by clearly drawing a line between langauge as "a self contained whole, a principle of classification" and contextual factors which began, in his view, with the speech act itself (1966:9).

When this approach to linguistics came to be used by Lévi-Strauss and others as the basis of a method of analyzing narrative, it resulted in decontextualizing the narrative. Since ancient narratives have often been decontextualized by history so that their author and provenance are no longer known with certainty, this new method, at first, seemed to offer a fruitful way of gaining access to the meaning of narratives despite the lack of historical, contextual knowledge we might have of them. But when these narratives are examined more closely, an internal problem with the method is encountered in that these narratives are almost always composed of both third person speech (the narrator's discourse) and the direct speech of the characters. How is one to analyze, semantically, the direct discourse of characters with a method that does not have a place for the contextual factors in the narrative framework which may, e.g., transform a simple straight utterance into sarcasm or irony?

Not all linguists have followed Saussure into his separation of language from acts of speech, but, on the contrary, some have chosen to begin with the act of speech in their attempt to understand language as a whole. Because I view the relationship of direct discourse to the narrative framework as central for analyzing the structure of narratives, and a speech act approach to semantics seems to allow a more sensitive treatment of the direct discourse and narrative framework in narratives, I will bring together some theoretical semantic perspectives from this viewpoint, and then apply them to the Joseph story in the Book of Genesis, focusing on the beginning of the story in Genesis 37.

According to a general semantic theory espoused by Eugenio Coseriu, the sign consists of two axes, the communicative axis and the referential axis (1974:66). It is the communicative axis that relates the sign to the grammatical structures which embody the symbolic reflection of the community (the action of self-reflective consciousness upon langauge itself which endows it with a signifying order). These in turn imply agreements to which each speaker becomes a party in order to communicate within a particular language community. A direct line thus leads from the communicative axis of language to the order of society, since acceptable grammar varies not only with each separate language community, but with ethnic classes and regional sub-groups within the same language community. Even the referential axis of terms is supported by implicit agreements between speakers regarding the object or definition which a term denotes; and these may vary for the same term with each sub-group within a single language community. It is thus obvious that decontextualizing a speech act dissolves the network of semantic constraints which normally control the meaning of words and presents the author with a semantic *tabula rasa* upon which he may begin to compose a new system.

This becomes clearer if we look at the work of the French linguist, Oswald Ducrot, who has rigorously analyzed language from the viewpoint of the semantic significance of contextual speech acts. Every statement has a context which includes its act of utterance or production, and extends to the associated physical, temporal, social and psychological conditions under which its production occurs. Ducrot argues that the context of a statement is of such fundamental semantic importance that the goal of pursuing the "literal sense" of sentences must be renounced. In his view, the "sentence" is an abstraction created by linguistics on the basis of the operation of even more abstract rules of syntax, lexical definitions, etc., brought together outside of the context of ordinary discourse. Words acquire their meaning only in the context of sentences, and sentences only in the context of longer units of discourse (1980:9). He proposes to place at the center of his linguistics the term, "statement" (*énoncé*), which will always be a particular sentence uttered by a speaker to a hearer. For him "language (as a theoretical object) must contain a reference to this which is for Saussure, *la parole*" (1978:108). When semantic analysis begins with the statement so delineated, then the ways in which the situation of discourse shapes its meaning becomes clear (1978:7, 8). The role of linguistics becomes that of providing hypotheses of the meaning of words and sentences which can be used deductively to interpret the meaning of texts (1980:10). This necessary inclusion by every statement of a reference to the act which produced it, causes the statement to embody an aspect of self-reference which imbues it with illocutory force. As he writes: ". . . the illocutory aspect of the activity of *parole* confers on it a necessary reference to itself and permits already the recognition of itself as the indispensible 'primacy' to its structural study" (1978:114).

In Ducrot's early work on the semantics of the enunciation, *Dire et ne pas Dire* (1972), he categorizes these contextual factors under the heading of "implicit signification" which he contrasts with "literal signification" (1972:10). The implicit can be broken down into a number of different types all of which need not detain us here. All of these flow from the concrete act of speech production and pertain to what the speaker assumes about the way in which his speech will be received by the hearer. The implicit thus refers to certain usually unspoken, and perhaps even unconscious views which he shares with his interlocutors because of being a part of the same linguistic community. He calls these views the "*sous-entendu*" (implication, innuendo of discourse [1972:8]). A person may simply state that, "It is eight o'clock," but the implication of this is that it is time to go. Whether the person "catches" the implication depends upon the extent to which he shares the same view of the situation as the speaker. By expressing himself in this indirect fashion, he allows the addressee the freedom to choose to stay longer without explicitly opposing the speaker's opinion. He allows himself the freedom as well to deny that it was his intention to go, in the event that he does elicit a negative response to his implications. This permits the speaker to say something while at the same time assuming no responsibility for having said it (Ducrot, 1972:11). The interpretation of the implication is placed in the hands of the hearer. Ducrot describes the situation as viewed from the perspective of the enunciation thus: "He has said X to me, but one says X only if Y; thus he has wanted to say Y" (1972:12). This form of implication would be distinguished from the logical presupposition which a statement, e.g., John is no longer married, implies, i.e., that John was married. This means that the hearer may draw an implication from the statement that is totally unexpected by the speaker. It might be that the hearer is under a doctor's treatment and has been given instructions to take a pill at eight o'clock, and he will thus respond by leaving for the kitchen. Ducrot sees the literal meaning of the sentence thus as conveying a minimal content which says ". . . only what it is necessary to do in order to discover the sense . . ." (1980:17). The sentence implies a context, a situation, which itself provides the meaning to the hearer. The situation, however, is always very complex because a single situation ". . . comports an infinity of givens from which the interpreter is able to draw in a multitude of different ways (in a 'situation of discourse,' there are, among others, all the beliefs and intentions of the interlocutors; one makes the reading vary as much as one wants depending upon which is taken into account and which is rejected in interpreting a statement)" (1980:18).

This deep network of implications rooted in the social setting that each act of discourse draws upon causes each utterance to be formulated in light of the way in which it will be "taken" by the hearer. It thus, in Ducrot's opinion, is not possible to separate the thought of others from one's own thought, since ". . . the thought of this is constitutive of mine, and it is impossible to separate them radically" (1980:45). Even when you refer to the opinion of another, e.g., "others think that p," this is not unrelated to the statement, "I think that p," as logic would require, since, in Ducrot's view, ". . . one would not be able, in effect, to envision a foreign opinion without giving in it, from this fact, a *certain degree of adhesion*" (his emphasis, 1980:45). In discourse, as distinct from logical reasoning, even those statements or views towards which a speaker maintains a distance still are related to his own interest and perspective and thus are invested indirectly with his own voice (thereby imparting to them as well illocutory force). It is this field of implications within which a sentence is positioned that renders language polyphonic.

Francois Flahault, in his work, *La parole intermédiare*, more broadly describes the source of Ducrot's "implicit" dimension of discursive language as an "effect of place." Flahault locates the source of human subjectivity in the events of mutual recognition between subjects where each partner finds himself confirmed by the other in dialogical encounter. It is here that he finds the illocutory effect of the discursive implicit. Every dialogue assumes that each partner occupies some position of power relative to the other—i.e., at least some capacity to give pleasure to those who support and confirm his global discursive position and inflict pain on those who reject or disdain it. As Flahault says, "Every desiring subject, in effect, bears the mark of an absolute subjection to the criteria according to which recognition is operated in the intersubjective network of which he constitutes one of the links" (1978:48). With the initiation of dialogue, the speaker presumes that the hearer will accede to the position which he assumes for himself. This position operates within the subject on four "registers" according to Flahault: The unconscious, the ideological (hierarchical, social system), the constraints of the situation of the specific utterance, and the circulation of signs within the dialogical interchange between the allocutory partners which effects the previous three (1978:137–52). The speech act thus, in requiring accession to the first three homologous positions by the hearer, requires an implicit agreement by the hearer to these conditions. If the hearer does not accede to them in the fourth register of the dialogical process, then the conversation will soon be terminated. This implicit agreement is what Flahault calls the illocutionary effect of the implicit factors in discourse. They represent unconscious and conscious effects of the interpersonal, social experiences of the speaker which have created in him a real or imaginary subjective sense of his place within the social and historical or cosmic system. For the speaker to accede to his sense of place indicates a shared world of discourse, an intersubjective bond that gives meaning to the utterances by providing their implications.

From these perspectives it is then possible to see precisely what occurs in the narrative form. The character's discourse, by displacing the direct discourse of the narrator, has been deprived of a *place* with a given network of social relations, and temporal events, thereby eliminating all implicit meanings which would normally be provided by that network. This frees the sign/personage from all utilitarian contacts and poses him in a state of complete subjective openness. The narrator, speaking through the mask of the third person, returns to fill in, to one extent or another, this missing network of implications. Since, as we have seen, these implications reach, along the communicative axis, to the horizon of the social or cosmic system within which the personage must be accorded place, the narrative framework thus serves epistemologically to control the ultimate horizon of meaning within which the character's discourse can be understood. Roland Barthes can thus say that in proportion to the degree that the third person position is established in the narrative, "existence becomes fate" (1970:36).

This process by which the narrative personage emerges replicates, at a secondary (symbolic) level, the trauma by which language was originally established in consciousness. The posing of the "he" beyond the constraints of speech imposed upon the real author by his place in a community is a performative act, the meaning of which stems from the effect of the act itself (Barthes, 1966:21). Just as the author is negated, the personage who exists in his absence is a pure empty form, devoid of referential content, and thus able to embody the subjective tensions produced in the actual author and his reader by the primary displacement which permits the operation of the sign in human consciousness. As Kristeva says, "He [the personage] appears as the refuge of subjectivity very near to zero" (1970:84).

It becomes clear then that the way in which this narrative framework is constructed in relation to the discourse of the characters is of decisive semantic importance for the entire narrative. The narrator, in the first instance, poses his characters by means of a third person pronoun, *he* or *she*, which have as their object reference only an instance of speech designated by the pronoun "I," i.e., the source of the direct discourse of the characters. Since the "I," as an instance of speech, is a word whose meaning arises fundamentally from the communicative axis of the sign, and the "he" depends entirely upon the referential axis of the sign for its meaning, the juxtaposition of the "he" and the "I" in the narrator's and character's discourse in the narrative places these two functions of the sign into tension with each other for dominance. On the basis of this analysis one might predict that these tensions might produce different types of narratives which would be dependent upon the way in which the author had chosen to deal with this tension.

No narrative in the Pentateuch is a more enlightening example of the significance of the relationship between the narrative framework and the direct discourse of the characters than the Joseph narrative. None of the preceding narratives in Genesis have the lengthy third person framework found in the Joseph story. If the narrator in the third person framework supplies the semantic world of his characters with its communicative axis, and thereby fills in those implicit meanings and forces which determine their words and actions, the question of the way in which the extensive narrative framework in the Joseph story relates to the world of discourse of the characters (i.e., the living world of the characters themselves internal to the narrative framework) becomes central for understanding the meaning of the narrative.

For the purposes of this article I would like to describe the types of relation between the narrative framework and the character's discourse by utilizing two categories of literary presentation developed by Stanley Fish. In his analytical reading, especially of seventeenth and eighteenth century poetic and narrative literature, Fish has discovered two kinds of literary presentation which he describes as "rhetorical" and "dialectical." The rhetorical presentation is closed, the end corresponding to the beginning, whereas the dialectical approach is open. This openness is achieved in a way that might be described as inartistic or even anti-artistic, i.e., by pointing "away from itself to something its forms cannot capture"

(1974:4). By pointing beyond itself, it becomes "a vehicle for its own abandonment" (1974:3), or a "self-consuming artifact." What is this transcendental goal? It is the transformation of the reader's mind itself so that it is "congruent with the Reality it would perceive" (1974:21). He terms this a dialectical process, and sees it put to the service of a number of different realities from pure reason, the idea of the good, the inner light, to faith. He calls this "anti-art-for-the-sake-of-art because it is concerned less with the making of better poems than with the making of better persons" (1974:4). Among the religious works in which he finds this dialectic at work are Milton's *Paradise Lost (Surprised by Sin)* and some of the works of Augustine, John Donne, and Bunyan (*Self-Consuming Artifacts*). While Fish is concerned with the effect of the literary work upon the reader, I will be pushing the investigation back one further stage to the origin of this tension between "rhetoric" and "dialectic" in the way in which the relation of the narrative framework (the closed "rhetorical" aspect of narrative in Fish's sense) to the discourse of the characters (the "dialectical" open aspect of narrative) is formed. I will be proposing a homology between what Fish means by a closed "rhetorical" presentation and the narrator's discourse, and between his transformative dialectical presentation and the discourse of the characters. The process of a narrative "consuming itself" will then take the form of the content of the closed perspective of the narrative framework being taken up into the direct discourse of the characters and subordinated to the ongoing dialogical process which prevents the narrative from achieving closure.

In the standard rhetorical narrative we must assume that the plot is constructed from the viewpoint of its ending which is known by the narrator from the outset. The characters themselves are defined, imbued with qualities and placed in a circumstantial situation not of their own making. This given world, provided by the narrator, thus provides the implicit meaning of their first utterances. The characters themselves may not be aware of much in this given world known by the narrator (and reader), or if aware, can do little to change it. The author, in the narrative framework, is making the reader aware of those emotions and forces which are behind the words and actions of the characters that constitute some sort of explanation which makes the characters understandable. Such "explanations," rooted in the given circumstances of a character's world, presuppose a system (psychological, social, mythic, etc.), the ultimacy of which will be reconfirmed by the success or failure of the character at the end through conformity to it, rebellion against it, or unconscious determination by it.

The dialectical narrative, on the other hand, is constructed so as to imbue the dialogical discourse of the characters with a dynamism stemming from the effects of the spoken language upon themselves and others. This verbal dynamism, usually produced by what J. L. Austin has called the illocutionary and perlocutionary effects of language, stands in tension with the closed semantic systems of the narrator's explanations of his characters which refer to non-verbal circumstances and forces that operate according to their own impersonal laws. When the discourse of the characters ascends to the point of perceiving the hidden forces operating in the circumstances of thier lives, and incorporates those forces into their discourse so as to subordinate them to the open dynamics of discourse, then, I will contend, the narrative has become dialectical. It is this process which I see occurring in the Joseph story, and which I will now attempt briefly to outline. I am aware of the many incongruities and irregularities in this story which have given rise to suspicions about its unity. I will not stop here to argue each of these points because none of these discrepancies have been so self-evident as to achieve unanimity among critical scholars. This study, stemming from a new perspective, needs to be carried through without presuming the conclusions of previous source-critical analysis, as a means of developing new evidence not shaped by previously held views.

The particular questions which will guide this investigation are: to what extent is the end of the narrative known? To what extent are the words and actions of the characters explained in the narrative framework in terms of circumstances, forces or emotional impulses which lead inevitably to a predictable end? Or, on the other hand, to what extent do the words and actions of the characters arise unpredictably from the mystery of their own being and produce the effects which form their contingent future? Another way of putting this might be: to what extent does the perspective of the narrator, who knows the end of the story, coincide with that of a character so as to permit the character to participate in the shaping of that future?

These questions open up a surprisingly varied landscape in the Joseph story. The answer to the first question regarding the end of the story depends, of course, upon what one regards as the end! Coats, in his study of the redaction history of this passage, argues that the actual literary end of the story in 50:22–26 "plays no integral role in a narrative but serves simply as a device to round off the Jacob-Joseph narration and bind it to a number of larger collections of tradition (Exod. 13:19; Jos. 24:32)" (1974:21). Since, however, it does constitute the end of the story as it now stands for the contemporary reader, it would be difficult to exclude it from this analysis.

In terms of this analysis the last three verses of this story constitute a most significant ending. They contain the transmission of the patriarchal promise of land from Joseph to his brothers (the first such transmission from one generation to the next by a human agent), and the extraction of an oath by Joseph from his brothers to carry his bones up from Egypt, presumably when this promise of land is fulfilled. Only the report by the narrator of Joseph's death, his age at death, and his burial follows. The transmission of a promise and the giving of an oath by the characters open a future which extends beyond the end of this narrative. Though Joseph's death and burial are reported, even this does not actually conclude the story of Joseph, since his bones will participate in the future of his people. The narrative thus, in every sense ends with uncertainty. Will this promise be fulfilled? Will Joseph's bones find their ultimate resting place in the land of the promise? These future-oriented words, spoken by a narrative personage, thus constitute the final horizon of meaning within which the preceding narrative should be understood.

If this is the end, then one must conclude that the preceding events have been ordered in such a way as to make this event possible, if not necessary. Is there an internal connection between this climactic event, the transmission of the promise by Joseph to his brothers, and the foregoing narrative? One of the most frequently recurring motifs throughout the narratives of Genesis has been intra-familial rivalry. The initial sin of mankind after banishment from paradise was Cain's murder of Abel. In the Abraham cycle, it is implied that the rivalry of his wives, Hagar and Sarah, extends to rivalry between their sons Ishmael and Isaac (Gen. 20:10). The proper transmission of the promise is threatened as long as Ishmael remains in Abraham's household, in Sarah's view, and Abraham expels Hagar and Ishmael (Gen. 26:1–5). Similarly in the Jacob cycle, the problem of rivalry between Jacob and his brother Esau was resolved before the promise was transmitted to Jacob. The problem of rivalry thus occupies an important position in the primeval history, and in both the Abraham and Jacob cycles. One might also conclude that it is never satisfactorily resolved. In each case one of the rivals is simply forced outside the pale of God's blessing.

In the Joseph narrative the problem of rival brothers is placed in center stage and explored in depth. One reason for this may be the unprecedented critical problem posed by sibling rivalry for the transmission of the promise which must take place here at the end of the patriarchal history. No longer can the promise be transmitted to the chosen son, and his rival brother pushed to the sidelines of sacred history. The promise must now be transmitted to the prototypical form of the nation, the "Sons of Israel." But to have to transmit it to the whole body of sons poses the problem of sibling rivalry as a central obstacle, since no rival can now be simply rejected.

An additional problem arises because the promise cannot be transmitted by God to a collective entity, as he had transmitted it to Abraham, Isaac, and Jacob in private visions. It might have been transmitted by the last patriarch to all of his sons, but that would not have dealt forthrightly with the complex problem of rivalry which the biblical writers had always acknowledged as having its roots in the parental habit of favoring one son above the other(s). Is Jacob then to be exempted from this pattern so evident in the tales of the previous patriarchial families? But if not the patriarch, then who? The brilliant solution to this problem, one which is both continuous with the previous narratives, and yet boldly new, is for Jacob to choose his favorite son for the transmission of the promise, thereby precipitating the problem of sibling rivalry. Then, in the course of the narrative, a solution is devised which will enable the favorite son, acting as a patriarchal-type figure, to transmit the promise successfully to his brothers. After this it would then be vested in the traditions of each tribe and family in the nation-to-be (Van der Merwe, 1966).

I would like to propose then that there is indeed a profound link between the concluding verses of the Joseph narrative and the events which precede it; and that in fact, it is the conclusion reached at the end of that narrative plot in 50:21 that makes possible the climactic event, the transmission of the promise, for the first time, from one brother to another. It will then be the task of the following analysis to show the beginning of the complex logic of this plot in chapter 37 which makes possible the transcending of brotherly rivalry.

The narrative framework which serves as the formal closure of the major unifying theme of the Joseph narrative is the concluding statement of the narrator in 50:21b: "Thus he comforted them and spoke of the concerns of their heart." This sentence corresponds in its narrative position, function, and thematic content to 45:15. Both represent generalizing summaries by the narrator at the conclusion of critical encounters between Joseph and his brothers in which Joseph, using the same general arguments, has persuaded his brothers to trust him. 50:21 indicates a restoration of the relation of intimate trust described by the narrator in 45:15: "And he kissed all his brothers, and he wept upon them, and afterward his brothers spoke with him." The significance of this concluding sentence stems from its reversal of the concluding sentence in the narrator's introduction in 37:1-4, where he reports that the brothers "could not speak *shalom* to him." These three sentences, positioned as they are at critical junctures in the narrative, reveal the narrator's unifying framework extending from the beginning to nearly the end of the narrative. Sentence A (37:4c) reveals the problem to be resolved; sentence B (45:15) indicates the resolution of that problem; sentence C (50:21b) reaffirms the state reached in sentence B due to a new threat arising from other sub-motifs in the plot. Sentence C then constitutes the necessary basis for the transmission of the promise by Joseph to his brothers in 50:24.

These three sentences from the narrator's framework reveal the form of the closure which is being imposed on the words and actions of the characters. Examination of this framework will reveal the underlying system in terms of which the characters are motivated.

The narrator can determine the course of events not only through the internal motivation of his characters, however. Other factors can impinge upon a character's world of discourse from outside so as to shape his action. Chance circumstances are one such type of external force at the disposal of the narrator which our narrator here uses liberally (famine, chance encounters with the Ishmaelite caravan, chance sale of Joseph to a highly placed governmental official). Another significant influential force in this story which stands midway between internal motivation and external chance is the dream. Beyond this is the totally external power of the divine to influence the course of events which always may relate to chance occurrences. Each of these which might, in itself, become a major explanatory system, is finally subordinated to and made to serve the dynamics of the communications theme. We will now see the way in which the plot unfolds through the interplay of tension between the narrative frame and the discourse of the characters in chapter 37. The remaining episodes must be made the subject of a later analysis.

The most complete and powerful explanatory system offered by the narrative framework is found in 37:1-4. In these few verses (but *many* for the reticent biblical narrator) a system of forces and influences is outlined which defines the characters and explains the forces at work in the interpersonal, familial relations. The seventeen-year-old Joseph is out watching sheep with his half-brothers but brings to his father reports of their undescribed evil behavior. The reason for this 'tattling' by a seventeen-year old (which must be presumed to be unusual) is indirectly accounted for by reference to two factors. Joseph was not born of the same mother as the brothers he was betraying, and he was loved by his father more than the other sons, though the connection between these two factors is not made in this narrative for the reader (i.e., that Jacob favored Joseph's strangely unnamed mother more than his other wives). Joseph's actions are thus explained by reference to his father's attitudes. But lest the father's attitude appear arbitrary and ungrounded, it is then explained that Joseph was the בן־זקנים "son of his old age" (This explanation is apparently preferred by the writer to the son-of-the-favorite-wife explanation—thus the omission of the name of Joseph's mother). This accounts for Jacob's preferential treatment and thus makes his actions, as well as those of Joseph, understandable in light of the system of circumstances and consequent emotional forces operating in the family.

No mention has yet been made of the brother's responses to this state of affairs. Perhaps the brothers do not know, for a fact, that Joseph is bringing these "evil reports." The father, however, next makes his preferential feelings for Joseph public by bestowing upon him an unusual robe with sleeves (or stripes, depending upon the translation of פסים).

Then the narrator reports, "his brothers *saw* that it was he that their father loved above all his brothers." With this objectification of the father's partiality, the narrator then reports that "they hated him, and were not able to speak *shalom* to him."

The narrator has thus outlined a system of emotional forces in the family, over which no one has control, and its consequences. Jacob is hopelessly attached to this son of his old age, and this inevitably intrudes into Joseph's relations with his brothers. When this state of affairs is flaunted openly before the face of the brothers, their response of hatred is also to be expected. This system of emotions then constitutes the motivating force behind most of the actions which follow in chapter 37, leading to the near murder and expulsion of Joseph by his brothers.

Before the brothers are permitted to give expression to their hatred, the narrator introduces another influential system of forces. Joseph unexpectedly becomes the recipient of two dreams which, in thinly veiled symbolism, portray him as ruling over his brothers, and even his parents. This dream is obviously related to the emotional situation outlined in verses 1–4, but, as a dream, cannot be too simply equated with Joseph's own subjective feelings. One does not willfully dream, as he would willfully tattle on his brothers. The dream is conventionally considered to contain fateful knowledge of the future, not merely individual subjective fantasy. As a narrative device, the dream is a medium that permits knowledge which is normally possessed only by the narrator to enter in symbolic form into the consciousness of a character, i.e., knowledge of the end of the story. The dream can thus become the vehicle of another explanatory system depending upon the way in which the characters relate to it. It could be used as the narrator's means of articulating an ideology of fate by suggesting to the characters that their lives are determined in advance by transcendent forces beyond their comprehension.

Here, however, in anticipation of an even bolder dialogizing of cosmic determinism, the dreams are not attributed to God as their source, but exert influence on events as they become speech acts. It is the response to the *report* of the dreams which shapes the course of events and leads eventually to their fulfillment. This perspective the narrator makes clear in his introductory statement to the dream reports: "And Joseph dreamed a dream, and *when he told it* to his brothers, they increased all the more, their hatred of him" (37:5). And after the first report the narrator says, "And they again increased their hatred of him because of his dreams and *because of his words*" (37:8). The reporting of the dream to his father precipitates even *his* "rebuke" as characterized by the narrator (37:10). The dream thus is presented by the narrator not as a mysterious cosmic force, but as a speech event which has profound effects upon the network of personal relations in the family. When now this thinly disguised arrogance of Joseph expressed in his words is added to the public symbolism of the robe, the brother's hatred escalates to a new level of intensity. But even more significantly, the narrator now portrays even Jacob as angry with Joseph over these words. If the dream had been disclosed only in the narrative framework, and not in the direct discourse of a character, its significance in the plot would be entirely different.

The narrator's concluding comment to this scene is significant: "And his brothers envied him, and his father noted the saying (הדבר)." This reference to Jacob's reflective inner response to the dream report is a sign of its future significance in the plot. It is not to be merely a negative stimulus to the envy of the brothers. It also positively foreshadows future events. It thus appears ambiguous at this point with regard to its influence upon the course of events.

As a totally unmotivated intrusion into the consciousness of a character with what is taken to be information about the future, it is either a deception which presupposes a critical stance by the narrator toward dreams, or it is a symbolic presentation of knowledge of the future course of events usually held only by the narrator.

The evidence here points more to an ironic than critical standpoint on the part of the narrator. The irony in the narrator's use of these dreams stems from their two levels of meaning. On the one hand, they serve as genuine revelations of the future; but on the other, they mirror Joseph's consciousness of infinite superiority. The brothers, not seeing the larger purpose which will be served by Joseph's ascension to power over them, interpret the dream altogether in terms of the latter, i.e., the emotional system of sibling rivalry in the family. Previously the familial emotional system has been expressed only indirectly through acts of betrayal (Joseph), symbolic gestures (Jacob), and strained communication (the brothers). Now, however, the narrator incites the direct expression of those buried emotions by allowing the material end toward which this system is leading to be disclosed at the outset. He then uses the benighted reaction of the brothers to this disclosure to set in motion the plot mechanism which will lead to its realization. The supreme irony of this strategy is that by inciting the brothers to take action against the "dreamer" and his dreams, the familial system of jealous hatred is made to serve the very end of Joseph's ascendency which it seeks to defeat.

It would seem, however, that such incitement would be precisely the wrong thing to do, since such knowledge in the hands of the opponents of the dream's protagonist would enable them to thwart the plan. This was, in fact, the completely reasonable thinking of the brothers (37:20). But by posing, in the discourse of the narrative, two closed systems in opposition to each other—the system of Joseph's ascent to power represented by the dream vs. the system of intra-familial hatred (which logically leads to the death of Joseph)—the narrator enables the logic of the plot to develop in the dialogue of the characters, and thus causes their emotions to be disciplined by that dialogue. First, the brothers sarcastically question him about the meaning of his dream. Then Jacob, when faced with an open statement that not too indirectly articulates the implications of his treatment of Joseph, also cannot accept it, and rebukes him before his brothers. The entrance of his dream report into the discourse of the family thus has the effect of pushing the latent problem into an open crisis. Not only does the hatred of his brothers increase; Joseph now has strained relations with his father as well. Without the support and approval of Jacob, Joseph is made totally vulnerable, suspended now between his father's rebuke and his brother's hatred.

The narrator then portrays life as continuing on in what is presumably its normal pattern, with the brothers going out to pasture their flock and Jacob sending Joseph along later to bring him another report on the brothers (v. 14). Now, however, the context has changed, and an ominous air pervades this event. The reader might wonder why Jacob was sending Joseph again to perform an action which could only result in the further inflamation of his brother's hatred. Coming, as it does, after Jacob's rebuke, further questions are suggested about Jacob's own motivation.

These suspicions which the reader might have are confirmed by the interjection of the mysterious vignette in 37:15–17, where it is reported that, "A man found him, and behold, he was wandering in the field, and the man asked him saying, 'What are you seeking?'" Here the narrator gives us a portrayal of Joseph behaving strangely. Why did *Joseph* not seek the man to ask him about his brothers? Why did he not return home to report that he couldn't find his brothers? Rather, Joseph is suspended between the two worlds of his father and his brothers, not wishing to seek his brothers and not willing to return home. He was thus "found wandering in the field."

The narrator reports in some detail the arrival of Joseph at his brothers's camp (37:18). Because they see him coming at some distance they are able to conspire against him. Coupled with the brother's physical separation from Jacob, this device of the porolonged arrival of Joseph provides a situation where the brother's feelings about Joseph can now find expression. That they *could* see him "from afar" (מרחק) is doubtless meant to allude to the unusual robe he was wearing which would make recognition possible at a great distance. Insulated by distance now from both Joseph and Jacob, the brothers, inflamed by at least the memory of the robe and the dreams, announce Joseph's coming with pointed sarcasm: "Behold, the dream lord has come."

This sarcastic reference to his dream identity and the plans which follow are spoken by the collective voice of all of the brothers. In this way no single brother is transformed into a villain by taking the responsibility for initiating the action. This is the collective "they" which articulates the feelings which have until now been only latent.

It is significant that it is in the form of sarcasm that this first open articulation of their feelings occurs. Their first response to his dream was in the form of shocked, doubting, rhetorical questions. They were overtly dubious as to whether Joseph would come to rule over them. Now, by using sarcasm, they admit into their speech the positive content of the dreams as they refer to him as a "dream lord." They further declare their future expectations: "We will see what will become of his dreams." The sarcasm of these statements arises from their proximity to the plan to kill him (and to "cover up" their deed), which they assume will be the end of both the dreamer and his dreams. But it is precisely their plan to kill him and cover up their crime that will set in motion the events leading to the fulfillment of the dreams. Already in these words the dream is a force working both to incite and to gather up into itself the emotions of the family system which it will transform.

With this statement of the brothers, the system of the family emotions and that of the dream are brought, through sarcasm, into discourse. This opens the possibility then for other words to be uttered about the matter at hand, and thus for a conscious dialectical process to begin to move the plot forward. Just as Joseph's dream, by articulating the implications of Jacob's bias toward him, evokes even from Jacob a negative reply, so now the expression of the ultimate logical consequences of the deep-seated feelings of the brothers evokes an objection from one of the brothers (the eldest, Reuben), thereby breaking up the unified collective voice. As the eldest (and the writer must assume that the reader is aware of this), he would be the single one upon whom the responsibility for this deed might fall. As the natural heir, he is also the one whose motivations would be the most suspect since his own position in the family would be the most directly threatened by Joseph's ascendency. There are thus, within the family system, forces at work which would predictably break down the solidarity of the brothers behind the proposal to murder their hated younger brother. These forces (assumed by the narrator) thus produce Reuben's objection in principle to taking the life of Joseph (v. 21), followed by a more qualified and acceptable (to the brothers) suggestion that they "shed no blood," but merely cast him into an open pit, the unspoken assumption being that he would be left there to die (37:22). But the narrator then adds that the secret intention of Reuben was to return later and free him so that he could return to Jacob, revealing a significant tension at the level of unspoken assumptions.

This short exchange thus lifts up two contrary possibilities for the brothers: instant and certain death to Joseph with the burden of blood guilt vs. slow death to Joseph and no blood guilt, with the possibility that he might escape (or be delivered).

The opposition of Reuben thus creates a dilemma for the brothers, since if they kill Joseph without Reuben's support, he might well divulge it to their father. On the other hand, if Joseph survives to return another "bad report" of what has happened to their father, this is equally unacceptable. A decision must be made now because something must be done with him. Reuben did not raise his objection until the initial attack against Joseph had occurred. These options thus arose only *after* he was *in* the pit.

Faced with this dilemma, the narrator, amusingly, has them sit down to eat, presumably to think it through. Reuben's plan is, surprisingly, as much a dilemma for the narrator as for the brothers, since Joseph cannot be permitted to return to Jacob after a successful rescue by Reuben. This would not only abort the planned rise of Joseph to power in Egypt, but create an impossible dilemma for Jacob. What would he do with a report of what the brothers have already said and done to Joseph? Those who have seen the second proposal by Judah as an unnecessary repetition of the good-brother role have, in my opinion, not given careful enough attention to the underlying logic of this passage.

To resolve this dilemma, a compromise proposal is needed which will have the advantage of permanently ridding the family of this young, arrogant, spoiled brother, while not requiring his death. Since the materials for such a compromise are not obviously at hand, the narrator, utilizing his powers as a *deus ex machina*, brings a caravan of Ishmaelites on stage in the course of their journey into Egypt. Judah, then, seeing the opportunity this caravan presents, offers his proposal to sell Joseph into slavery and avoid responsibility for his death, "for," he adds with more than a hint of cynicism, "he is our brother, our flesh" (37:27). There was also a new factor which had not been a part of the brother's thinking up until this point, i.e., silver. Not only would the sale of Joseph rid them of him bloodlessly, but would actually produce a "profit" (בצע). Joseph in their midst would be replaced by silver in their coffers, an appealing prospect indeed! Thanks to the timely appearance of the Ishmaelites, a third possibility has thus arisen that has the virtues of both the previous proposals while lacking their respective disadvantages. Within the possibilities presented by these circumstances, a dialogical process has developed which carries the brothers away from the ultimately self-destructive system of rivalry toward an open unknown end.

The so-called "theft" of Joseph by another set of Midianite traders, possibly implied by 37:28a, would constitute a bizarre and illogical element in the progress of the narrative. In addition, if it were the Midianites who sold Joseph to the Ishmaelites, then this would break the connection between the motif of silver here and later, where it plays a major role in the drama of the reunion of Joseph and his brothers in Egypt. It is more reasonable to identify the Midianites with the Ishmaelites (Judg 8:24; Gunkel, 1964:409). In other instances the writer presupposes some knowledge on the part of his readers about such details, e.g., that Reuben is the eldest son, that Jacob and Israel are the same person, that Yahweh and Elohim are the same God).

The narrator then depicts for us the return of Reuben to the now empty pit. His response is both in action and in word. He rends his garment as a symbolic expression of his grief over the disappearance and presumed death of Joseph, and he complains to his brothers, "The lad is gone; and I, where shall I go?" This is a poignant moment giving rise to many questions and uncertainties. If indeed Reuben's action and plan confronted the brothers with a near-insoluble dilemma, it is dramatically reasonable for him to be absent from the brother's contemplation of that dilemma in 37:25. By his action Reuben separated himself from the collective voice of his peers, and thus lost his place in their continued conspiracy against Joseph. One solution for them would have obviously been to kill Reuben as well as Joseph, thereby eliminating the possibility of Reuben reporting their crime. With such possibilities in the air, Reuben had no place in the discussion. It is thus not necessary to assume, as does Rudolph, that Reuben was present for the conspiracy, and was shocked in verse 29 because of the unplanned theft of Joseph by the Midianites, rather than because of the execution of the brothers' own plot (1933:154). Nor is it necessary to assume that his absence from the plot discussion is an indication of a fissure in the redaction of independent sources. He reacts directly to the shocking discovery that he has returned too late, that the brothers have acted first. Reuben's complaint, "Where shall I go?" expresses the impossibility of his own position as an elder brother unable now to account for a younger brother. He is aware already of the forthcoming emotional encounter with Jacob, something which has not figured in the other brothers' detached calculations for their cover-up. His words thus point forward to the traumatic encounter of all the brothers with Jacob.

The question he raises also indicates his own surrender to the brother's treachery. Reuben is caught between his responsibility to his father and his solidarity with his brothers. The brutal murder of Joseph before his face might well have turned Reuben against his brothers, but the disappearance of Joseph from the pit, though suggesting his death (see 42:22), provides no concrete evidence of it. Lacking the evidence, Reuben thus is reduced to silence as he apparently watches the fabrication of the false evidence, and as the evidence is presented to Jacob (vv. 31, 32). Rather than accuse his brothers, he simply wishes to disappear. His voice now fades back into the collective as they say, "This, we have found. Examine it now to see whether it is the robe of your son or not." Reuben's role is not totally pathetic and ironic as Redford has said, however, since Reuben's proposal, though unsuccessful, initiated and set the terms for the brothers' discourse about Joseph's life and death

(1970:74). This discourse led to Judah's plan, which at least preserved Joseph's life and left the future open for the realization of the dream.

The final scene centers on the intense emotional reaction of Jacob to the reception of the robe. The brothers carefully do not lie in words. They present deceptive evidence, the bloodied robe, and let Jacob draw his own conclusion, a conclusion which was nearly inevitable because of the unusual singular nature of the robe. Note that the evidence they bring pertains not to "our brother," but to "your son." Jacob himself then describes what apparently happened almost exactly in the words of the brothers in the original conspiracy (37:20). The narrator then describes his physical reaction to the death of his son and the futile attempts of the sons and daughters to comfort him. He speaks of what may be the imminence of his own death: "I shall go down to Sheol to my son, mourning." No plan had been made to deal with the deep grief of Jacob over the presumed death of Joseph. But no one of the brothers is so moved by pity as to tell Jacob the truth that Joseph is not dead. They obviously consider him to be dead so far as their family life is concerned. But this knowledge which they have that cannot be shared with Jacob becomes a barrier in their communication that must be overcome. How could Jacob transmit his blessing and promise to his sons under these circumstances?

To return now to the question of the significance of contextual factors in the analysis of narrative, we have seen that the narrator of the Joseph story has given this story two possible contextual frameworks or systems which could determine the words and actions of the characters, i.e., the emotional system of brotherly rivalry/parental favoritism, and the system of future-prognosticating, dream images. He has posed them in such a way that the logic of each runs counter to the other, one leading to the death of Joseph, and the other to his ascendance to ultimate power over all his opponents. By couching the glorious end as a dream and allowing it to be introduced first in the direct discourse of the characters, he uses the dream to evoke into language the emotional system of rivalry. When articulated, it comes under the constraints of discourse, which deflects the course of its trajectory from its logical end toward an open, though certainly not promising, future.

This orientation of the narrator toward the direct discourse of the characters as the final determining process of the narrative is made explicit in the concluding statements by the narrator of the introductory and two concluding scenes (37:4; 43:15; 50:21) where the central tension of the plot is defined in terms of broken communication between brothers, and its resolution depicted as the restoration of communication. The means by which he narrator achieves this end thus also must be direct discourse (though not without utilization of the prerogatives of a *deus ex machina* at times).

As the systems of necessity are brought into the discourse of the narrative, they are "consumed," i.e., they cease to operate according to their own closed internal logic, and are subordinated to the open logic of spoken discourse. As at the conclusion of chapter 37, the system of family emotions has been "consumed," i.e., deprived of its logical end and rendered open. The mystical logic of the dream has been partially dismantled in that the force moving the plot toward its envisioned end is no longer hidden, occult, mysterious, but largely dialogical. A mystical element remains operative, however, namely in the *deus ex machina* events of the plot. This feature becomes more dominant in the early Egyptian experiences of Joseph depicted in chapters 39-40. The incorporation of the mystical dimension of the plot does not occur until the climax of the reunion scene in chapter 45. This complex sequence in chapters 41-45 cannot be analyzed now in detail, but only a suggestion given of the conclusion to which an analysis would lead.

After the final disclosure by Joseph to his brothers of his identity, there is no instant restoration of brotherly intimacy and communication. The narrator depicts the brothers as too shocked, guilt-ridden, and fearful to be able even to speak again to Joseph (45:3) in spite of his warm entreaties. In order to overcome these emotions, Joseph tells them, "Now do not be grieved or angry with yourselves because you sold me here, for God sent me before you to preserve life" (45:5, similarly repeated in 45:8 and again in 50:20). Though the dream was not attributed to God, here the uncanny circumstances which resulted in Joseph's descent into Egypt and his rise to power are now revealed to be a divine plan. The dream system is thus incorporated into a larger deterministic, mystical perspective which virtually negates the meaning of the conscious intentions of the brothers. They are being confronted with the knowledge that they have been victims of what John Milton called a "good temptation" wherein a temptation to sin that overcomes the will of the righteous may have a positive role to play in the divine plan:

> A good temptation is that whereby God tempts even the righteous for the purpose of proving them, not as though he were ignorant of the disposition of their hearts, but for the purpose . . . of lessening their self-confidence, and reproving their weakness, that . . . they themselves may become wise by experience. (Fish, 1971:40)

But this story goes beyond Milton's providential view of the divine will, since this view is being presented to the brothers in direct discourse as a means of persuasion. It is not being offered in the narrative framework as a final "explanation" for the curious turns in the plot, but rather is a part of a plot that is not yet concluded. The end of the plot, so far as the narrator is concerned, is the restoration of communication between the brothers, a matter which is uncertain, and not at all pre-determined by God. It is the utterance by Joseph of this statement which releases the power to bring about this end. Thus even the most encompassing explanation is subordinated to (and thus "consumed" by) the open dialogical process.

It might then be argued that the dialogical perspective itself, characteristic of the writer, which reaches its climax in 50:20, is finally an ideological system which imposes its own closure upon the narrative plot. This is true if one does not take into account the transmission of the promise in 50:24. The brothers have transcended their rivalry sufficiently to trust one another, and to receive the promise now from their formerly hated rival. But what will be the future of this promise, and of these quarrelsome brothers? The final utterances which have been made possible by the restoration of trust and dialogue between Joseph and his brothers thus open a future which is certain only to the eyes of faith. Every system utilized by the narrator to explain the actions of his characters, including the drive toward the restoration of broken communication between Joseph and his brothers, is thus finally subordinated to the uttered promise and its open future.

WORKS CONSULTED

Barthes, Roland
    1966   "Introduction à l'analyse structural des récits." *Communications* 8:1–27.
    1970   *Writing Degree Zero and Elements of Semiology*. Trans. A. Lavers and C. Smith. Boston: Beacon Press.

Coats, George, W.
    1974   "Redactional Unity in Genesis 37–50." *Journal of Biblical Literature* 93: 15–21.
    1976   *From Canaan to Egypt: Structural and Theological Context for the Joseph Story*. Washington, D.C.: The Catholic Biblical Association of America.

Cosieru, Eugenio
    1974   *Synchronie, Dichronie und Geschichte*. München: Wilhelm Fink Verlag.

Ducrot, Oswald
    1972   *Dire et ne pas dire*. Paris: Hermann.
    1974   *La Preuve et le Dire*. Paris: Mâme.
    1978   "Structuralisme, énonciation et sémantique." *Poétique* 33: 107–25.
    1980   *Les Mots de discourse*. Paris: Les Editions de Minuit.

Fish, Stanley E.
1967   *Surprised by Sin. The Reader in Paradise Lost*. Berkeley: Univ. of California.
1974   *Self-Consuming Artifacts: The Experiences of Seventeenth-Century Literature*. Berkeley: University of California.

Flahault, Francois
1978   *La parole intermédiare*. Paris: Éditions du Seuil.

Gunkel, Hermann
1964   *Genesis*. 6th ed. Göttingen: Vandenhoeck & Reprecht.

Kristeva, Julia
1970   *Le Texte du roman*. Paris, La Haye: Mouton.

Merwe, B. J. van der
1966   "Joseph as Successor of Jacob." Pp. 221–31 in *Studia Biblica et Semitica*, Th. C. Vriezen Festschrift. Wageningen: H. Veenmen Zonen.

Redford, Donald B.
1970   *A Study of the Biblical Story of Joseph Genesis 37–50*. Leiden: E. J. Brill.

Rudolph, Wilhelm
1933   "Die Josephgeschichte." Pp. 142–83 in Paul Volz and Wilhelm Rudolph, *Der Elohist als Erzähler, Ein Irrweg der Pentateuchkritik*. Giessen: Alfred Topelmann.

Saussure, Ferdinand de
1966   *Course in General Linguistics*. New York: McGraw-Hill.

Seebass, Horst
1978   *Geschichtliche Zeit und Theonome Tradition in der Joseph-Erzählung*. Gütersloher Verlagshaus Gerd Mohn.

Text and Reality: Aspects of Reference in Biblical Texts
Bernard C. Lategan, Willem S. Vorster

The authors explore some of the possibilities opened up by recent developments in literary theory for the interpretation of biblical texts. The discussion touches on the following aspects: text and history, the role of redescription in the transmission of texts, reader-response (the reception of texts), the problem of reference in biblical texts, and the relation between text and reality. Theoretical concepts are constantly illustrated with examples drawn from biblical material.

Code: 06 06 14   Cloth $14.95 (9.95); paper $9.95 (6.75)*

The Limits of Story
George Aichele, Jr.

Informed by both structuralism and post-structuralism, this study is a critical exploration of the logical and metaphysical limits of narrative and of the theological implications of those limits. The six chapters approach the question of limits from different but interrelated angles and draw from literary and philosophical sources as diverse as Borges, Kafka, Crossan, and Derrida.

Code: 06 06 13   Cloth $15.75 (10.50); paper $10.50 (6.95)

The Workings of Old Testament Narrative
Peter D. Miscall

Maintaining that Old Testament narrative is complex and elusive because of, not in spite of, the concrete details, Miscall engages in a close reading of selected passages from Genesis on Abraham and from 1 Samuel on David to show how OT texts defy definitive interpretation. Miscall's reading of these passages illustrates what it means to follow the text, to trace its workings, even if it should lead to "undecidability" and indeterminateness.

Code: 06 06 12   Paper $8.95 (5.95)

*( ) denotes price available to members of sponsoring societies and subscribers to Scholars Press journals. Write for information. Prepayment (check, M/C or Visa) required. GA residents add 4% sales tax. Postage/handling: first item $1.00, $.50 for each thereafter; $4.00 maximum. Outside US $2.00 surcharge.

℘ SCHOLARS PRESS CUSTOMER SERVICES
P.O. Box 4869, Hampden Station, Baltimore, MD 21211

DOUBLE AND TRIPLE STORIES, THE IMPLIED READER, AND REDUNDANCY IN MATTHEW

Janice Capel Anderson

ABSTRACT

This article shows how double and triple stories chart the role of the implied reader of Matthew. These stories are episodes which are essentially repeated two or three times. They involve substantial verbal repetition. The repetition, arrangement, and location of the stories shapes, in part, the reading process. Double and triple stories play an integral role in the development of plot and character in the gospel. The repetition of an episode has a powerful rhetorical effect in which anticipation, retrospection, and repetition with variation are involved. The context in which the stories are found also contributes to their effect upon the implied reader. The final section of the article introduces the concept of redundancy used by information theorists. It suggests that redundancy may help to explain the reading process described in more ordinary terms in the first part of the article.

Introduction

Plunging into the realm of reader-response criticism is like plunging into a thicket of terminology and critical categories. One is apt to stumble around in the underbrush, emerging tired and scratched, but with the reward of a bucket full of huckleberries. Unfortunately, when you try to describe the location of this huckleberry patch to friends, they find your directions incomprehensible. Recognizing that reality, this article contains a limited number of critical terms, most of which are already familiar to readers of *Semeia*. These include implied author, implied reader, narrator, and narratee. With the exception of the implied reader, the definitions offered by Seymour Chatman in *Story and Discourse* are assumed. For the implied reader, Wolfgang Iser's definition which includes *both* the textual structure to be realized and the structured act of realization is preferred (1974, 1978). Or to put it more simply, the implied reader is made up of the set of directions formed by the text and the stance that an actual reader takes as he or she creatively reads. In the final section of the article, one new term will be introduced: redundancy. The concept will be explained as clearly as possible. It is used because it helps to explain the reading process described in more ordinary terms in the first part of the article.

All of the elements of the Matthean narrative—character, plot, setting, etc.—help to chart the role of its implied reader. Some elements are fairly transparent means by which the implied author molds the implied reader's response. Direct or explicit commentary (Booth, Chatman) from the gospel's reliable narrator to its narratee is the most obvious element used. Examples of direct commentary include (a) the Heading (1:1), (b) the Genealogy (1:2–7), (c) Fulfillment Quotations (1:22–23, 2:15, 17–18, 23; 4:15–16, 8:17, 12:17–21; 13:35; 21:4–5; 27:9–10 and 3:3 without formula introduction), (d) Explanatory glosses (translation, 1:23; 27:33, 46; cultural, 22:33; 27:15–16; etiological, 27:8; 28:15b; parenthetical, 7:29; 10:2f; and 12:8), (e) Wink to the Reader (24:15) and (f) Labels such as "the one called Peter" or "the betraying one." Since the implied author and reliable narrator and implied reader and narratee are so closely aligned in Matthew, the narrator's addresses to the narratee are in effect, if not in fact, addresses from the implied author to the implied reader.

Other means of shaping the implied reader's response are more subtle, but just as important. The use of double and triple stories is one such means. This article will explore how the repetition, arrangment, and location of these stories powerfully shape the reading process.

Double and Triple Stories

Double and triple stories are stories which are essentially repeated two or three times. They involve substantial verbal repetition. Some are almost carbon copies. Others are repeated with greater variation. Some episodes are reduplicated and then expanded. The placement and arrangement of these stories are crucial to the development of both plot and character in Matthew. The implied reader's response is guided by the arrangement. The first occurence anticipates the second (and third) and the latter recalls the former. The implied reader reads each episode in the light of the other, in prospect and retrospect. The similarities between the episodes are important in their own right. They engage the implied reader's memory and at times emphasize an aspect of characterization or an element of the plot, etc. However, the similarities are also important because they cause variations between episodes to stand out in relief. The implied reader must account for the variations. The response of the implied reader to double stories is also affected by what has transpired between episodes and the contexts in which they are found. Further, the overall arrangement of these episodes will shape his or her reading. The order in which the events appear is important.

On the level of plot and characterization it will be suggested below that one of the most important effects of Matthew's double and triple stories is that the implied reader compares and contrasts the various character groups as the plot moves forward. The major character groups: the disciples, the crowds, the Gentiles, the supplicants, and the Jewish leaders, serve as foils for one another./1/ Their attitudes toward Jesus and Jesus' attitudes toward them (as the reliable protagonist closely aligned with the narrator in important ways) provide the implied reader with crucial information for creating a reading of the gospel.

Expanded Doublets

Two examples of expanded doublets are the stilling of the storm incidents in 8:23-27 and 14:22-33 (seventeen words in common) and the healings of demoniacs in 9:32-34 and 12:22-?7 (twenty-two words in common). The first stilling of a storm follows several teachings on the difficulty of discipleship and precedes the exorcism of the Gadarene demoniacs. It is a miracle, but as Bornkamm has put it, the focus is on discipleship (54ff.). On a boat journey, the disciples frightened by wind and wave, wake Jesus saying, "Lord, save, we are perishing." Jesus responds: "Why are you fearful little faiths?" Afterwards the men marvel, "What sort of man is this that even the winds and sea obey him?" They call Jesus "Lord," a title used only by persons who have faith in Jesus. yet they do not have enough faith to trust that they will be safe. Jesus, therefore, calls them "little-faiths," an epithet he uses to label them in 6:30 and 16:8 as well as here and in the other stilling of the storm story. he also uses the closely related "of little-faith" in 17:20. The second incident occurs later in the gospel after the watershed of 13:35 when Jesus begins to devote more time to preparing the disciples for their future role. It follows the feeding of the Five Thousand paralleling that story's emphasis on the faith *and* weakness of the disciples. Again the disciples are at sea, but this time their fright is caused by the appearance of Jesus walking on the water. Peter, exhibiting faith, walks on the water toward Jesus. However, his gaze falters, he fears the wind, and begins to sink. Just as the group cried out in the first incident now Peter cries out, "Lord, save me." Jesus again responds, although in the singular, "Little faith, why did you doubt?" This time, however, the ones in the boat *worship* Jesus and make one of the three human confessions of Jesus as Son of God in the gospel./2/ Verbal repetition links the two stories. When the implied reader reads the second story, he or she recalls the first and compares the two. The similarities and differences are highlighted. The fear and doubt of the disciples have not disappeared. They are still little-faiths.

Nonetheless, as the plot moves forward they have made some progress. Peter exhibits a great deal of faith, before he falters. All have grown in their understanding of Jesus' identity. The disciples confess Jesus as Son of God in the second episode. The response of the men in the first was to wonder what sort of man Jesus might be. The first episode occurs before the watershed of chapter 13 where Jesus contrasts those who see and hear, blessing the disciples, with those outside who do not. The second with its focus on Peter and the disciples' closing confession appropriately follows chapter 13 where Jesus begins to focus more upon the disciples. The variations in the second story help to build toward Peter's confession and rebuke in chapter 16.

The second example of an expanded doublet is the exorcism of demoniacs in 9:32–34 and 12:22–37 (twenty-two words in common). These episodes develop Jesus' conflict with the Pharisees and the struggle for the hearts of the crowd. In 9:32–34 Jesus exorcises a dumb demoniac. The crowd marvels, "Never was anything like this seen in Israel." But the Pharisees respond, "He casts out demons by the ruler of demons." This is the first time that the Pharisees openly oppose Jesus. With this open opposition a section of miracles and questions concerning Jesus' identity and activities is brought to a close. It also foreshadows events to come. It plants in the implied reader's mind seeds of a conflict which will come to flower later in the gospel. Lest the reader forget, he or she is reminded of the conflict a few verses later. In 10:25 Jesus warns the disciples that opponents who identify him as "Beezeboul" will malign them as well. This also anticipates the second member of the doublet when the Jewish leaders again will charge Jesus with exorcising by the power of the ruler of demons. There they add the name Beezeboul. The interpretation of 10:25 as retrospective as well as prospective assumes that the implied reader knows that Beezeboul is the ruler of demons./3/ If the reader does not, the meaning of the term becomes a puzzle which will only be solved when the second story is read. It would then be an anticipation whose meaning only becomes clear in retrospect. This would draw even more attention to the stories and to 10:25. It would also highlight the controversy with the Jewish leaders over exorcism. The controversy comes to a head in chapter 12. There, after two incidents of Sabbath breaking, the implied reader learnes that the Pharisees have now had it with Jesus. They are plotting to destroy him (12:14). Jesus withdraws. The narrator indicates that his withdrawal fulfills Isaiah 42:1–4. This prophecy of the chosen servant echoes God's words in the baptism and foreshadows God's words in the transfiguration. The Pharisees plot against God's own son. The prophecy also offers hope to the Gentiles who, unlike the Pharisees, accept the servant.

The stage is set for a replay of the demoniac incident with several significant variations. Jesus' healing in 12:22ff. is even more miraculous. This demoniac is blind as well as dumb. The crowd is not only amazed, but wonders if Jesus is the Son of David. They have grown in their openness and are willing to entertain the possibility./4/ This accords well with the fact that crowds follow Jesus, drawn by his healing and authority. The Pharisees, however, persist in their misunderstanding and opposition. Uniting the phraseology of 9:34 and 10:25 they claim, "It is only by Beezeboul, ruler of demons that this man casts out demons." This time, instead of withdrawing, Jesus explodes in condemnation. The Pharisees have recognized neither the power of the Holy Spirit nor the dawn of the kingdom of God. They are enemies who will not be forgiven (12:30-32). Jesus castigates them in words which echo John's charges in 3:7ff. and his own warnings against false prophets in 7:15-20. The Pharisees are a brood of vipers, bad trees yielding evil fruit. Similar invective will reappear in chapters 15 and 23. The demoniac may have been physically blind, but the Pharisees are spiritually blind (15:14, 23:16-22, 26). The opposition of the Jewish leaders is emphasized by the repeated story. This brood of vipers blasphemed against the Holy Spirit, not once but twice, claiming twice that Jesus' power to exorcise came from the ruler of demons. The implied reader sees Jesus' lengthy condemnation after the second story as warranted. The implied reader will also compare the similarities between the Jewish leaders' responses in both stories and the difference in the two responses of the crowds. The Jewish leaders persist in their opposition—indeed there are other indications between the first and second episodes (such as 12:14) that their opposition has grown. The crowd's openness has increased even though their sight is not clear as indicated by Jesus in chapter 11 (see 11:7-24).

Nearly Identical Double Stories and a Triad

Turning to more nearly identical doublets, similar contributions to the development of plot and character can be observed. A careful arrangement of these stories is also apparent. This arrangement allows the characters to be seen even more clearly as foils for one another, and moves the plot along.

If one simply lists the rest of the gospel doublets as they appear in the narrative, a chiastic pattern emerges. The pattern can be expanded by the inclusion of one further episode, the Canaanite woman (15:22-28):

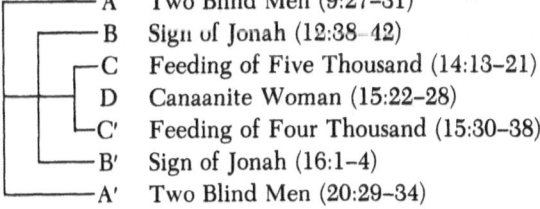

A   Two Blind Men (9:27-31)
B   Sign of Jonah (12:38-42)
C   Feeding of Five Thousand (14:13-21)
D   Canaanite Woman (15:22-28)
C'   Feeding of Four Thousand (15:30-38)
B'   Sign of Jonah (16:1-4)
A'   Two Blind Men (20:29-34)

The Canaanite woman episode follows the same pattern as the blind men doublets: cry for help, (attempt to silence), renewed request—questioning by Jesus, healing on the basis of faith. It also contains the same request for help:

> cried out saying: "Have mercy on me Lord, Son of David (15:22)."
> cried out saying: "Lord, have mercy on us, Son of David (15:22)."
> cried out and saying: "Have mercy on us, Son of David (9:27)."
> "Yes, Lord (9:28)."

Thus, the three healings form a triad. The Canaanite woman episode is the fulcrum of the chiastic pattern. A real reader need not perceive that a chiastic pattern exists in order for it to affect him or her.

The pattern, encompassing a central section of the gospel, highlights the contrasts between the five major character groups: the outcast suppliants, the Jewish leaders, the crowds, the disciples, and the Gentiles. Although the same contrasts are made readily apparent in the rest of the narrative, repetition makes them quite crisp here. The stories move from a focus on (Jewish) supplicants, to the Jewish leaders, the disciples, a Gentile woman aligned with the other supplicants, then back to the disciples, the Jewish leaders, and finally to supplicants again. The linking of the blind men with the Gentile woman is particularly significant. It is they who exhibit the most faith, not the Pharisees who would reject contact with them both, nor the disciples whose faith and understanding waivers. One of the main themes of the gospel is the extension of the mission to the Gentiles; what better way to justify that extension! Other functions of the pericopes included in the chiastic pattern can be seen in a detailed examination.

The Triad: Blind Men and Canaanite Woman

The chiastic pattern begins with the healing of two blind men in 9:27–31. This episode occurs in a series of miracles preceding the missionary discourse. It immediately precedes the healing of the dumb demoniac. In the episode two blind men cry out, "Have mercy on us, Son of David." Jesus questions them, "Do you believe that I am able to do this." They answer yes, identifying Jesus as Lord, a title only those who have faith in him use. Their eyes are opened. Jesus charges them to remain silent, but they spread his fame throughout the entire district. As they leave the dumb demoniac (the second of the expanded doublets discussed above, 9:32–34) is brought to Jesus. The crowds marvel and the Pharisees charge him with exorcising by the power of the ruler of demons.

The second episode in 20:29–34 follows the request of the mother of the sons of Zebedee for a place of honor for her sons. It occurs just prior to the entry into Jerusalem. The cry of the blind men is the same, but this time *the crowd* rebukes them. They cry out all the more repeating the same phrase, "Lord, have mercy on us, Son of David (20:29, 31)." Jesus asks them what they want. They reply, "Lord, let our eyes be opened." This time, however, there is no injunction to silence and no disobedience. Instead they follow Jesus.

When the implied reader comes to the second member of the doublet, he or she reads it in the light of the first and vice versa. Verbal repetition draws the reader's attention to the similarities between the episodes engaging the reader's memory. At the same time it also puts the variations in relief. The two major differences are the differing responses of the pairs of blind men to being healed and the role of the crowds which appears only in the second story. In the first story the blind men exhibit faith but not enough. Jesus touched their eyes (ὀφθαλμῶν) and healed them according to their faith (9:29). Their eyes were opened, but unlike the second pair, they did not truly "see" and failed in obedience. The second set was healed when Jesus touched their ὄμματα, a poetic word for eyes which often occurs in the phrase "the eyes of the soul" (Gibbs: 459). The narrator explicitly states that they "saw." They then "followed" Jesus. If the second pairs' "following" indicates discipleship they have made a transition that the first pair did not. At least nine actual reader—commentators have interpreted the stories in that way./5/ Other readers read "following" as an indication that the men joined the group marching toward Jerusalem with Jesus, but not as a metaphor for discipleship./6/ In either case, the second group of blind men is pictured more favorably than the first who disobey./7/ The second major difference that emerges when each story is read in the light of the other is the role of the crowd. In the first episode the crowd is not present, but immediately following it are marveling at Jesus' ability to exorcise. In the second episode, the crowd rebukes the blind men.

Both of the major differences, the response of the blind men to being healed and the role of the crowd are related to the locations of the stories in the narrative. The first story is part of the series of miracles which precede the missionary discourse. These miracles emphasize Jesus' healing power and the spread of his fame, factors underscored by the encircling summaries of 4:23-25 and 9:35. They also highlight the faith of the supplicants. The faith of the blind men is seen in their request to Jesus as Lord and Son of David. The injunction to silence and their disobedience underlines the spread of Jesus' fame and the gathering of persons about him. The blind men are favorably contrasted with the Jewish leaders who attribute Jesus' power to the ruler of demons in the following episode. This pair and the second pair of blind men may be physically blind, but the Jewish leaders are spiritually blind (15:14; 23:16-22, 26). The crowds, although not mentioned in the story, marvel at Jesus' power in the following story, "Never has anything like this been seen in Israel (9:33)." The supplicants and the crowds gather about Jesus. The disciples are being groomed to serve them. In the missionary discourse Jesus commissions them to preach and heal as he has done. They are warned that they also will be opposed by the Jewish leaders who have called their master Beezeboul (see especially 10:17-25).

The second episode takes place immediately prior to Jesus' entry into Jerusalem. It follows the final passion and resurrection prediction, emphasizing the Jewish leaders' role in Jesus' death, and the squabble over places of honor initiated by the request of the mother of the sons of Zebedee. When Jesus enters Jerusalem and the temple, his healings and the cries "Hosanna to the Son of David" (21:14-15) anger the Jewish leaders. The fact that the second pair of blind men follows Jesus rather than being enjoined to keep silence and disobeying as the first pair is appropriate since he is about to enter Jerusalem. The confrontation with the Jewish leaders about Jesus' identity is about to come to a climax. The differences between the first and second pairs also enhance the contrast between marginal characters and various character groups. As the close of the narrative draws near marginal characters such as the blind men, women and Gentiles like the Canaanite woman and Roman centurion of 27:54 respond more and more positively to Jesus. The Jewish leaders, on the other hand, grow more hostile; the crowd shifts from initial attraction to calling for Jesus' death; and the disciples' understanding and loyalty waiver. These three groups of characters all appear in an unfavorable light compared to the blind men in the immediate context. As noted above, the Jewish leaders' antagonism to Jesus is stressed in the passion and resurrection prediction which precedes the episode and by their reaction to his entry into Jerusalem. The disciples do not fully understand the passion prediction and dispute among themselves about places of honor following the request of the mother of the sons of Zebedee. The crowds rebuke the blind men within the story itself. Shortly after the first member of the doublet they marveled at Jesus' ability to exorcise (9:33). Later they wondered if he might be the Son of David (12:23). Now their rebuke, which stands out in relief as a variation between the two blind men episodes, casts them in an unfavorable light. It foreshadows their eventual switch to the side of the Jewish leaders. They understand Jesus as a prophetic Son of David (21:9-11), not a Lordly one. They do not treat the blind men with compassion (σπλαγχνισθείς, 20:34) as Jesus does—a compassion he had earlier shown toward them (ἐσπλαγχνίσθη, 9:36; ἐσπλαγχνίσθη, 14:14; and σπλαγχνίζομαι, 15:32).

The third episode which must be considered in tandem with the healings of the two blind men is that of the Canaanite woman (15:22-28). It forms the center of the chiastic pattern of double stories. It is sandwiched between the two feeding stories. It immediately follows the condemnation of the Pharisees' teaching on defilement and precedes the feeding of the Four Thousand. Linked to the healings in 9:27ff. and 20:20ff., this pericope also has ties to the healing of the centurion's slave in 8:5-13 ("Truly I say to you, not even in Israel have I found such faith") and Jesus' injunction to go only to the lost sheep of the house of Israel in the missionary discourse (10:6 = 15:24, six words in common). It gathers together many threads in the gospel, offering a particularly vivid justification for and anticipation of the extension of the mission to πάντα τὰ ἔθνη in 28:19. Jesus reiterates, at first, the limitation to Israel and then breaks it because of the woman's great faith.

As noted above, the repetitive triad creates several meaningful contrasts. The faith of the Jewish outcasts and Gentile woman can be seen synoptically and contrasted with that of the Jewish leaders, disciples and crowds. It may be, however, that the faith of this Gentile woman is to be seen by the implied reader as even greater than that of the blind Jews, especially that of the first pair who disobey Jesus. As a Gentile and a woman she has doubly marginal status. Yet this Gentile woman recognizes Jesus as both Son of David and Lord. She calls Jesus Lord three times and *worships* him. She must overcome objections from the disciples (not just the crowds as in 20:31) and even Jesus himself ("I was sent only to the lost sheep of the house of Israel"). Her faith wins out and her daughter is healed *from that hour.*

If the blind men pale by comparison, the Jewish leaders are hopeless. The context of the episode underlines this. Jesus' condemnation of the Jewish leaders' teaching on defilement (15:1-20) immediately precedes his approval of the woman's faith. Their second request for a sign follows shortly thereafter. It serves as a transition to Jesus' condemnation of their teaching on leaven in 16:5-12. Even the disciples cannot stand comparison. They attempt to silence her. Their little faith and difficulty in understanding in the feeding stories of 14:13-21 and 15:30-38, and in 16:5-12, are readily available for the implied reader to observe. She is willing to receive "bread-crumbs" while the disciples do not understand about bread and the loaves of the Five Thousand or the Four Thousand (16:5-12). The motif of bread which ties these episodes together with that of the Canaanite woman and heightens the contrast will be discussed further below.

The Sign of Jonah

The next doublet related in the chiastic pattern is the Pharisees' request for a sign (12:38-42 = 16:1-4, twenty-four words in common). The initial request for a sign follows the second Beezeboul episode and precedes Jesus' rejection of his mother and brothers, forming a climax to the rejection of Jesus' words and deeds prior to chapter 13. The scribes and Pharisees answer Jesus' charges by saying, "Teacher (διδάσκαλε), we wish to see a sign from you."/8/ Jesus answers: "An evil and adulterous generation seeks a sign; but no sign shall be given to it except the sign of Jonah, the prophet." He interprets the sign as the Son of Man remaining in the heart of the earth three days and three nights. "This generation" will be condemned because they do not listen to a "greater thing" than either Jonah or Solomon. Jesus drives home his point with the story of the unclean spirit, illustrating what will happen to "this evil generation" (12:39 and 12:45b form a sort of inclusio around Jesus' condemnation). Jesus' tirade is brought to an end only by the appearance of his family. Although his anger is specifically directed at the Pharisees, 12:46 indicates the crowd has been present the whole time.

The second episode provides a bridge between the feeding of the Four Thousand and Jesus' warnings about the leaven of the Pharisees and Sadducees (16:5-12). The only audience present are the Pharisees and Sadducees (see 15:36 and 16:5). This time the Jewish leaders' request for a sign is specifically identified as an effort to *test* or *tempt* Jesus. The implied reader, reading the second episode in light of the first, sees the Jewish leaders becoming more perverse in the course of the narrative. The first request may have been genuine; the second is not. Jesus' answer also includes a reference to the ability of the Pharisees to read the signs of the sky, but not the signs of the times (16:3). There is no interpretation of the sign of Jonah. None is necessary. The implied reader learned its meaning from the first episode and is expected to recall it in retrospect. The Pharisees have not learned a thing. For the implied reader suspense is created and sustained—when will the sign of Jonah appear and what exactly will it be? So far, there have been no clear passion and resurrection predictions. Yet both episodes tie the sign together with the opposition of the Jewish leaders. The second episode, preceded by the Canaanite woman (15:21-28), the healing of the dumb, maimed, lame and blind (15:29-32) and the feeding of the Four Thousand (15:32-39), also provides a contrast between the perversity of the Jewish leaders, the faith of the Gentile woman who called Jesus, "Son of David" and "Lord," and the amazement of the crowds who marvel at Jesus' power and glorify Israel's God. It leads naturally into Jesus' warnings about the leaven in 16:5-12. Reinforced by the echo of the first episode it helps to ensure that the implied reader will understand what the disciples initially do not, the meaning of the leaven.

The Feedings

The final episodes to be considered are the feedings of the Five Thousand and the Four Thousand (14:13-21 = 15:30-38, fifty-six words in common) and the related question concerning the leaven of the Pharisees and

Sadduccees in 16:5-12. The first feeding is set in a wilderness place (14:13) with a mountain nearby (14:23); the second, on a mountain near the Sea of Galilee (15:29). In both stories Jesus feeds large crowds with a few loaves and fishes. The disciples serve as mediators, giving the food to the crowd. The existence of the first story, however, effects the reading of its double. The implied reader asks why the disciples wonder where the loaves to feed the crowd will come from when they have participated in a similar situation so recently. The repetition underscores the waivering faith and understanding the disciples display in the intervening stories. Those stories include the second stilling of the storm episode and their lack of intelligence (ἀσυνετοί) concerning the Pharisees and defilement in 15:12-20.

Differences between the two feeding episodes are also significant. There is repetition with variation. In the first story the disciples approach Jesus when evening falls, asking him to dismiss the crowds to go into the villages to buy food since "the place is wilderness and the hour already passed" (14:15). In the second story Jesus speaks to the disciples first: "And Jesus calling forward his disciples said: 'I am filled with tenderness over the crowd, because they remain with me now three days and do not have anything they may eat; and to dismiss them without food I am not willing lest they fall in the way'" (15:32). In the first story, Jesus' reply to their request is to tell them to give the crowd something to eat. Their reaction is to say they have nothing except five loaves and two fishes. In the second story, the disciples' reaction to Jesus' statement that he is unwilling to dismiss the crowds is to ask: "Whence, *to us* in a wilderness enough loaves to satisfy so great a crowd?" They seem to have at least learned that they are to provide the food, but do not know where to get enough. Jesus asks them how many loaves they have. They reply, "Seven and a few fishes." The fact that Jesus expresses his concern for the crowd to the disciples highlights their role as mediators. It also underscores their failure to understand fully what had occured in the first story.

The disciples' waivering faith and understanding is driven home not only by the repetitive feeding stories, but also by the context in which they are found. The second stilling of the storm episode where Peter walks on the water yet falters as a "little-faith," the disciples' failure to understand Jesus' teaching on defilement, and the Canaanite woman episode intervene between the two stories. As noted above, the Canaanite woman's willingness to receive *bread*-crumbs is part of a motif of bread introduced in the first feeding story. This motif comes to a climax in 16:5-12. There the disciples do not understand why Jesus warns them of the *leaven* of the Pharisees and Sadducees. This warning is clear to the implied reader and ought to be clear to the disciples. The second request for a sign has just occurred, the only incident intervening between the second feeding and Jesus' warning. Jesus rebukes the disciples with a favorite Matthean label, "O little-faiths" (16:8 = 6:30 = 8:26

= 14:31; cf. 17:20). He asks, "do you not yet perceive? Do you not remember the five *loaves* of the Five Thousand . . . ? Or the seven *loaves* of the Four Thousand . . . ?" Then reminded by these echoes, they do understand. Immediately following, Peter is able to make the confession of Jesus as "The Christ, the Son of the living God." Even though Peter does not understand yet all that this entails, he and the other disciples are on the way to becoming the church with power to bind and loose (16:18–19 = 18:18–20). The implied author uses the doublet of the feeding and its sequel, the leaven of the Pharisees, to show the disciples in transit, in all their weakness, on the way to true discipleship.

We have seen that double and triple stories play an integral role in the development of plot and character in the Gospel of Matthew. The repetition of a similar episode is not merely an additional episode. It has a powerful rhetorical effect in which anticipation and retrospection and repetition with variation are involved. There is a complex texture of interlocking echoes forcing the implied reader to read one episode in the light of the other. The contexts in which the stories reverberate contribute to their effect.

Repetition and Redundancy: Information Theory

In recent years information theory has influenced studies of literature, rhetoric and reading. At bottom, information theory treats communication as the transmission of a message between sender and receiver. The same basic model has been used in much of reader-response criticism. It is therefore, not surprising that several studies utilizing information theory have implications for understanding double and triple stories and the role of the implied reader in Matthew (Wittig, 1973, 1978; Suleiman, Smith). A key concept in each is the concept of redundancy. Redundancy is the availability of information from more than one source. Information is necessary for a receiver properly to interpret (or decode) any message. He or she must choose from various alternative interpretations. For example, a reader presented with the visual image "read" must decide whether the meaning is past or present tense. Redundancy increases predictability by decreasing the number of possible alternatives. This reduces uncertainty, facilitating the communication process (Cherry: 18)./9/ One form of redundancy is the use of both oral and visual clues. In the above example when presented with oral and visual representations uncertainty is almost entirely eliminated. There are many other types of redundancy, usually involving information the receiver already possesses, and which is acquired through previous experience. Repeated exposure to the English language teaches, for example, that nouns usually follow "the." The occurrence of a noun is expected; it is predictable.

Susan Wittig makes use of this insight in studying formulas in written verse narratives. "The element of predictability demonstrably present in formulaic verse is a feature known to information theorists as *redundancy*; that is some words or groups of words, some syntactical and metrical patterns, have a high probability of occurence in a given context" (1973:126). She offers the example of the Middle English two-verse formula:

> When he awoke and speke myght
> Sore he wept and sore he syght

After having heard or read the formula several times, the Middle English audience could predict (or anticipate) that when the first verse appeared it would be followed by the second (Wittig, 1973:125)./10/ She also notes redundancy on the level of the larger narrative verse formulas of motif and scene: ". . . many of the narratives will be seen to be structurally redundant in terms of plot as well as verseform; that is, having heard or read the first scene, made up of a number of obligatory motifs, an audience familiar with several narratives in the same genre can predict the composition of the second scene, and so on, through the course of the narrative" (1973:127). She is noting both focal expectations, relating to the immediate context and global expectations, extending over larger sections including the whole course of a work. Global and focal predictions are made simultaneously and influence one another (Smith: 168-72). They provide another form of redundancy.

Susan Suleiman writing about realistic narrative, specifically, the *roman à thèse*, concentrates on global expectations which affect the text as a whole. Suleiman presents the hypothesis that redundancy is highly characteristic of "readable" texts, especially realistic narratives./11/ Adopting a schema based on the work of A. J. Greimas and G. Genette, she offers a detailed classification of the types of redundancy possible in realistic narratives on the level of the story, the discourse, and between story and discourse. She goes on to suggest which of these types are prevalent in the *roman à thèse*, the high degree and types of redundancy serving to partly define the genre. While both Wittig and Suleiman are interested in types of redundancy characteristic of genres, many of Suleiman's categories focus on redundancy within a text. For example, "A1.1 The same event or same sequence of events happens to a single C [character] n times" or "B.2 The narrator pronounces n times the same commentary about the character, an event or a context." For Suleiman repeated commentary may be characteristic of a genre, but the content repeated may vary. Each succeeding repetition teaches the reader the same lesson. The reader does not *necessarily* know from the genre what the lesson will be.

Redundancy And The Implied Reader In Matthew

What are the functions of redundancy? How does this concept shed light on how double and triple stories shape the role of the implied reader in Matthew?

Redundancy increases the intelligibility and cohesiveness of a message and the reliability and speed of its transmission./12/ It enhances the psychological efficiency of the response (Wittig, 1973:127; Carpenter: 62–63)./13/ It allows the receiver to overcome any *noise* or distractions in the communication channel./14/ Redundancy also has a persuasive function. In relation to formulaic narratives Wittig writes:

> The creation (either consciously and deliberately or unconsciously and unintentionally) of a multi-level set of expectancies not only allows the audience to predict the occurence of successive items [whether "the next word in a linear sequence of words, or the next stanzaic sequence, or the next motif or scene in a plot sequence" (1973:130)], but also provides for that audience's *assent* to the sequence, for if the listener can predict the next item (perhaps he may repeat it silently before it occurs) he will be more likely to accept it and agree to it. . . . The persuasive effect of such familiar lexical-syntactical-metrical patterns has been recognized by rhetoricians for centuries, and is the basis of much current advertising theory. (1973:131)

Suleiman makes a similar point about redundancy in the *roman à thèse*: ". . . it is by means of redundancy that plural meanings and ambiguities are eliminated and a single "correct" reading imposed" (120). Redundancy may be supplied by a message itself or by the competency of the receiver in linguistic or generic codes or both. The implied reader of a narrative, for example, may expect a character to act a certain way in a given situation because he or she has done so two times already or because this type of character always acts that way in the genre involved.

The concept of redundancy can help to explain the reading process in Matthew, and particularly some of the functions of verbal repetition, the simplest and most obvious form of redundancy. In the case of double and triple stories, verbal repetition increases predictability, creates expectations, eliminates noise, persuades, and reduces alternative interpretations. Verbal repetition teaches the implied reader how to "read" the text. When the opening lines of a repeated story reveal the similarity to a previous story, the implied reader predicts what will occur next; in many cases the exact words which will appear. The information is easily assimilable. The stories often confirm one another. The two sign of Jonah episodes, for example, convey essentially the same information in almost the same words. The implied reader can be in no doubt about the nature of the Jewish leaders. The "noise" resulting from the length of the gospel is reduced by these repetitions which engage the reader's memory. They have a persuasive function as well. The repetition of the sign of Jonah stories disposes the implied reader to view the Jewish leaders in a certain light.

The way in which redundancy creates expectations also helps to explain the importance of repetition with *variation*. After the implied reader recognizes similarity, variations stand out. When the expected pattern is broken new information appears which cannot be easily assimilated. It creates uncertainty and requires the implied reader to make choices. Why do the disciples point out the crowd's hunger in the first feeding story, while Jesus does so in the second? Why are the Jewish leaders described as "testing" or "tempting" Jesus in the second sign of Jonah episode, but not the first? Thus, the implied reader's views of character, plot and themes develop. Anticipation and retrospection become especially important parts of the reading process. There is also room for diversity in real readers' actualizations. For example, the variation in the endings of the two blind men stories (9:27–31 = 20:29–34) has become an interpretive crux for actual readers. The fact that the first pair of blind men disobeys Jesus' charge to remain silent, while the second pair "follows," him receives various interpretations.

Finally, redundancy helps to explain the importance of context in relationship to double and triple stories. Context "cues" the implied reader's response. In addition to the stories themselves, the context provides another source of information. It reduces the alternatives. Thus, the focus on the disciples' waivering faith and understanding in the feeding stories is reinforced by the context in which they are found. Peter's faltering walk on water, the disciples failure to understand Jesus' teaching on defilement, and the Canaanite woman story intervene between the feedings. The leaven incident with its retrospective references to the two feedings almost immediately follows the second feeding in 16:5–12.

In conclusion, it can be said that he concept of redundancy contributes to an understanding of how double and triple stories help to create the role of Matthew's implied reader. Much of what was discussed also applies to the many other examples of verbal repetition in the gospel. In addition, the description of redundancy offered suggests that other forms of redundancy might be fruitfully investigated. This would include not only forms of redundancy located within the text like verbal repetition, but also extra-textual competencies required by the text. What forms of prior knowledge does the text assume? What aspects of the text, including types of redundancy, may be part of a generic code the implied reader is expected to know?

NOTES

/1/ Although various sub-groups of the Jewish leaders are named, there are no sharp distinctions made and all function together as Jesus' opponents (see Van Tilborg: 1–7).

/2/ The others are Peter's in 16:17 and the centurion's in 27:54.

/3/ The exact historical meaning of the term is uncertain (Allen: 107–8; McNeile: 143–44).

/4/ Even if Kingsbury (1978:61) is right in asserting that the *meti* anticipates a negative answer. Duling (401) notes that the *untrusting* statement of the Pharisees "implies there could be a positive answer, at least for Matthew's reader." See also Kingsbury (1976:600) and Gibbs (458).

/5/ Kingsbury (1978:57) lists eight, to which add Gibbs (454–55, 460).

/6/ Kingsbury is an important proponent of this reading. He argues that "following" only indicates discipleship when Jesus and not the narrator speaks (1978:58, 61). He also argues that two factors must be present, (a) "personal commitment" where Jesus calls disciples or addresses those who are already disciples and (b) "cost," which involves sacrifice or abandoning one's former life (1978:58). With the exception of 8:19 and 19:20–22, this limits him to contexts involving members of the character group, "the disciples."

/7/ Part of the difference in interpretation depends on whether discipleship is defined as becoming a member of the character group, "the disciples," or as the response of faith. The blind men respond to Jesus, but do not appear in the narrative again as members of the character group. They are united with other supplicants and the narrator in calling Jesus "Son of David," something the disciples never do. The disciples and supplicants do both call Jesus "Lord." Only members of "the disciples" and the narrator call Jesus "Christ" and along with the voice from heaven and the Roman centurion in 27:54, "Son of God." Perhaps most telling is the fact that if the blind men became disciples, it would not be possible to contrast them (along with the Canaanite woman) with that character group.

/8/ Teacher as a title for Jesus is used only by members of the Jewish establishment (8:19, 12:38, 19:16, 22:16, 22:24, 22:36; see also "your teacher" in 9:11 and 16:24b).

/9/ Cherry (18–19) defines redundancy as follows: "Briefly, redundancy is a property of languages, codes, and sign systems which arises from a superfluity of rules, and which facilitates communication in spite of all the factors of uncertainty acting against it."

/10/ Wittig (1973:125) notes that syntactical and metrical patterns underlie the lexical repetitions. Formulas may vary on the lexical level and remain the same on the other levels as in:

$$\left\{\begin{array}{l}\text{he}\\ \text{she}\\ \text{he}\\ \text{thou}\end{array}\right\} \text{ were never so } \left\{\begin{array}{l}\text{nobyll a knyght}\\ \text{fayr ne whyte he}\\ \text{kene}\\ \text{prest}\end{array}\right\}$$

/11/ In employing the term "readable" Suleiman (119) is working with R. Barthes' distinction between readable (*lisible*) and writable (*scriptible*) texts. The former limits meaning, employing traditional grammar, structure and logic. It is analyzable. The latter is modern, extremely open, and plural. The reader becomes the producer of a writable text rather than a consumer.

/12/ Smith makes these points throughout his book. Smith and Wittig both note the importance of contextual clues and the receiver's prior knowledge. For example, if unrelated letters are flashed on a screen only four or five may be reported by a receiver; if words are flashed two or three consisting of about twelve letters may be reported; if there is a sentence the four or five words consisting of about twenty-five letters may be reported (Smith: 30). Speed of identification also increases. Smith (32) gives the following illustrations: If a single letter A is flashed on a screen and a reader is given no prior clues, the reaction time can be as long as five hundred milliseconds or half a second. If the reader is told the letter is A or B, reaction time may be as little as two hundred milliseconds.

/13/ Carpenter (64-67) suggests that certain rhetorical devices including the repetitive antithesis, paromoeosis, and formal climax increase redundancy and efficiency of psychological response.

/14/ The classic illustration of overcoming *noise*, Colin Cherry's "Cocktail Party Problem" (Cherry: 227-78), is cited by Smith (202) and Wittig (1973:129). Listeners in crowds can overcome the distraction of many voices—noise—and concentrate on one speaker. Noise in reading can consist of such things as a bad print face, distracting thoughts, or even the reader's forgetfulness (see Smith: 14; Suleiman: 122).

WORKS CONSULTED

Abrams, M. H.
    1981   *A Glossary of Literary Terms*. 3d ed. New York: Holt, Rinehart and Winston.

Allen, W. C.
    1977   *A Critical and Exegetical Commentary on the Gospel According to St. Matthew*. 3d ed. ICC. Edinburg: T. and T. Clark.

Anderson, Janice Capel
    1981   "Point of View in Matthew: Evidence." SBL Symposium on the Literary Analysis of the Gospels and Acts. SBL Annual Meeting.

Book, C. L., Albrecht, T. L., et al.
　1980　　　　　*Human Communication: Principles, Contexts and Skills.* New York: St. Martin's.

Booth, Wayne
　1961　　　　　*The Rhetoric of Fiction.* Chicago: University of Chicago.

Bornkamm, Günther
　1963　　　　　"The Stilling of the Storm." In *Tradition and Interpretation in Matthew*, pp. 52–57. By Günther Bornkamm, Gerhard Barth, and Heinz-Joachim Held. Philadelphia: Westminster.

Carpenter, Ronald H.
　1970　　　　　"Stylistic Redundancy and Function in Discourse." *Language and Style* 3: 62–68.

Chatman, Seymour
　1978　　　　　*Story and Discourse.* Ithaca: Cornell University.

Cherry, Colin
　1957　　　　　*On Human Communication.* Cambridge: M.I.T.

Duling, Dennis
　1978　　　　　"The Therapeutic Son of David." NTS 24: 392–410.

Fowler, Robert M.
　1981　　　　　*Loaves and Fishes.* SBLDS. Chico: Scholars.

Gibbs, James M.
　1963/64　　　"Purpose and Pattern in Matthew's Use of the Title 'Son of David.'" *NTS* 10: 446–64.

Giblin, Charles H.
　1975　　　　　"Structural and Thematic Correlations in the Matthean Burial—Resurrection Narrative (Matt. 27:57–28:20)," *NTS* 21: 406–20.

Iser, Wolfgang
　1974　　　　　*The Implied Reader.* Baltimore: John Hopkins University.
　1978　　　　　*The Act of Reading.* Baltimore: John Hopkins University.

Kingsbury, Jack D.
　1976　　　　　"The Title Son of David in Matthew's Gospel." *JBL* 95: 591–602.
　1978　　　　　"The Verb *Akolouthein* ('To Follow') as an Index to Matthew's View of his Community." *JBL* 97: 56–73.

Luz, Ulrich
　1971　　　　　"Die Jünger im Matthäusevangelium." ZNW 62: 141–71.

McNeile, Alan H.
　1915　　　　　*The Gospel According to St. Matthew.* New York: Macmillan; reprint ed. Grand Rapids: Baker Book House, 1980.

Minear, Paul S.
　1974　　　　　"The Disciples and Crowds in the Gospel of Matthew." *ATR Supp. Series* 3: 28–44.

Pierce, J. P.
1961 *Symbols, Signals and Noise: The Nature and Process of Communication.* New York: Harper & Row.

Sheridan, Mark
1973 "Disciples and Discipleship in Matthew and Luke." *BTB* 3: 235-55.

Smith, Frank
1978 *Understanding Reading: A Psycholinguistic Analysis of Reading and Learning to Read.* 2d ed. New York: Holt, Rinehart, and Winston.

Suleiman, Susan Rubin
1980 "Redundancy and the 'Readable' Text." *Poetics Today* 1: 119-42.

Van Tilborg, Sjef
1972 *The Jewish Leaders in Matthew.* Leiden: E. J. Brill.

Uspensky, Boris
1973 *A Poetics of Composition.* Berkeley: University of California.

Wittig, Susan
1973 "Formulaic Style and the Problem of Redundancy." *Centrum* 1: 123-36.
1978 *Stylistic and Narrative Structures in the Middle English Romances.* Austin: University of Texas. a

PROLEGOMENON TO READING MATTHEW'S ESCHATOLOGICAL DISCOURSE: REDUNDANCY AND THE EDUCATION OF THE READER IN MATTHEW

Fred W. Burnett
Anderson College

ABSTRACT

Redundancy is one way a text educates its implied reader. "Redundancy" refers to the probability of occurrence for a signal or group of signals. The Matthean text is redundant on both the story and discourse levels. One major redundancy in Matthew occurs with the name "Jesus." The text constantly reinforces the initial presentation of Jesus as "God with us." The redundant presentation of Jesus as "God with us" educates the reader to organize the reading of the whole gospel (both narrative and discourse material) by the redundant supersymbol "Jesus." In terms of the reading experience in the eschatological discourse, redundancies help create an aesthetic experience when reader expectations about Jesus are unfulfilled. The overall effect of redundancies on the implied reader, though, is to create a narrative world in which stability is primary. Everything in Matthew's narrative world occurs as the unfolding of the plan of God, and Jesus is the hero around whom the plan unfolds for the reader.

Reader-response critics agree that reading is a temporal, sequential process (Fish, 1980a:73–74; Iser, 1980a:278; Lanser: 238–39; Mailloux, 1977:426). This does not mean, of course, that reading is only an irreversible, linear experience. Readers will often be required to repattern earlier parts of the text as well as hazard guesses about what will happen in later parts (what Menakhem Perry calls "retrospective patterning": 59–60). The sequential nature of the reading process, though, does require one to understand what has preceded the part of the text which one wants to describe or interpret. Thus, if one wants to describe the reading process in Matthew's eschatological discourse, then one must first read the "horizon" of the discourse (cf. Iser, 1980a:278).

The material preceding Matthew 24-25 is important also for reader-response critics because it constitutes the reader's "education." The text not only selects a model reader through the linguistic code, literary style, and encyclopedic competence it presupposes, but it also seeks *during the reading process* "to build up, by merely textual means, such a competence" (Eco: 7-8). The text provides the reader with techniques and interpretive habits which he or she can use in reading later passages. Describing the process of how the reader learns to read the text is so important that Steven Mailloux calls it "the paradigmatic move of reader-response criticism" (1979:106). This paper will attempt to describe how the reader has been positioned and educated to read the eschatological discourse in Matthew (24:3-25:36). By "reader" I mean a theoretical construct which is both encoded in the text and is an image of certain competencies presupposed or assumed by the text. Iser's definition of the implied reader is sufficient for my purposes: "This term [the implied reader] incorporates both the prestructuring of the potential meaning by the text, and the reader's actualization of this potential through the reading process. It refers to the active nature of this process—which will vary historically from one age to another—and not to a typology of possible readers" (1980a:xii)./1/ I will focus on only one aspect of the reader's education in Matthew, the repetitions, or, more precisely, the redundancies. ("Matthew" will refer to the text of the Gospel rather than to the actual author.)

Repetition has long been recognized as a technique of folk-literature both in its oral and written stages (Lohr, Kelber, Eichenbaum, and Greene). The ostensible function of repetition in biblical literature is to organize and unify disparate material (Lohr: 404-5; cf. Alter: 92-97; and Tannehill, 1975:43). This is also true of Matthew. It has often been noted how the repetitive and highly schematic nature of Matthew's Gospel constitutes its primary structural feature (e.g., Lohr: 408-34; Ellis). In terms of reader-response criticism, I would suggest that redundancy is one of the most important ways in which the Matthean text educates its reader.

For those who are utilizing reader-response criticism, this suggestion may take on additional importance in light of recent work on redundancy in information theory. The consensus of information theorists is that redundancy is essential to *any* communication process—oral, written, or electronic. Since reader-response critics assume virtually the same basic communication model for narrative fiction as information theorists do for any type of communication, redundancy would seem to be an important feature to describe both in terms of the reader's education and of its effect on the reader (e.g., Iser, 1980b:107,111). To the best of my knowledge, no one in biblical studies has explored redundancy within the context of reader-response criticism, and very few have broached the issue in terms of narrative fiction generally./2/ Iser has some comments on the importance of redundancy (1978:93-99). Susan Suleiman has taken an important, yet tentative, step in exploring redundancy within narrative. She has proposed a very helpful classification of the types of redundancy which are possible—on both the levels of story and discourse—in realistic fiction (1980b:119-42). Her proposal, however, is tentative because she recognizes that there is as yet no general theory of textual redundancy (121).

For folk-literature (*Kleinliteratur*) like Matthew (cf. Beardslee: 5; Talbert: 3-4), whose compositional redundancies reflect both oral and written stages, Susan Wittig has succinctly stated the problem and one solution with regard to reader-response criticism:

> Discussions of formulaic styles usually focus on the composer of the formulaic tale, and characterize the style as a product of the conditions of oral delivery. However, such an approach cannot account for the presence of formulae in texts composed in writing, nor can it describe the effect of stylistic and narrative redundancy on the audience. Information theory provides a framework for a larger discussion of the psychological, social, and artistic functions of redundancy in literature. (123)

In appropriating Wittig's suggestion, my procedure will be threefold: (1) the basic understanding of redundancy in information theory will be summarized; (2) one type of redundancy in Matthew will be highlighted, namely, redundancies involving the name "Jesus"; and (3) redundancies on both story and discourse levels in Matt. 24:3 will be examined in order to suggest how they align the reader to understand the following discourse.

1. *Redundancy in Information Theory*

For information theorists "redundancy" is the element of predictability in any form of communication. ("Communication" is usually defined very broadly "to include all of the procedures by which one mind may affect another" [Weaver: 95].) Basically, redundancy means that some signal or group of signals has a high probability of occurrence in a given context./3/ Although redundancies are superfluous, they are not to be removed because they are considered essential to the communication process. The function of redundancies is to overcome interference on the channel ("noise") and to ensure the reception of the message which was transmitted./4/ Information theorists agree that every communication channel, regardless of its physical properties, is subject to noise. Therefore, as John Lyons says, "a certain degree of redundancy is essential, not only in language, but in any communication system in order to counteract the disturbing effects of noise" (1:44; cf. Bolinger: 57, and Pierce: 164)./5/

The basic principle of modern information theory, as far as redundancy is concerned, "is that any message which has a high probability of occurrence conveys little information" (Young: 4). The word "information," however, in information theory should not be confused with its ordinary usage as "meaning." The word *information*, rather, "relates not so much to what you *do* say, as to what you *could* say. That is, information is a measure of one's freedom of choice when one selects a message" (Weaver: 100). There is, thus, an inverse relationship between redundancy and information. If *information* is one's freedom of choice in selecting a message, then the "greater this freedom of choice, and hence the greater the information, the greater is the uncertainty that the message actually selected is a particular one. Thus greater freedom of choice, greater uncertainty, greater information go hand in hand" (Weaver: 109). In effect, redundancy reduces the effort of choice for both the sender and the recipient of the message by reducing the number of discriminations to be made (cf. Whatmough: 132).

This would seem to present an insurmountable problem, in narrative poetics, of appreciating redundancy. Even in ordinary speech a message is considered important in proportion to the amount of information (as content) it carries, but in poetics the "unfamiliar" (*ostraneniye*), the surprising, and the unique, have been valued in one form or another (e.g., Shklovsky). When a reader has a high probability of predicting what is coming in a narrative (because he or she has read the same phrase or encountered a character performing the same narrative function *n* times), this does not seem to lend itself to the anticipation-correction schema so valued by reader-response critics. A redundant text like Matthew would seem to lend itself more to Roland Barthes' conception of a "readable text," i.e., one which is didactic and singular (3-9). As Suleiman contends, "[for Barthes] it is by means of redundancy that plural meanings and ambiguities are eliminated and a single 'correct' reading imposed" (1980b:120). As we have seen, redundancy facilitates recognition on the reader's part, but it is important to note that in didactic texts like Matthew redundancy not only allows the reader to anticipate with a high degree of probability. It also readily wins the reader's *assent* because it has the effect of reinforcing the reader's "world." Wittig identifies this reinforcement as the most important function of redundancy:

> But the ability to predict the next word in a linear sequence of words, or the next syntactical pattern in a stanzaic sequence, or the next motif or scene in a plot sequence, has another function, the implications of which seem to have more significance

> for the understanding of formulaic narrative than those we have discussed.... The creation (either consciously and deliberately or unconsciously and unintentionally) of a multi-level set of expectancies not only allows the audience to predict the occurrence of successive items, but also provides for that audience's *assent* to the sequence, for if the listener can predict the next item (perhaps he may repeat it silently before it occurs) he will be more likely to accept it and agree to it. (130–31)

This means cognitively that "formulaic style presents the world as completely recognized and finally achieved. As ritualistic language, unhesitatingly spoken and accepted as truth, it provides a declarative, definitive statement about the nature of knowledge. Therein, for its audience, lies its beauty and utility" (133).

There is no question that Matthew is formulaic and redundant in the senses defined above. However, as we have seen, *no* communication—even in the sense of an aesthetic experience—occurs without some degree of redundancy. In Matthew's case redundancy seems to be important in the reading experience precisely because it "lulls the reader to sleep" and aligns him or her to expect the familiar. Of course, in some cases in Matthew the expected does not follow, and this forces the reader to reevaluate his or her expectations (cf. Tannehill, 1975:43–44). There would be few "aesthetic gaps" in Matthew were it not for the redundancies which lead the reader to expect the familiar. It will be contended below that this is true in certain respects of the eschatological discourse.

2. Redundancies with the Name "Jesus"

Given the sequential nature of reading, reader-response critics realize that one way a text educates its reader is simply by positioning certain items before others. The information (as content), attitudes, characters, etc. presented at the beginning of a text will be retained by the reader, and he or she will interpret every subsequent item in their light (the "primacy effect") *unless* the text "sets up a mechanism to oppose them, giving rise, rather, to a recency effect" (Perry: 57; cf. Minear's remark that "it was the habit of biblical people to find at the outset of a story a kind of preview of all that would follow" [38]). As Perry says, there are some texts "in which meanings, constructed at the beginning of the text as a result of the distribution of information in the text-continuum, will remain stable until the reading is over simply because *once constructed there is nothing in the sequel of the text to contradict or undermine them so as to cause their final rejection*" (48). In other words, because of the "recency effect," if "the text intends the effect of its initial state to prevail throughout, it must keep reinforcing it" (57). In terms of information theory, in order for a text to maintain the primacy effect, it must be redundant.

It is recognized generally that the first character to be introduced in a text will be regarded "as the protagonist for as long as it has not been displaced in the center by another character" (Perry: 53). By "character" I mean simply "any individual agent or potential agent of action whether human or non-human" (Suleiman, 1980b:125, n. 4). There is little doubt that the initial focus of Matthew is upon Jesus, and that he is certainly the protagonist against whom the reader will judge all other characters. Further, in terms of the primacy effect, the first in a series of qualities presented about a character is decisive for the reader in determining the overall impression or trait of that character (Perry: 54). In Matthew Jesus is presented first to the reader as "God with us" (1:23). It is my contention that this description of Jesus as "God with us" becomes paradigmatic for all later scenes involving Jesus, and it is what the Matthean text continually reinforces (cf. Genette: 72).

At the beginning of the text an omniscient, heterodiegetic narrator (Genette: 248) takes the reader back generations to confirm that Jesus is the culmination of (for this text) the messianic lineage./6/ The reader is informed that Jesus' birth is the fulfillment of prophecy (1:22), and that Jesus is "God with us." Matthew 1:23 thus qualifies as *direct characterization* because it (1) comes from the most authoritative voice in the text and thus implicitly forces the reader to accept the quality, and (2) it even gives the *cause* for the name Emmanuel, "he will save his people" (cf. γάρ, 1:21). This determines Jesus' role in the story. As Tomashevsky says: "In uncomplicated story forms it is sometimes enough to give a character's name and no other characteristics (a character in the abstract) in order to define his necessary role in the story" (88; I take αὐτός to refer to Jesus, not God, and understand Jesus in 1:21 to parallel Emmanuel in 1:23). The reader is thus informed *by the most authoritative voice in the text* who Jesus is, and the reader of a classical text like Matthew will align himself or herself with the position of the omniscient narrator (Belsey: 77–78). The whole narrative is now focused on Jesus as the "hero." As Scholes points out: "The hero, once named, is the subject of a narrative as a substantive may be the grammatical subject of a sentence . . ." (108).

Although the reader does not know precisely what "God with us" means, he or she does know that Jesus is the fulfillment of God's plan and that "history" in Matthew is the progressive fulfillment of the Divine Plan. This initial impression has at least two important consequences for the reader./7/ One is that Jesus will be a "flat" character, i.e., one which does not develop in the course of the narrative. To use E. M. Forster's words, flat characters in "their purest form . . . are constructed around a single idea or quality" which can usually "be expressed in one sentence" (75). Jesus' character "trait" is established at the beginning of the narrative as "God with us"; it would be very difficult by any first or second century code to imply that a character who is God (in any sense) could develop. If "trait" can mean simply a "relatively stable or abiding personal quality," then Jesus' name is a "stasis statement" and his identity is established at the beginning of the narrative (Chatman: 126; cf. 32–33). "The very name *Jesus*," as Minear says, "symbolized his later work, which would be to 'save his people from their sins'" (33). Jesus' words and deeds in the narrative will unfold for the reader more precisely what "God with us" means./8/ In that sense Jesus is for the reader an enigmatic character because the "not-yet-named traits abide in the proper name of the character as a mysterious residue" (Chatman: 130; cf. Barthes: 190–91). The advantage for the reader is that a flat character is recognized easily and is predictable (Chatman: 132; Ewen: i–ii). Each time Jesus appears the reader will understand that "where Jesus is, there God is" (Minear: 33)./9/

A second consequence of the narrator's portrayal of Jesus is that the reader knows (in contrast to the characters in the narrative world) that Jesus will be the reliable commentator throughout the narrative (Booth: 18; cf. Tannehill, 1977:391; Lanser: 138–39; Thomashevsky: 75; Suleiman, 1980b:128). The reader, then, will evaluate all other characters vis-à-vis their responses to Jesus' words and deeds or his responses to them. The ideology, or the "general system of viewing the world conceptually," is presented here from a single, dominant point of view, that of the narrator-focalizer. All other evaluations (ideologies) in the text "will in turn be reevaluated from the more dominant position" (Uspensky: 8–9; cf. 22). In terms of Genette's hierarchy of narrative levels the comments of the narrator would be at the highest possible narrative level (248; cf. Lanser: 151–54, 210).

Barthes suggests that reading (in the classical text) depends upon nomination and its repetition. Reading is "nomination in the course of becoming" (11; cf. 93. For Barthes any "readerly text" is a "classic text" [41]). Barthes comes close to elevating the semic code (character) over the proairetic code (actions) when he says: "As soon as a Name exists (even a pronoun) the semes become predicates, inductors of truth, and the Name becomes a subject: we can say that *what is proper to narrative is not action but the character as Proper Name . . .*" (Barthes: 191 [italics mine]; cf. Scholes: 108–10). The proper name, then, is *the* cohesive factor during the reading process. If this is the case, then the function of the proper name "Jesus" becomes a very important one in Matthew. In Matthew Jesus' name even parallels morphologically his character trait so that the reader transfers the saving presence of God to the name "Jesus" (cf. Hamon: 147–50)./10/ In this sense, as Chatman says, "The proper name, like the definite article, is deictic, establishing individual specificity" (221; cf. Tomashevsky: 88). Each time the reader encounters the name "Jesus," he or she can construct the same, saving character (Barthes: 67; Todorov: 77).

In information theory messages are encoded under one supersymbol by "block encoding," i.e., "encoding a sequence of symbols together" (Pierce: 287). The purpose for creating such a supersymbol is "to add redundancy to non-redundant messages so that they can be transmitted without error over a noisy channel" (Pierce: 164). The consistent use of a name for a character in narrative can function in a way which is analogous to a redundant supersymbol (cf. Pierce: 90). The proper name functions as a cohesive factor for the reader, and he or she can read more efficiently the material which the supersymbol introduces. One could contend that the cohesive supersymbol for the reader in Matthew's narrative/discourse structure is the name "Jesus."

3. *Redundancies in Matthew 24:3*

Interpreters agree that 24:3 is the interpretive crux for reading the eschatological discourse in Matthew. The reader must decide how 24:3ff. (the Parousia) relates to 24:1–2 (the prediction of the temple's destruction). A decision on this point will determine how one understands the disciples' question(s) in 24:3c: "when will these things ($\tau a \hat{v} \tau a$) be?" Commentators have concentrated most of their energy on 24:3c in order to *interpret* the discourse. The chief question has been: does $\tau a \hat{v} \tau a$ refer to what precedes (the predicted destruction) or to what follows ("what will be the sign of your *parousia* and the consummation of the age?") or to both (Burnett: 198–226)? In light of what I have claimed for redundancy, however, 24:3a (Jesus sits on the mountain) and 24:3b (the disciples approach Jesus) may be more important than 24:3c is for *describing the reading experience*, since the redundancies here align the reader to process what follows.

The reader's attention in 24:3 is focused exclusively on Jesus (the pronoun $a\dot{v}\tau\acute{o}s$ can function in narrative as a proper name [Barthes: 191]). Verse 3 is backgrounded by Jesus' emphatic departure from the temple which culminates in his pronouncement of judgment (24:2; cf. 23:38; see Burnett: 112–32; 160–64). For the reader this indirect characterization suggests that God's presence has left the temple with the departure of Jesus. In indirect characterization such as this the reader deciphers in reverse (Rimmon-Kenan: 64–65). Thus, Jesus abandons the temple; therefore God has abandoned the temple. A new introduction begins the scene at 24:3 (Burnett: 209–26), and this has the effect on the reader of causing him or her to recall all of the previous scenes about Jesus which have been introduced in this highly stylized and redundant fashion. Redundancies do not cause the reader to *repattern* previous material; they only reinforce in a non-contradictory manner all previous meanings or effects (Perry: 57–59; cf. Iser, 1980a:49).

It has often been noted how stylized, almost formulaic, the introduction in 24:3a, b is. It is commonly known that in this Gospel Jesus "sits" (κάθημαι) when he teaches (5:1, 13:1–2, 15:29; cf. 23:2). As Fenton says: "Jesus sits to teach; this was usual, but is emphasized in this Gospel" (77). Within the Gospel itself, but certainly against the background of its cultural codes, a divine figure like Jesus assumes a sitting posture as a sign of his or her teaching ability and deity (cf. Schneider: 441–42). Jesus' authority and dignity are enhanced by the fact that he is seated upon a mountain. In Matthew a mountain is usually the place for messianic teachings (chaps. 5–7, 24–25), for messianic decision-making (14:23, 26:30), for exercising messianic power (15:29), and for disclosures of Jesus' transcendent authority (17:1–9, 28:16–20; see Minear: 43). Jesus' authority and dignity are also enhanced by the fact that his disciples, his intimate followers, approach him reverently (see Burnett: 133–45; and Kingsbury, 1969:40–41).

In terms of reader-response criticism, there are several redundancies in 24:3a, b which operate *simultaneously* on the levels of story and discourse./11/ First, the context is metonymically redundant with the character (Jesus). As the presence of God, Jesus is seated authoritatively upon a place (the mountain) which is appropriate for his authority (cf. Burnett: 367–68). Secondly, several characters (the disciples) accomplish the same syntagmatic function for the sixth time, i.e., they reverently approach Jesus for his instruction (5:1; 13:10, 36; 15:12 [cf. 15:15]; 18.1; cf. 28:17). Thirdly, a single character (Jesus) accomplishes the same function (sits to teach) for a fourth time (5:1–2, 13:1–3, 15:29). Finally, the actantial role of a character (Jesus as the hero/revealer) is redundant with his qualities implied in the scene and given explicitly to the reader elsewhere. For example, he is "God with us" (1:23), he has been given "all things" (ταῦτα) by the Father (11:25–27), he is the Wisdom of God (cf. 11:2 and 11:19), he is the lord of the Sabbath (12:8), and he is the Messiah-King (21:4–5).

The educated reader knows that there is a high probability that Jesus is about to deliver another discourse. The reader will sense also that the pace of the narrative is about to decelerate as it usually does for discourses./12/ This expected (and probable) deceleration, particularly in light of Matthew's redundant narrative/discourse structure, gives the reader a sense of stability which, in turn, lends effect to the stability of the hero or Jesus (cf. Eichenbaum: 116–20). In this respect Matthew almost qualifies for what Scholes calls a "self-regulating structure" (186–87).

Matthew 24:3a, b then is the "device laid bare" (cf. Tomashevsky: 94). The reader is aligned to receive a discourse from Jesus whose stability as "God with us" has been reinforced in several ways. The redundancies, or the schemata of the first code, have conveyed little aesthetic (or second code) information to the reader (cf. Iser, 1978:92–93). However, the sole function of the redundancies is to reinforce the familiar and thus "provide an unmistakable setting for the [aesthetic] information that is to be imparted" (Iser, 1978:94).

The disciples ask Jesus in 24:3c: "Tell us, when will these things be, i.e., what will be the sign of your advent and the consummation of the age?" (cf. Burnett: 198–208). The disciples' use of *"parousia"* and "consummation of the age" should evoke in the reader ideas of the *eschaton*, the divinely appointed "end" of this world-order. Although the word παρουσία has not yet occurred for the reader, the phrase "consummation of the age" has occurred (13:39, 40, 49). It is a stereotypical apocalyptic phrase with which the reader should be familiar (Burnett: 218–24), but the words still constitute a gap which the reader must naturalize in terms of generic expectations within his or her cultural code (Culler: 147; Scholes: 130–31; Perry: 36; Iser, 1980a:56). As used in the disciples' question, either a farewell discourse (especially in light of 23:39) or an apocalyptic discourse could be implied (Burnett: 185–93).

For our purposes it is sufficient to note that the reader has no reason to doubt that Jesus can answer the question of *when* (πότε) these things will occur. There has been no limitation of any kind on Jesus' knowledge up to this point in the text. In fact, Jesus has had foreknowledge of events (e.g., 16:21, 27–28; 20:18–19), and the thanksgiving in 11:25–27 implies, albeit ambiguously (ταῦτα), that Jesus has been given eschatological secrets (cf. 11:24) which he can reveal to anyone he chooses. The setting in 24:3 is an intimate one (κατ' ἰδίαν), and the reader, on the basis of prior reading (cf. 13:36), would certainly think that the "discourse is a secret revelation to a chosen few" (McNeile: 344; cf. Ellis: 118) The next verse is presented explicitly as Jesus' answer to their question (ἀποκριθείς). The disciples' question and every redundancy in 24:3 lead the reader to expect an answer *in temporal terms* (πότε) from an apparently omniscient character.

Jesus, however, never explicitly answers the question, unless verses 14 and 29–30 could be indirect and ambiguous answers. The most disconcerting thing for the reader's hypothesis, though, is that Jesus admits that he does not know when that day will come (24:36)./13/ The situation becomes even more perplexing if the reader tries to relate 24:14 to 10:23 (cf. Iser, 1980a:283). If the τέλος of 24:14 is synonymous with the coming of the Son of man mentioned in 10:23, then the reader is put in the difficult position of having the same Jesus predict the *parousia* but change the extent of the disciples' missionary task (from Israel to the οἰκουμένη). The reader knows with the disciples that *Jesus* is the Son of man ("*your* parousia," 24:3), but he continues in this discourse to speak of the Son of man in the third person.

The seven parables (24:32–25:46) reiterate two themes—be ready for the *parousia* and redeem the time. This "expanding indeterminacy" in terms of a precise time for the End may prompt the reader to ask: "What is the purpose of waiting?" (cf. Iser, 1980a:271). The scene in 25:31-46 answers that question by giving the reader insight into what lies beyond the τέλος, namely, salvation. After reading 25:31-46 the reader has been educated to understand that the End is not a goal in itself. Jesus' lack of knowledge about the time of the End has not only functioned as defamiliarization for the reader's view of Jesus; it has also, so to speak, almost "abolished history in favor of eschatology." The eschatological discourse, as prolepsis, has created a gap between story time and the predicted time by leaving out any unequivocal temporal depiciton of the stages between the first narrative and the predicted future. If the disciples as narratees have forged a link with the implied reader (cf. Dewey: 102-3), then the reader, with the disciples, stands "in the middest" of "an imaginatively predicted future" and must complete his or her understanding of the gap as best as he or she can (especially since the disciples make no reply to Jesus; see Kermode: 8). The reader knows, though, that his or her time, like that of the disciples, stands under the Divine δεῖ which will lead without fail to the appointed End (24:6, 8, 14, 22, 36; cf. 25:34).

4. Summary and Conclusions

The reader of the eschatological discourse does not have everything revealed to him or her. Although he or she has occupied a superior place throughout the narrative by knowing more than the characters, in this reading instant the reader knows no more about the End than do the characters (including Jesus). But surely the reader believes that the narrator knows the answer to "when"—after all the narrator is "omniscient!" The reader experiences the truth of the cliché that "to know All is not to tell All." The reader of the eschatological discourse, perhaps because of the redundancies in 24:3, has overshot the mark along with the disciples in their question. This failure is an important form of reader education (cf. Iser, 1980a:288).

For the subsequent reading experience the reader is still in a superior position to the disciples. He or she still knows that Jesus is "God with us" and that the divine plan which guides Jesus' history cannot be thwarted./14/ Thus even though the reader knows that Jesus' death must come to pass (e.g., 20:18-20) and that Jesus future is guaranteed, there is a suspense in the reading of the Passion Narrative (26:1-28:20). The reader knows what is going to happen, but he or she cannot communicate that knowledge to the disciples, with whom he or she has been aligned in the eschatological discourse (cf. Chatman: 59).

The ending of the Gospel (28:16-20) brings the reader back to the beginning (1:23). In redundant fashion the ending calls attention to all of the major themes of the Gospel./15/ The disciples once again approach Jesus reverently on a mountain (28:16-17), and the use of the proper name (28:18) tells the reader that the resurrection, which the reader expected (e.g., 17:9; 20:18-19), has not changed Jesus' identity. He is still the supersymbol by which the reader can encode the entire Gospel. The Gospel closes with Jesus' statement to the disciples: "and, behold, I am with you ($\mu\epsilon\theta$' $\dot{\upsilon}\mu\hat{\omega}\nu$) always, until the consummation of the age." The $\mu\epsilon\theta$' $\dot{\upsilon}\mu\hat{\omega}\nu$ converges for the reader the discourses of the narrator and of Jesus. The reader now receives in direct discourse from Jesus himself what he or she had received from the narrator in 1:23 (Jesus is God with us). As the last item in the text (the "recency effect") it confirms and reinforces the first items which the reader received about Jesus. Lohr's conclusion is instructive:

> The use ... which the Evangelist makes of *inclusio* in interconnecting his materials has not been observed. The conception of Jesus and his redemptive work dominates his Gospel. His characteristic title for Jesus is Immanuel—a name foretold by Isaiah (Is 7,14) and explained by Mt at the outset of his Gospel as meaning "God with us" (Mt 1, 23). At the very close of his book, the Evangelist records the promise of the glorified Christ ... "I will be with you always, to the very close of the age" (28, 20). Thus we have an *inclusio* which gives the spirit of the whole work. (410)

In other words, the reader's position now seems aligned with that of the omniscient narrator (cf. Belsey: 70-79).

The one remaining gap for the reader is the doubt of the disciples (28:17). Will there be closure for them? Will the events of the story and the narrator's discourse become fully intelligible to them? The reader cannot be certain that "in the middest" the disciples will carry out their commission, endure to the End, and be saved (cf. 24:14; see Richard A. Edwards).

NOTES

/1/ Iser's definition has the advantage of viewing the text as a system of "reconstruction-inviting structures rather than as an autonomous object" (Rimmon-Kenan: 119). Such a definition, however, does not escape the circularity involved in all interpretation. As Suleiman rightly notes: "I construct the images of the implied author and implied reader gradually as I read a work, and then use the images I have constructed to validate my reading" (1980a:11). Perhaps Mailloux is right. After surveying most of the theoretical definitions of the "reader," he concludes: "*In actual critical practice* [italics mine], all of these theoretical constructs become identical to the 'intended reader,' the person

/2/   Tannehill has pointed out how repetitions can disclose the points of emphasis and aid in interpreting a text (1975:43). Fowler has shown how repetition is one means by which a narrator can establish reliability (229: n. 23).

/3/   E.g., when the word ἵνα occurs, the probability is very high that either a subjunctive or an infinitive will follow. The probability that οἶκος will follow ἵνα is very low. In more technical terms, *redundancy* is the amount of certainty or uncertainty that a certain signal will occur. If there is only one possible outcome, uncertainty vanishes. "Uncertainty" refers to both the source and the recipient of the message. The recipient of a message, in other words, knows what he or she has received, but he or she cannot be certain that the message received was the message transmitted. On the other hand, the sender of the message cannot be certain that the message he or she transmitted was the one received. As J. R. Pierce puts it: "From the sender's point of view, the uncertainty of the recipient as to the true message is the uncertainty, or entropy, of the message source plus the uncertainty of the recipient as to what message was transmitted *when he knows what message was received*" (163–64). (For the mathematical formula of redundancy and an explanation of it see Elwyn Edwards [42–43].)

/4/   *Noise* means "any disturbances or defects in the communication system which interfere with the faithful transmission of signals" (Lyons, 1:44). "Noise" in a written text could be a misspelled word, the ambiguity of a word (is παρουσία "presence" or "arrival?"), another textual possibility (is one to read ἔχομεν or ἔχωμεν in Rom. 5:1?), etc.

/5/   Modern information theory, particularly this view of redundancy, is based on the work of Claude E. Shannon. For a slightly different definition of redundancy see John F. Young (58).

/6/   At the beginning of a text there are no expectations of the reader other than cultural ones (Perry: 53). Each text is projected onto a cultural text, i.e., the world view of a given time and place (Lanser: 56).

/7/   All of the ways in which the text reinforces the reliability of Jesus as "God with us" cannot be detailed here. The fulfillment quotations (1:22; 2:15, 17, 23; 4:14; 8:17; 12:17; 13:35; 21:4; 26:56; 27:9-10), the angel of God (1:20), the action of God Himself through dreams (2:12, 19), the star's guidance (2:9-10), the testimony of John the Baptist (3:14), and the voice from heaven (3.17; cf. 17:5) all function redundantly in the early parts of the text to reinforce the reader's initial impression of Jesus and educate him or her about how to read the rest of the text. Once the text has established a few deterministic interpretations, it can forego them in later parts of the text because the reader will continue to interpret the way he or she has been taught (Todorov: 75–76).

/8/   The christological titles only add to the reader's view of Jesus; they do not change it. One character can have a variety of titles; this is important for

'whose education, opinions, concerns, linguistic competencies, etc. make him capable of having the experience the author wished to provide'" (1979:95; the definition is Stanley Fish's [1980b:174]).

point of view, but not necessarily for the development of the character (cf. Uspensky: 25).

/9/ While 1:23 does predetermine certain conclusions for the reader and leaves little room for him or her to maneuver with regard to Jesus, there are still important gaps which the reader must attempt to fill. E.g., who are "his people," and what does it mean that he will "save" them (cf. Iser, 1980a:50, 121)? To say that the text "educates" the reader, then, does not mean that all of his or her reactions and decisions are predetermined. The reader "is simply offered a frame of possible decisions" (Iser, 1980a:55).

/10/ Cf. 1:1. The name Ἰησοῦς is the LXX rendering of "Joshua," but behind it stands the Hebrew for "YHWH saves." It seems that Greek readers would be familiar with Ἰησοῦς as "YHWH saves" by "popular etymology" (e.g., Acts 4:12, Philo's *De mutatione nominum* xii, 121; see Brown: 130–31).

/11/ Suleiman points out that since redundancies are an "essential means of creating syntactic and semantic *coherence*," they can operate simultaneously on multiple levels to create a "set of interrelated codes." She concludes, then, that it is extremely difficult to separate schematically the levels on which redundancies function, especially since there is as yet no general theory of textual redundancy (1980b:121–23).

/12/ It is, of course, virtually impossible to measure text-duration vis-à-vis story time, since the rate of reading is an unknown factor (cf. Genette: 86). Perhaps the comparison should not be between narratives and discourses but between the discourses themselves. If the discourses are arranged chiastically, the reader will sense that they "are artfully balanced both in length and subject matter" (Ellis: 14).

/13/ The phrase οὐδὲ ὁ υἱός has been a difficult one for readers to accept (cf. the textual apparatus). In terms of what the implied reader has been led to expect, the phrase is the most difficult reading.

/14/ Unless the disciples gained this information at 18:20 (and they show little indication that they did), they still do not know as much about Jesus' fulfillment of God's plan as does the implied reader.

/15/ There is general agreement that 28:16–20 summarizes the major themes of the Gospel. See Michel, Lohmeyer, Vögtle, Bornkamm, and Kingsbury (1974).

WORKS CONSULTED

Alter, Robert
    1981   *The Art of Biblical Narrative*. New York: Basic Books.

Barthes, Roland
    1974   S/Z. New York: Hill and Wang.

Beardslee, William A.
1970 *Literary Criticism of the New Testament.* Philadelphia: Fortress.

Belsey, Catharine
1980 *Critical Practice.* New York: Methuen.

Bolinger, Dwight
1971 *Aspects of Information Theory.* New York: Wiley Interscience.

Booth, Wayne C.
1961 *The Rhetoric of Fiction.* Chicago: University of Chicago Press.

Bornkamm, Günther
1971 "The Risen Lord and the Earthly Jesus: Matthew 28:16-20." Pp. 203-29 in *The Future of Our Religious Past.* Ed. James M. Robinson. New York: Harper & Row.

Brown, Raymond E.
1977 *The Birth of the Messiah. A Commentary on the Infancy Narratives in Matthew and Luke.* Garden City, NY: Doubleday & Co., Inc.

Burnett, Fred W.
1981 *The Testament of Jesus-Sophia. A Redaction-Critical Study of the Eschatological Discourse in Matthew.* Washington, D.C.: University Press of America.

Chatman, Seymour
1978 *Story and Discourse. Narrative Structure in Fiction and Film.* Ithaca, NY: Cornell University Press.

Culler, Jonathan
1976 *Structuralist Poetics. Structuralism, Linguistics, and the Study of Literature.* Ithaca, NY: Cornell University Press.

Dewey, Joanna
1982 "Point of View and the Disciples in Mark." Pp. 97-106 in *SBL Seminar Papers.* Chico, CA: Scholars Press.

Eco, Umberto
1979 *The Role of the Reader. Explorations in the Semiotics of Texts.* Bloomington: Indiana University Press.

Edwards, Elwyn
1969 *Information Transmission. An Introductory Guide to the Application of the Theory of Information to the Human Sciences.* London: Chapman & Hall.

Edwards, Richard A.
1983 "Uncertain Faith: Matthew's Portrait of the Disciples." An unpublished paper presented to The Catholic Biblical Association.

Eichenbaum, Boris
1965   "The Theory of the 'Formal Method.'" Pp. 99–139 in *Russian Formalist Criticism. Four Essays.* Ed. Lee T. Lemon and J. Marion Reis. Lincoln: University of Nebraska Press.

Ellis, Peter F.
1974   *Matthew: His Mind and His Message.* Collegeville, MN: The Liturgical Press.

Ewen, Joseph
1971   "The Theory of Character in Narrative Fiction." *Hasifrut* 3: i–30.

Fenton, J. C.
1963   *The Gospel of St. Matthew.* Baltimore: Penguin Books.

Fish, Stanley E.
1980a   "Literature in the Reader. Affective Stylistics." Pp. 70–100 in *Reader-Response Criticism: From Formalism to Post-Structuralism.* Ed. Jane P. Tomkins. Baltimore: Johns Hopkins.
1980b   "Interpreting the *Variorum.*" Pp. 164–84 in *Reader-Response Criticism: From Formalism to Post-Structuralism.* Ed. Jane P. Tomkins. Baltimore: Johns Hopkins.

Forster, E. M.
1927   *Aspects of the Novel.* Baltimore: Penguin. Reprinted 1963.

Fowler, Robert M.
1981   *Loaves and Fishes. The Function of the Feeding Stories in the Gospel of Mark.* SBLDS 54. Chico, CA: Scholars Press.

Genette, Gérard
1981   *Narrative Discourse. An Essay in Method.* Ithaca, NY: Cornell University Press.

Greene, W. C.
1951   "The Spoken and the Written Word." *Harvard Studies in Classical Philology* 60: 23–51.

Hamon, Phillippe
1977   "Pour un statut sémiologique du personage." Pp. 117–63 in *Poétique du récit.* Ed. Roland Barthes. Paris: Seuil.

Iser, Wolfgang
1978   *The Act of Reading. A Theory of Aesthetic Response.* Baltimore: Johns Hopkins.
1980a   *The Implied Reader. Patterns of Communication in Prose Fiction from Bunyan to Beckett.* Baltimore: Johns Hopkins.
1980b   "Interaction Between Text and Reader." Pp. 106–19 in *The Reader in the Text. Essays on Audience and Interpretation.* Ed. Susan R. Suleiman and Inge Crosman. Princeton: Princeton University Press.

Kelber, Werner H.
    1983   *The Oral and the Written Gospel. The Hermeneutics of Speaking and Writing in the Synoptic Tradition, Mark, Paul, and Q.* Philadelphia: Fortress.

Kermode, Frank
    1967   *The Sense of an Ending. Studies in the Theory of Fiction.* New York: Oxford.

Kingsbury, Jack Dean
    1969   *The Parables of Jesus in Matthew 13.* Atlanta: John Knox.
    1974   "The Composition and Christology of Matt 28:16–20." *JBL* 93: 573–84.

Lanser, Susan Sniader
    1981   *The Narrative Act. Point of View in Prose Fiction.* Princeton: Princeton University Press.

Lévi-Strauss, Claude
    1967   "The Structural Study of Myth." Pp. 169–94 in *The Structuralists from Marx to Lévi-Strauss.* Ed. Richard and Fernande DeGeorge. Garden City, NY: Doubleday.

Lohmeyer, Ernst
    1951   "Mir ist gegeben alle Gewalt! Eine Exegese von Mt 28, 16–20." Pp. 22–49 in *In Memoriam Ernst Lohmeyer.* Stuttgart: n.p.

Lohr, Charles H.
    1961   "Oral Techniques in the Gospel of Matthew." *CBQ* 23: 403–35.

Lyons, John
    1978   *Semantics.* 2 vols. Cambridge: University Press.

McNeile, A. H.
    1965   *The Gospel According to St. Matthew.* London: Macmillan.

Mailloux, Steven
    1977   "Reader-Response Criticism?" *Genre* 10: 413–31.
    1979   "Learning to Read: Interpretation and Reader-Response Criticism." *Studies in the Literary Imagination* 12: 93–108.

Michel, O.
    1950   "Der Abschluss des Matthàusevangeliums." *EvT* 10: 17–28.

Minear, Paul S.
    1982   *Matthew. The Teacher's Gospel.* New York: The Pilgrim Press.

Perry, Menakhem
    1979   "Literary Dynamics: How the Order of a Text Creates Its Meanings." *Poetics Today* 1: 35–64 and 2: 311–61.

Pierce, J. R.
    1961   *Symbols, Signals and Noise: The Nature and Process of Communication.* New York: Harper & Brothers.

Rimmon-Kenan, Shlomith
1983   *Narrative Fiction: Contemporary Poetics*. New York: Methuen.

Schneider, Carl
1965   "Κάθημαι." *TDNT* 3: 440–44.

Scholes, Robert
1974   *Structuralism in Literature. An Introduction*. New Haven: Yale University Press.

Shannon, Claude E.
1949   "The Mathematical Theory of Communication." Pp. 3–94 in *The Mathematical Theory of Communication*. Ed. Claude E. Shannon and Warren Weaver. Urbana: University of Illinois Press.

Shklovsky, Victor
1965   "Art as Technique." Pp. 3–24 in *Russian Formalist Criticism. Four Essays*. Ed. Lee T. Lemon and J. Marion Reis. Lincoln: University of Nebraska Press.

Suleiman, Susan R.
1980a   Editor, *The Reader in the Text. Essays on Audience and Interpretation*. Princeton: Princeton University Press.
1980b   "Redundancy and the 'Readable' Text." *Poetics Today* 1: 119–42.

Talbert, Charles H.
1977   *What Is A Gospel? The Genre of the Canonical Gospels*. Philadelphia: Fortress.

Tannehill, Robert C.
1975   *The Sword of His Mouth*. SBL Semeia Supplements, 1. Philadelphia: Fortress.
1977   "The Disciples in Mark: The Function of a Narrative Role." *JR* 57: 386–405.

Todorov, Tzvetan
1980   "Reading as Construction." Pp. 67–82 in *The Reader in the Text. Essays on Audience and Interpretation*. Princeton: Princeton University Press.

Tomashevsky, Boris
1965   "Thematics." Pp. 61–98 in *Russian Formalist Criticism. Four Essays*. Ed. Lee T. Lemon and J. Marion Reis. Lincoln: University of Nebraska Press.

Uspensky, Boris
1973   *A Poetics of Composition. The Structure of the Artistic Text and Typology of a Compositional Form*. Berkeley: University of California Press.

Vögtle, A.
1964   "Das christologische und ekklesiologische Anliegen von Mt 28, 18–20." *SE* II: 266–94.

Weaver, Warren, ed.
    1949   *The Mathematical Theory of Communication*. Urbana: University of Illinois Press.

Whatmough, Joshua
    1956   *Language: A Modern Synthesis*. New York: St. Martin's.

Wittig, Susan
    1973   "Formulaic Style and the Problem of Redundancy." *Centrum* 1: 123–36.

Young, John F.
    1971   *Information Theory*. New York: Wiley Interscience.

HISTORY AND TEXT:
THE READER IN CONTEXT
IN MATTHEW'S PARABLES DISCOURSE

Gary A. Phillips
Holy Cross College

ABSTRACT

Following structuralist exegesis has come a form of "post-structuralist" critical reflection that follows through with the structural impulse by submitting modern critical thought and practice to fundamental metaphysical and epistemological critique. The work of J. Derrida and M. Foucault provides resources for a different kind of critical practice to be employed by Biblical exegetes who find themselves dislocated by structuralism and disappointed with traditional ways of raising questions about text, context, history and reader. The following essay will examine elements of the post-structuralist thought of Derrida and Foucault and draw upon them in a reading of the Parables Discourse found in Mt 13. This reading represents a return of critical attention to the question of Matthew's text in relation to its reader and to its historical context.

History and Intertextuality

In the now well-publicized "Yale Manifesto" Jacques Derrida reflects upon the notion of borders, those lines of demarcation that constitute limits separating text from extratextual world, text from text, text from reader. He says:

> The question of the text, as it has been elaborated and transformed in the last dozen or so years, has not merely 'touched' 'shore,' *le bord* (scandalously tampering, changing, as in Mallarme's declaration, '*On a touche au vers*'), all those boundaries that form the running border of what used to be called a text, of what we once thought this word could identify, i.e., the supposed end and beginning of a work, the unity of a corpus, the title, the margins, the

signatures, the referential realm outside the frame, and so forth. What has happened, if it has happened, is a sort of overrun [*debordement*] that spoils all these boundaries and divisions and forces us to extend the accredited concept, the dominant notion of a 'text,' of what I still call a 'text,' for strategic reasons, in part—a 'text' that is henceforth no longer a finished corpus of writing, some content enclosed in a book or its margins, but a differential network, a fabric of traces referring endlessly to something other than itself, to other differential traces. Thus the text overruns all the limits assigned to it so far (not submerging or drowning them in an undifferentiated homogeneity, but rather making them more complex, dividing and multiplying strokes and lines)—all the limits, everything that was to be set up in opposition to writing (speech, life, the world, the real, history, and what not, every field of reference—to body or mind, conscious or unconscious, politics, economics, and so forth). (83-4)/1/

Using the concept of textuality defined in semiotic terms as a wedge, Derrida activates a full-scale effort at prying apart and exposing the private parts of the metaphysical system in the form of its literary and philosophical traditions. Against this backdrop his more particular concern in this essay is with the nature of the boundary questions that arise when such expressions as "that which lies outside of the text," the "referential realm outside of the text," and "the opposition to writing (speech, life, the world, the real, history . . . every field of reference)" are used. He does this by arguing the ridiculous and absurd case that the text overruns everything established as a limit to its working. What Derrida has in mind in raising the question of the text in history (western intellectual history) is to draw attention to the boundary implications of the textual/extratextual dichotomy. At one level Derrida's concern is clearly not to deny or to diminish what is other-than-text, since the logic of "difference" demands the "other," but to direct slumbering attention to the *border* and the *fact* of the border that separates text from what it is not. The question is: what do the boundaries signify? On what bases do we consent to distinguish text from extratext?

In raising the matter of borders Derrida shows this to be but the question of difference in yet another guise. Like Lacan's bar separating signifier from signified within the sign, the boundary separating the text from context ("speech, life, the world, the real") is an established border. For this reason "no border is guaranteed, inside or out" (78) on its own grounds but is authorized by some "*external* constraint;" all borders and relationships are arbitrary in some sense and can be violated. Derrida's major unfinished business is specifying the nature of this "external constraint;" for Foucault, by contrast, this matter lies at the heart of his historical writing.

A too-rapid reading of Derrida as a dismissal of the world by reduction to textuality fails to appreciate the problematic of borders that he presses: "I am here seeking to establish the necessity of this whole problematic of judicial framing and of the jurisdiction of frames" (88). In one sense this is not a call for total textualization of the world at the expense of context, history, referent or the other but a reaffirmation of difference as that which makes it possible before the fact to recognize the text/world relationship. Overrunning the border as he does with such statements as "Il n'y a pas de hors-texte" is part of an invasive strategy that underscores the necessity of difference/borders within history understood in the first instance as *textual history*. *Intertextuality*, the deferral of text to text, functions both as a confirmation of difference and the foreground for an understanding of the relation of text to historical truth. Once we recognize that the text consists of different traces that refer to other traces we can say with Riddel: "Derrida deprives us of literature in its relation to truth, only to give us back 'literature' in quotation marks, a text whose meaningfulness resides in its play of differences, including the insertion within of disruptive re-marks, other text, signs that are not filled with meaning but are always already doubles . . ." (247).

To understand the text within history is to comprehend its differential status in relation to other texts. Less convincing is the other side of this equation, namely that in order to understand history one must do so principally in intertextual terms, as a play of differences. Foucault will force the issue (1977:119–20). Derrida does not seek to dissolve boundaries (only to "spoil" them) nor "to extend the reassuring notion of the text to a whole extratextual realm and to transform the world into a library by doing away with all boundaries, all frameworks" (84). Rather, he problematizes the very notion of boundary and along with it the way we habitually think about text, meaning, reader, context, history, and so forth, by multiplying instead of leveling boundaries. Yet, a limited view of text as sign suggests the very position that he denies.

Hyperbole notwithstanding, why should Derrida's view of text and what it implies about the text's place within history be so disturbing? In part it is because he does not honor traditional boundaries which distinguish between literary criticism and literary history, boundaries which define the latter as a search for the cause, origin, goal, purpose of a text, an approach predicated upon the fundamental separation of text from history, text from reader, text from context. The more serious irritation, however, is the recognition that he forces of the metaphysical investment in these boundaries. The very idea of borders as an enigma is a blow to a tradition which views its borders as given. There is considerable reluctance in admitting that my borders are imposed (Isn't all history written by the winners?); that any separation of text from context is always an imposition (in the sense of "imposere"), which means deceit, an imposture ("impositus"): "It is always an *external* constraint that asserts a text in general . . ." (171).

Context is history viewed in terms of text and intertextual relationships. But what of the reader and the reader's role in this process of differentiation? First of all, there is no "ideal reader" who exercises a competence that connects text with text; no organized search for the spaces of indeterminacy to be mortared in so as to secure the text. Such a view implies a "right" sort of reader and an identification of the "right" borders. In the same way that historical context dissolves into texts, so the reader for Derrida gives way to the activity of writing, textual dissemination. This activity is neither a reactionary search for the true borders nor a radical overthrow of those that prevail: "No one inflexion enjoys an absolute privilege" (78). One would presume from this statement that it is a value-free activity. The reader is hardly more than an occasion for penetrating and expanding the network of texts that make up the literary intertextual chain; subjectivity is swallowed up by textuality. As an activity of reading the reader thus becomes a confirmation of an intertextuality that overruns those borders that have traditionally privileged the referent, the context, the cause, etc.; it is a strategy that at the same time gives the disseminating text free reign as signifier to cross the borders into other texts, and thus to show the signifying possibility of all texts with any context. The reader as controlling subject defers to the text. Moreover, whatever else we may want to say about them, the strategy of intertextuality dramatizes the force of difference that plays throughout history in the text. Whereas in the past we have been content to speak about literary history as genealogy from origin to telos because of the border separating text from context, now the semiotic nature of that imposed boundary is exposed and overrun to admit of the possibility of imposing a different distinction. We don't have far to go to see the reader as Bloom does as the opportunity for misreading, as the expression of the power of difference.

Thus we are forced to see in Derrida's notions of textuality and intertextuality that context and reader are not isolatable entities within an historical flow of events explainable simply in terms of cause/effect, accident, and the like, but are effects of textual differentiation. "The literary text is a play of textuality, not simply in the obvious sense that a 'work' of art always originates in the historical field of predecessors. Its own play of differences mirrors its displacement and reappropriation of other texts, and anticipates the necessary critical text which must 'supplement' it . . . " (Riddel: 98). In its relation to another text (to commentary, for example) neither preceding nor following text is superior or inferior, better or worse, *by nature*. From the point of view of differentiation, the critical reading as intertext is as necessary as the read text; it is a signifier/signified in relation to another sign, a supplement, a necessary complement. Derrida prefers to direct attention to the boundary conditions of texts; that for him is the way to address the question of context. Every text is best viewed as always already bound up within a systemic relationship with other texts, woven just as signifier is to signified, signifier to signifier, signified to signified. One text defers, differs from, is differentiated from another. In viewing all texts as supplements, as writing, the reader as individual voice disappears in favor of the effects of difference and the process of differentiation itself only to emerge in the guise of the new text. Textual history by this definition is not a search for an Ur-text that has founded all others but a demonstration of connections, of residual texts present by negative implication, by differences in not commonalities of source or intention. This means, of course, at the same time, that textual history is a series of gaps between text and text, text and reader in the same way that there are always gaps between signifiers and signifieds.

A work of literature from this perspective is but an interplay—to invoke Roland Barthes, a tissue, an interweaving, texture—in which there is always the possibility of finding and establishing a relationship with some other text, always a gap to be filled momentarily but never exhaustively, always more reading activity to take place, always room for one more reading. What this means for a literary history of the text is the short-circuiting of the search for the one meaning, the one signifier, the one stable mental content, the one voice, the ideal entity, the signified that one seeks to make present by invoking the proper method and technical hermeneutic. That texts are understood to camouflage a meaning only later to be reconstructed through careful interpretation is a traditional view of literary critical boundary conditions. But if we view "meaning" as continuous acts of dissemination, dispersion, spreading out, as functions of differentiation, interspersed through the myriad play of difference both within the text and between texts, the history of the text is an effort at displaying the boundaries/limits/conditions/differences that join and disjoin texts from one another.

"Il n'y a pas de hors-texte." One could read this as a denial of the external world and of history. But what we would say is that Derrida affirms the impossibility of escape on the one hand from the Western tradition and on the other hand from the play of differentiation, i.e., textuality. We cannot do with literature what Kant wanted to do but failed to do with philosophy—that is make it a science of knowledge, to get outside of our representation to some high ground of apodicticity where we can determine *the* truth about the text, its meaning and context; there is no respite from the process of differentiation. Derrida's contribution to the study of the history of the text, it seems to me, is that he helps us to see the hopeless philosophical efforts to escape and to search for some foundation (of truth, meaning, language, or subject), and the equally hopeless efforts of textual critics who do the same with their texts either by separating texts from other texts or divorcing texts from their readers. There can be neither escape from the Western tradition and its boundaries nor an overlooking of these borders, only an overrunning of the limits. Yet, what can Derrida's textual strategy say about these "external constraints?" Precisely because the reading subject is decentered, how are we to describe the structures that organize and effect the production and reception of texts? Derrida gives us a textual history outside of culture and cultural praxis that leaves us with far too many gaps.

History and Discourse

The cultural history practiced by Foucault, Said, and others contrasts sharply with the textual history that characterizes Derrida and other deconstructionists. If we admit to the limitations inherent in either situating the text outside of culture or in textualizing culture itself, but insist upon the importance of structur*al* thinking, then we must think of history in a different post-structuralist way. Foucault's notion of history as discourse moves us in that direction.

For Foucault history is defined in terms of discourse: history is an "immense panoply of heterogeneous discursive practices" (Leitch: 148). To describe history is to identify the discursive rules and procedures for writing and thinking characteristic of a particular field of knowledge within a cultural space as a whole. The way one goes about describing such rules of discourse is by a type of archeological excavation that attempts to disclose the distinctive layers of discursive rules operating within a particular era. This is done not by finding the universal forms of order covering a given period of time but the extant forms of disorder; by concentrating upon the discontinuities and differences of discourse within and between eras, the faults that separate one discursive practice from another. Archeology thus makes *discontinuity* a "positive" descriptive tool: it helps to restore to "our silent and apparently immobile soil its rifts, its instabilities, its flaws" (Foucault, 1970:xxiv).

Discourse is the key to a description of cultural history, for if we can identify the *rules* that make certain ways of speaking/writing possible, we can recover those unacknowledged structures that permit one kind of knowing to be practiced and not another. Discovery of these rules enables us to explain why then certain objects and concepts appear and others do not, why certain theories take shape, change, disappear, etc. Knowing the discursive rules means understanding how it is possible for thought and action to assume the shape that they do in a given historical era. History is disclosed through an identification of shifting discursive rules and practices over time.

The discursive rules that prevail at particular moments and contribute to a culture's distinctive character do not fall under the control of individual speakers or writers. In this sense, when it comes to understanding a text, Foucault is not at all concerned to identify generic constraints and rules of literary expression that individuals can choose to employ or not, but with what he calls the "positive unconscious" that underlies any individual expression and is at the same time responsible for the possible discursive practices of that individual. On this score Foucault shows his indebtedness, like Derrida, to the structural turn in that for him too the subject is "decentered" in relation to the discontinuities and regularities of the range of different discursive practices in a given historical period. (This is no less so in the post-modern period; we are simply more cognizant of it.) With the subject removed from the center the rules that govern discursive practice move to center stage. No longer can the historical critic simply identify the subject's thoughts, desires, intentions, background, and the like—though Foucault acknowledges that this research remains a possibility for others; rather, he/she must also investigate the *system of formation* that regulates discourse and makes it possible for the subject to be subject, thus to be able to know and to speak in a certain way (see Foucault, 1982:186-90).

Within each discourse (viewed as a "discipline" in the modern period), the statements that are uttered follow the rules peculiar to that discursive time and space. Those rules have their locus regionally in what Foucault calls the "archive," that is the "general system of the functions and transformation of statements" (1982:130) whose regularities make a volume of discourse organized and understandable. The archive is that set of rules "which gives what we say—and to itself, the object of discourse—its modes of appearance, its forms of existence and co-existence, its system of accumulation, historicity and disappearance" (1972:130). As such, historical investigation is an identification of various archives in force and the differences or discontinuities that exist between one set of rules and another. It is in this sense that Foucault can assert, "History becomes 'effective' to the degree it introduces discontinuity into our very being" (1977:119-20).

Importantly, the archive is not reducible to textual functions. Though Foucault concentrates upon the discursive character of knowing, "its forms of existence and co-existence," non-discursive aspects of culture, namely institutions, social relations, economic conditions, etc., which escape discursive reduction, occupy an important place. For Foucault discourse and non-discourse stand in a complementary relationship. Whatever non-discursive realm there is is knowable precisely in and through the practice of discourse which conditions the knowability of things. In contrast to proponents of a textual history that concentrate on intertextuality, Foucault argues for a notion of context that is discursive in nature, the system of cultural rules responsible for the production and reception of discourse. While in fact texts do defer to other texts, the rules and regularities that make the praxis of deferral possible constitute the suitable object of historical investigation. This is not to deny at some level the free play of texts and criticism but to situate it with respect to conventions and forces that operate at the level of a culture's being (see Said: 703-14). Texts and interpretations of texts, including their textual *form*, function as means of institutional power. Whether we speak of producing or reading a text, Foucault insists upon locating the text within the network of discursive, i.e., social, practices. Unlike Derrida's free-floating signifier/text which maintains rules of operation reducible to *differentiation* between it and other signifier/texts, Foucault's signifier/text is situated within a constructed, reticulated system of rules, regularities, and discontinuities (see Leitch: 150).

The rules and regularities comprising a discourse have both a positive and a negative side to them. Within an archive, speaking about some issues and topics is as much prohibited as speaking about others is permitted and encouraged. Control over what can be said or not said lies within the network of institutional and societal forces which prescribe limits, define boundaries, and organize conditions by which the "truth" emerges. We can see this negative role, for instance, in the function of commentary or criticism in so far as the critic reinforces by way of his/her interpretation, by his/her praxis, prevailing discursive rules and institutional controls: explaining, disallowing interpretations, determining meaning, all share in the larger activity of critical reading whose very form and presence acts to exclude alternative forms of reading, explaining, interpretation, etc. Discourse is a praxis and as such an exercise of social control. The exclusionary side to the archive points to the conflictual nature of the power that takes its shape in the form of the rules themselves. Knowledge and speaking are modes of power and conflict.

Clearly such a view of the exclusionary character of the archive affects the way Foucault understands the reader of the text. Foucault's notion of discursive constraints contrasts with Derrida's view of the hedonist reading by which the text is dissemination and speaking about the text, a self-indulgent act with seemingly little self-conscious cultural significance. Since the archive enforces negative speaking rules, reading is far from an unfettered exercise on the reader's part of the play of the signifier for all it's worth, but a regulated activity with fixed limits and enforced borders as regards what can and can't be said. Moreover, the limits placed discursively upon the reader signal an inclusion of the reader within history in another way. Since either production or analysis of a text is always a matter of cultural power being employed in one way or another, reading always exceeds a strictly individualistic play of differences between texts and assumes a *place* within the life and praxis of a culture. Reading is an act of power. Thus if we take seriously Foucault's description of the text as imbedded within a matrix of discursive rules and institutional power flow, then a reading is far from groundless or abysmal; it occupies a place within that given cultural archive./2/

These different orientations toward context and reader should not obscure what Derrida and Foucault have in common. Each in his own way prescribes a form of critical openness and theoretical ingenuity that generates a different kind of knowledge about texts. Also each situates the critical task on even footing with literary production itself, subject to the same forces of differentiation as "literary" texts. And finally, each attempts to locate a critical space that tries to avoid what Said calls the "self-confirming operations of culture and the wholly predictable monotony of a disengaged critical system" (Said: 682). The fact that Foucault does not completely succeed, and Derrida even less so, in making criticism an openly contentious cultural praxis ought not deter us from drawing insights from both in exploring the historical character of Matthew's Parables Discourse.

Matthew 13 as Intertextuality and Discourse

A brief overview of the contents of chapter 13 is in order. In this third of five major discourses by Jesus, Jesus speaks to the crowd and to the disciples on the matter of the Kingdom of Heaven. In the first half of the chapter Jesus presents four parables to the crowd who are identified in verse 2 as his listeners. However, the disciples' questioning in verse 10 indicates that they too have heard his discourse. Jesus seemingly speaks in two ways: first in an obfuscating manner to the crowd, and second in a clarifying way to the disciples. After verse 36 Jesus turns from the crowd to the disciples, now Jesus' exclusive hearers, both to explain the meaning of the parable and to offer three additional Kingdom of Heaven parables. At the end of the chapter Jesus speaks a final parable about a scribe trained for the Kingdom of Heaven (verses 51–52).

Matthew 13 displays a number of curious features: first the rapid and sudden change in hearership from crowd to disciples after verse 36; the matter of intentional obfuscation with respect to the crowd; the significance of the disciples' hearing and the contrast with the crowd's non-hearing; the presence of seven Kingdom of Heaven parables and an eighth non-Kingdom parable, and the function of the chiastic pattern broken by the Scribe text; the use of the Old Testament citations on the one hand to explain Jesus' speaking, and on the other the role of narrative discourse in explaining the Old Testament citations. This latter point raises the important question of the relationship of text to text, of "discourse to discourse," in the chapter and of the overlapping and interpenetration of enunciations on the part of various characters within the text (Isaiah, Jesus, the narrator, for instance). Using the notion of intertextuality and discourse we will make an effort to address certain of these questions.

Viewing Matthew 13 as a series of related texts, we can identify three different categories of texts contained within the chapter: (1) traditional Scripture (Isa 6:9-10; Ps 78:2); (2) Jesus' parabolic Kingdom texts (parables of the Sower, Wheat and Tares, Mustard Seed, Leaven, Treasure, Pearl, and Dragnet); and (3) Matthean narrative commentary (Sower allegory and Wheat and Tares allegory, Scribe parable, indeed the narrative as a whole). At the same time, we can associate with these different categories of texts different speaking or enunciating voices, different speaking times and different enunciative relationships. In the first instance, the enunciators of the Old Testament texts are identified as "prophets" (vv. 14-15, 35), though in the case of the Isaiah citation it is actually Yahweh who speaks; in the case of Jesus' Kingdom parables Jesus is the enunciator; and in the third instance the narrator "Matthew" is the one who speaks. Since the text belongs to the narrator, the narrator is in one sense enunciator of all the discourses. But it will be important to identify those moments when the narrator chooses to speak covertly and at other times overtly. As we will see, the superposing of enunciations works with the intertextual relationship among texts to create a narrative with depth of voice and of ear.

Using the notion of sign to explain the interrelationship of text to traces of texts, we can say that the intertextual phenomenon is fundamentally semiotic in nature: sign in relation to sign. Following Peirce's triadic model of the sign, the sign structure is made up of sign/ground (more or less equivalent to Saussure's "signifier"), object and interpretant (equivalent to Saussure's "signified"). According to Peirce, each and every sign can become an element within or for another sign by virtue of the functional relationship of the elements of the sign to one another: sign/ground, object and interpretant or a combination of these elements in one sign can become sign in its own right, each with its sign/ground, object and interpretant; and each of these elements may become a further sign with its own triadic elements, and so forth, ad infinitum. So, for example, the sign/ground—object relationship in one sign can become the object for a second sign which transforms the first interpretant into a new sign/ground demanding *its* interpretant. We can represent this semiotic process as follows:

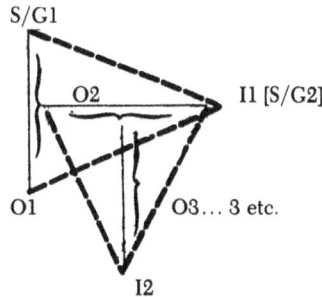

Fig. 1. Basic Triadic Sign

The intertextual process whereby texts defer to other texts can be explained in semiotic terms as the generating or producing of a new text-as-sign onto a previous text-as-sign. In the case of Matthew's text this process can be charted through the text as a serial production of different texts (represented often as different discourses) acting as interpretants for previous texts (both inside and outside of Matthew's gospel narrative). In this way the narrator "builds" her text and also the competence of her reader at one and the same time. The use of the triadic schema has the advantage of allowing us to describe not only the relationship of Old Testament texts to Jesus' parables to Matthew's narrative interpretation of both but also of showing how the interpenetration and overlapping of different speaking voices takes place, or the way different levels of discourse operate in relation to one another throughout the chapter.

In the schematic description to follow, we will concentrate attention upon the intertextual development and connections that are formed by various discourses within Matthew's text. Much more could be said about the narrational structure and the semantic organization of the text, but for the moment we will focus upon certain semiotic aspects of the text's structure. We will also point out ways in which the different levels of texts and of voices overlap and the effect achieved with respect to the reader, understood here to be the narrator's discursive partner. The case that we will argue is that the reader of Matthew 13 is manipulated by the narrator into acquiring a cognitive and pragmatic ability to hear and to speak Jesus' parables and to engage in a praxis that produces both word and deed (to become a "Scribe equipped for the Kingdom of Heaven," v. 51).

After some initial narrative description situating Jesus vis-à-vis the crowd, the narrator offers an interpretive comment about Jesus' parable-speaking to the crowd: "he told them many things in parables." This seemingly bland observation from the narrator's omniscient, bird's-eye perspective awaits further specification. We can represent the relationship of the narrator's interpretation to Jesus' Sower parable as follows:

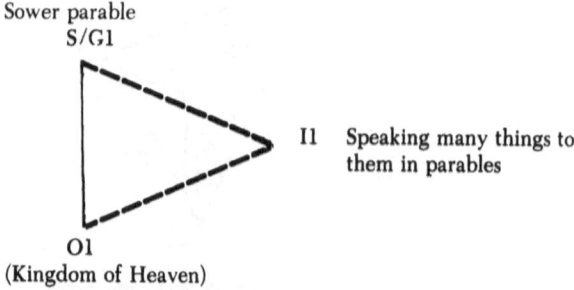

Fig. 2. Sower Parable as Sign

The narrator's description functions as an interpretant from the narrator's perspective to Jesus' parable-speaking, though the text leaves the object of the parable-as-sign ("Kingdom of Heaven") unspecified. In verse 24 the narrator will make it clear retroactively that the illustrand of the Sower parable is the "Kingdom of Heaven." The delayed identification is good narrating technique that forges anaphoric links between what precedes and what follows in the text. In this sign two enunciative levels are connected: the narrator's with Jesus'. It is also worth noting that the interpretive remark paraphrases the Prophetic words in verse 35b; only after verse 36 will it become clear that the Psalm text is cited proleptically in verse 3.

The narrator's remark in verse 10, "then the disciples said to him . . ." introduces a new textual element in the discourse in which a different interpretant of Jesus' speaking to the crowd is offered. This explanation, enunciated by Jesus (but also by the narrator), is an interpretation not of the parable per se but of the narrator's interpretation (I1) *speaking in parables to the crowd* (see Fig. 3). This new interpretation (I2) is two-fold: a blessing upon the disciples and a curse upon the crowd. The object within this second sign (O2) is the Sower parable-Kingdom of Heaven relationship, and the sign/ground is the narrator's previous interpretive remark about Jesus' speaking to the crowd (I1/[S/G2]). Textually speaking, the explanation operates as an interpretant at two levels: on the one hand *inside* the narrative time, space and events as Jesus' commentary directed in response to the disciples' question; on the other hand *outside* of narrative time of Jesus in the narrator's time as commentary addressed to the reader about what has just preceded. We may represent the textual relationship and development as follows:

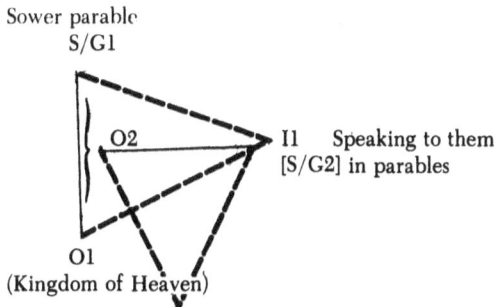

Fig. 3. Sower Parable and Explanation as Sign

Viewed rhetorically, the explanatory discourse displays a chiastic structure which moves from curse to blessing to blessing back to curse:

Those who have will have more	(v. 12a)
Those who have not will have less	(v. 12b)
Isaiah paraphrase (Isa 6:9-10)	(vv. 13b, 14-15)
"Q" eschatological prophecy (Matt 25:29)	(vv. 16-17)

In intertextual terms, the explanation is a double-text curse and blessing comprised of paraphrase and cited text (and in the case of the blessing a double citation). To know many things in parables is both good news and bad news: the good news is that knowing the meaning of what it means to speak/hear the parables leads to abundance and then some; the bad news is that speaking/hearing the parables leads nowhere—no further understanding, commentary, interpretation—nothing and less. The contrast between the two types of hearing and speaking relationships to Jesus is intensified when Jesus *stops* speaking to the crowd (i.e., leaves the crowd and turns to the disciples, v. 36) but *continues* speaking about speaking/hearing and about the Kingdom of Heaven to the disciples. From the point of view of the reader the explanation extends the parabolic text. The allegory of the Sower text extends it further, thereby constituting textual proof that right hearing/speaking is continued speaking/hearing. Within the narrative events the crowd never speaks, while the disciples continue to ask questions; outside of those events the reader is provided with a pragmatic example of abundance in the continuing form of the intertextual development of the narrative itself. When we come to the Scribe parable at the end the issue of the metalinguistic and pragmatic implication of the parable will come to a head. Will the *reader* be able to continue to speak as instructed?

In semiotic terms the Sower parable as sign yields two different interpretants, two different texts. On the one hand the good news explanation by Jesus is repeated by the Q prophecy, which defers to yet another text (the parable of the Talents, Matt 25:29). A fragment from one parabolic text is used to interpret the meaning of speaking in parables itself. We have a textual loop: parable text unfolds parable text. In a similar way the bad news expressed as a paraphrase of Isa 6:9–10 is repeated in the Isaiah citation. Textual duplication has often been cited as a Matthean literary technique. Here we see an instance of it described in semiotic terms.

The Isaiah text also serves an important double function as sign. Within the narrative events at the level of Jesus' discourse with the disciples, the Isaiah text is used by Jesus to interpret Jesus' speaking relationship to the crowd (as curse). At the level of the narration, the narrative of Jesus' parable-speaking functions as an interpretant of Isaiah's text (as fulfillment of Scripture). Sign/ground in the first instance becomes interpretant in the second. Within the narrative events Scripture interprets story; while outside narrative time story interprets Scripture. The reversible flow in interpretation and in the textual relationship illustrates Derrida's point that the borders separating texts can be crossed and are dependent upon an external point of view.

In the allegorical interpretation of the Sower parable (vv. 18–23) an interpretant of a different sort is introduced into the narrative flow. Unlike the explanation of parable-speaking/hearing to the disciples in verses 10–17, the allegory of verses 18–23 interprets the parable proper as sign and functions interpretatively at the same enunciative level as the narrator's remark in verse 3 (I1). In order to distinguish visually between the two interpretants and their respective contents, we will place the allegorical text to the left side of the initial triad schema. We will also see that the function of the allegory as interpretant is pragmatic, while that of the initial interpretation and subsequent interpretation in the explanation is cognitive.

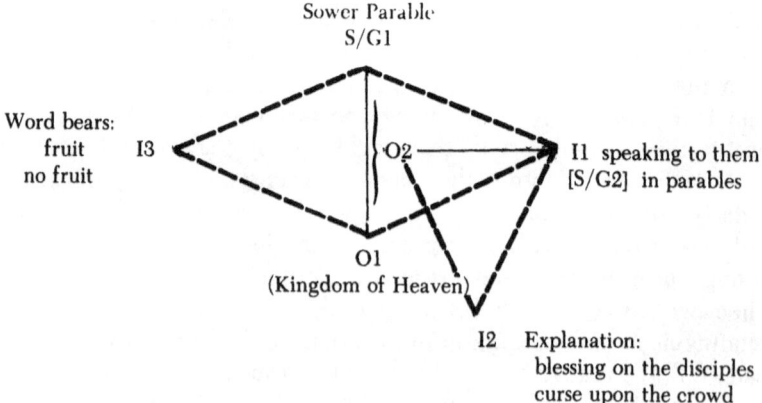

Fig. 4. Sower Parable, Explanation and Sower Allegory as Sign

Several comments are in order. First, the parable-as-sign can yield two different interpretants. While such interpretive productivity has been traditionally linked with the parables, by no means is it an exclusive property of the narrative or trope; interpretive productivity is a characteristic, as Peirce has shown, of all signs. Second, the allegorical interpretation turns the meaning of the Sower parable in a different direction: away from *speaking/hearing* as a *cognitive* response to *pragmatic responses* to parable-speaking/hearing. The parable admits of different types of interpretants (both cognitive and pragmatic). We can anticipate that successful speaking/hearing produces both hearing, word and action; unsuccessful speaking/hearing only silence and aborted action.

Following the allegory the narrator asserts her presence within the flow of the text once again with the stitching comment "Another parable he put before them" (v. 24). Over the course of the next nine verses the narrator will make two more such comments and offer three more parables of the Kingdom of Heaven. The object of the parable-as-sign is identified retroactively (to v. 3). Intertextually, the Wheat and Tares, Mustard Seed and Leaven texts produce a textual loop that operates in two ways. First, within the narrative events Jesus returns to the initial discursive situation with the crowd and repeats without success his word; second, aside from the good story-telling technique, at the narrator's level the reader is returned with considerably more information than the crowd to the start of Jesus' discourse. The crowd remains at a cognitive zero point—no net increase in knowledge; indeed with the physical separation of Jesus from the crowd in verse 36 Jesus is discursively separated as well. The reader, by contrast, has supplementary texts, multiple interpretants, connections with Scripture. The return to the starting point provides the reader with the opportunity now for a kind of competence check: with whom is the reader to be discursively identified—crowd or disciples? Which speaking/hearing relationship and praxis will be assumed? The reader is positioned as "critical" reader, in the sense of Webster's second definition—to be situated in a decision-making post—now to know cognitively that the parable means more than itself. The allegory at the same time brings the reader to know that parable hearing/speaking will have a pragmatic interpretant which the second half of the discourse will develop.

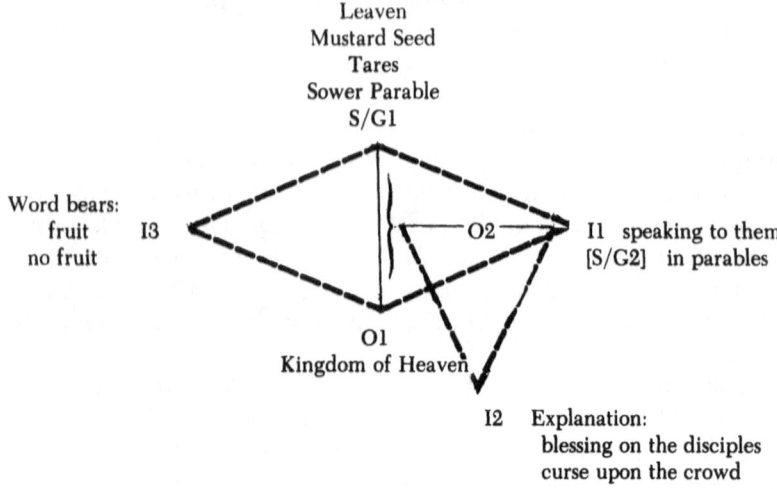

Fig. 5. Sower Parable, Explanation, Sower Allegory
and First Parable Triad as Sign

Following the three Kingdom parables the narrator intrudes decisively with a commentary upon all that has preceded and effectively brings to a close the first half of the discourse. No longer speaking through Jesus, the narrator postures herself in an omniscient way once again (cf. v. 3a) and interprets what speaking to the crowd in parables therefore means. The narrator's description and cited text, Ps 78:2, function like Isa 6:9–10 as an interpretant both inside and outside the narrative events to interpret Jesus' parabolic speaking and the narrator's own interpretive development of the textual tradition. So far within the narrative two types of speaking/hearing relationships with Jesus are contrasted: the crowd as not hearing/speaking and so cursed, the disciples as hearing/speaking and blessed. The disciples' blessed hearing is one that opens up ears and mouths to new hearing/speaking rather than leaving one deaf and mute. At the narrator's level the reader is given to understand that successful speaking/hearing is itself continued parabolic speaking, continued Psalm speaking, continued Isaiah speaking, continued speaking of Yahweh's word (cf. Isa 6:8), continued narrative itself: different, interrelated, and complementary texts.

But intertextuality *also* means praxis—a productivity that yields fruit as word (metalinguistic word about the Word) and as deed. Thus parable hearing is more than a cognitive operation that extends the Word through the production of interpretation or deferral to another text, though it is that to be sure. It means producing a harvest of action which the second half of the discourse will go on to develop. Cognitive competence as understanding and parenesis as praxis of the word are equally and necessarily interpretants of the parabolic word. From the narrator's point of view as enunciator of Ps 78:2, the meaning of parable-speaking is, to repeat, the production of the allegorical text and the extended narrative of this whole process. Here again we have textual recursivity. Opening the mouth in parables (v. 34) is an interpretant of the allegory of production of word as fruit; conversely, the allegory interprets the Sower parable. Word interprets act; act word. Borders are crossed and recrossed. Like the Isaiah citation before it, the narration of speaking in parables is interpreted as Ps 78:2, and conversely the meaning of Ps 78:2 is the narrative of speaking in parables, of opening the mouth in parables as is done in the Scribe parable of verses 51–52.

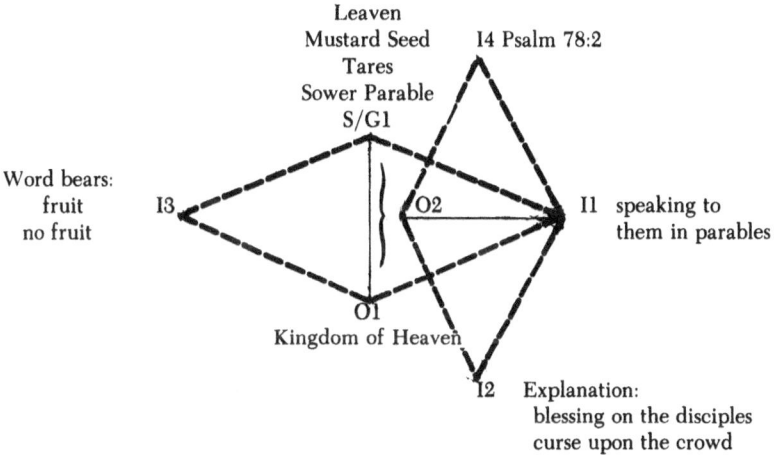

Fig. 6. Psalm Citation and Matthew 13 as Sign

What has the reader learned? She has received both parables and interpretation of the parables in the form of allegory, explanation and narrative of parable speaking/hearing. At minimum she can conclude that the parable as text is always incomplete; the parable demands to be supplemented by other texts, parabolic and non-parabolic. Conversely parables of the Kingdom are supplements to Scripture and to commentary, a network of signs and texts.

In the second half of the chapter the interpretive focus shifts from cognitive competence (being the right kind of hearer/speaker) to praxis (doing the right kind of deed), though the interpretants are never completely separated from one another, as the Sower and Wheat and Tares interpretants illustrate in Fig. 7. If the first triad of parables functioned to reveal the enigmatic character of parable-hearing/speaking, the second triad in verses 44–50 illustrates the parenetic significance of Jesus' speaking.

In verses 36–42 the narrative shifts back to a previous discursive relationship, in this instance with the disciples. At the level of the narrative events the narrator's description of Jesus' leaving the crowd in verse 36 closes the book on the Jesus-crowd discursive relationship and opens up a new chapter with the disciples. At the level of the narration, the reader repeats the act of returning to an earlier moment of the narrative in which the parable of the Sower is replayed (in v. 24), though now it is the parable of the Wheat and the Tares. For this reason we can place the Wheat and Tares allegory in a comparable semiotic relationship to the Wheat and Tares parable as the Sower allegory to the Sower parable.

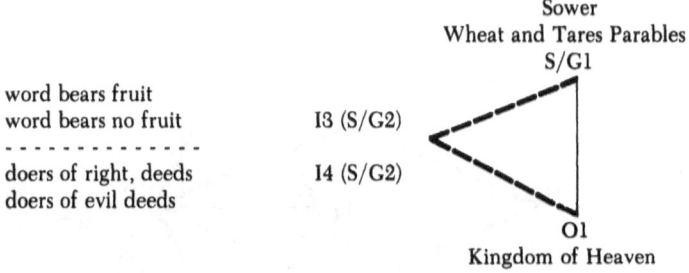

Fig. 7. Wheat and Tares Parable and Allegory as Sign

Like the Sower allegory in verses 24–20, the Wheat and Tares allegory functions directly as an interpretant of the parable-as-sign rather than as an interpretant of the meaning of speaking in parables. The Sower allegory concentrates upon an identification of praxis as related to the word; the Wheat and Tares allegory describes praxis in terms of right action.

The second triad of kingdom parables in verses 44–50 (Treasure, Pearl, and Dragnet) follows upon the Wheat and Tares allegory. Unlike the first triad (cf. Fig. 4), which functioned semiotically as a redundant sign of the Sower parable, the second triad functions as an interpretant of the Wheat and Tares allegory to make clear the meaning of doers of righteous deeds versus doers of evil deeds. If the discursive effect of the first triad was to underscore the enigmatic character of hearing/speaking (in relation to the crowd), the effect of the second is to underscore the praxis associated with the parables (in relation to the reader). Rhetorically the parable triads look the same (see Wenham: 517); intertextually, however, they work quite differently. Finally, note that the object of the parable-as-sign has shifted from the Kingdom of Heaven in the first half of the discourse to righteous/unrighteous doing in the second half. This parallels the movement that Jeremias has identified in the development of the parabolic tradition from word about God to word about the church.

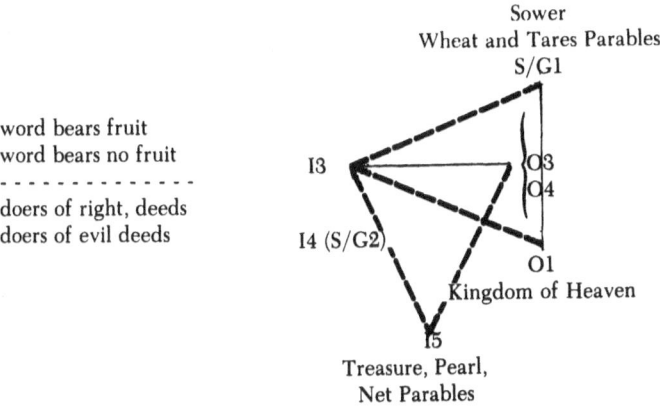

Fig. 8. Wheat and Tares Parable, Allegory, and Second Parable Triad

Addressed within the narrative to the disciples, the parable triad interprets righteous praxis, though unrighteous praxis is implicit in the Treasure and Pearl parables and explicit in the allegorical conclusion to the Dragnet parable. Outside the narrative events the reader sees how the interpretation of the interpretation of the parable is, in one sense, the parable itself: parable interprets parable. Jesus' enunciation at one level of the discourse functions to interpret the narrator's enunciation at another level. Borders are crossed.

The reader at this level is subject to an intertextual expansion of Jesus' parabolic discourse whose interpretation is enigmatic hearing/speaking in verses 3ff. but becomes productive word in verses 18ff. Matthew's narrative expands the meaning of parabolic speaking in the second half of the chapter from a discrimination between types of hearer/speakers to types of praxes. The import of this distinction will become clear in the final Scribe parable in verses 51-52.

Within the Dragnet text we encounter a third allegorical interpretant (vv. 49-50). Though brief in comparison with the two preceding allegories, the allegory of the Dragnet functions climactically in the intertextual unfolding of the chapter.

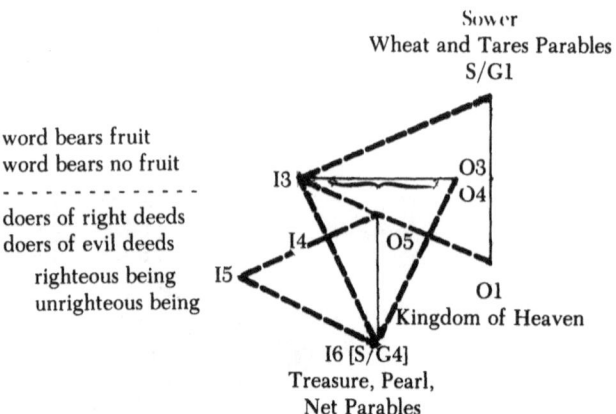

Fig 9. Wheat and Tares Parable, Allegory, Second Parable Triad
and Net Allegory as Sign

This allegorical interpretation is grafted onto the Dragnet parable in the same way that the Wheat and Tares and Sower allegories interpret their respective parables. Outside the narrative (though the indices of the narrator's intervention have all but disappeared, suggesting a possible merger of the enunciative levels), the reader receives this third allegory as reinforcement of the interpretive, intertextual technique. More importantly, verses 47–48 restate the meaning of what it means to act righteously (and unrighteously), while verses 49–50 interpret that praxis as eschatological consequence. The latter's focus is upon the results of righteous/unrighteous behavior in contrast to the allegory of the Wheat and the Tares in verses 37–43. If anything, the Dragnet allegory ignores the positive praxis and concentrates upon the negative (righteous being versus unrighteous being). Being and doing are interpretatively linked. Hearing/speaking the parables of the Kingdom entails considerable risk (both positive and negative) and serves as point of contrast to the bountiful eschatological blessing of verse 12 (and Q and Mt 25:29). The Dragnet allegory defers to a prior text both inside and outside of the narrative.

The Scribe parable in verses 51–52 functions as a concluding interpretant to what has been developed throughout the chapter. In the figure below we represent the Scribe text as grafted onto the Sower and Wheat and Tares allegories and, by implication, to the second triad of parables devoted to defining righteous/unrighteous praxis.

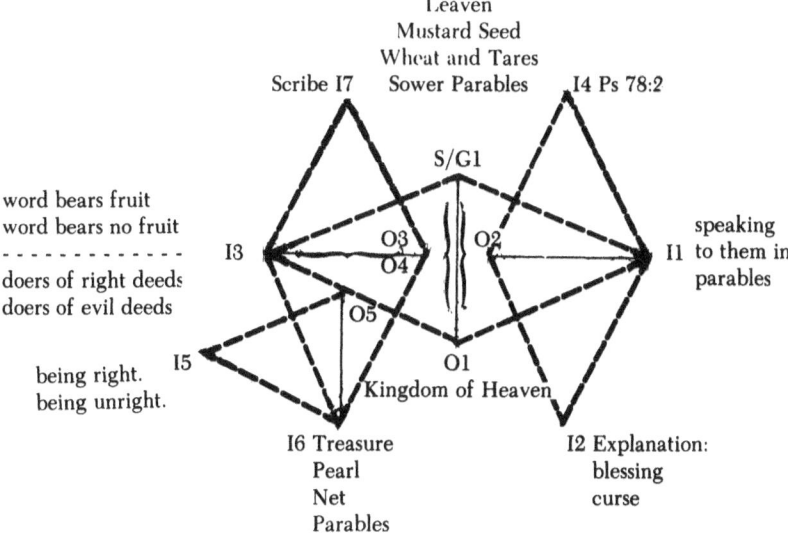

Fig. 10. Matthew 13 as Sign and Semiosis

Within the narrative events the Scribe parable functions as Jesus' concluding word to the disciples about what it means to interpret parabolic texts. Grammatically speaking, the antecedent to the pronoun "these things" in the question "Have you understood all of these things?" includes within the narrative not only the Wheat and Tares allegory but also the Sower allegory in verses 18–23, effectively connecting both halves of the chapter. At the level of the reader "these things" refers to the *entire* preceding narrative and is intended to ask: Have you understood what it means for the crowd to be unable to speak/hear the parables and for the disciples to succeed? Have you understood the cognitive and pragmatic meanings of the parable texts? The reader benefits from the position of having seen and compared the experience and outcome of the crowd's and the disciples' speaking/hearing. Like the Psalm text, the Scribe parable functions as a summary interpretant of all that has preceded: in the Psalm text the narrator speaks about speaking in parables; in the Scribe parable, she actually speaks in parables (the Scribe parable). She *produces* a parable as a response.

From one point of view we can say that the function of the Scribe parable is to turn the productivity of parable-hearing into the production of parables themselves, a metaparabolic production and a fitting conclusion to a discourse on the Kingdom parables; other types of discourse will be undertaken, as the eschatological discourse in chapters 24–25 and the farewell discourse in 28:18–20 will make clear. We have already noted that this is the only one of the eight parables whose illustrand is "a scribe trained for the Kingdom of Heaven." The contrast in parabolic comparison is marked: saying what the Kingdom is about to saying what someone who understands and follows the Kingdom is all about. The reader, as one who follows the action of the narrative from inside and outside, finds the designation of "You" implied in the verb "Have you understood" then to direct the question and the narrative text away from crowd and disciples to the reader herself. Are you able to produce Kingdom texts and interpretations and extend the intertextual process of the tradition in the way the narrator has? Are you able to unfold the parables of Jesus and the prophecies of Isaiah and the Psalmist and Q through a praxis that transforms word about the Kingdom speaking itself? Can you produce midrash upon the Kingdom text by following the narrator's example and producing a new interpretant that draws upon old texts and new texts to extend the parabolic text, Scripture, prophecy, God's word? If the reader says "yes" along with the disciples then the reader's own transformation itself becomes an interpretant to the narrative, a lived transformation not only of speaking parables/speaking about parables but also of becoming a righteous one equipped for teaching and preaching that is yet to come. Remember: we are only half way through Matthew's gospel. The intertextual process continues to unfold narratively, metalinguistically, pragmatically.

From what we have seen, intertextuality as defined along the semiotic lines of Peirce and illustrated in the unfolding text of Matthew's Parables Discourse is an expanded notion of text that includes praxis (righteous deeds) and the very transformation of the reading subject herself (a scribe trained for the Kingdom of Heaven). The notion of history as textuality in this expanded sense avoids the pitfalls associated with the deconstructionist view of text (grounded upon the dyadic model of sign proposed by Saussure) and brings us closer to the notion of text in context as a regulated praxis set forth by Foucault. In the latter sense the text and reader are configured within history as a result in part of particular discursive rules. Textuality as a function of semiosis defined in Peircian terms eclipses the limitation of textuality in Derrida's literary sense and inserts both text and reader within a history discursively defined. This is a history whose borders do not lie exclusively between literary texts but between texts and reading subject, texts and discursive rules, texts and institutional power, and the like.

Foucault's insistence upon an identification of discursive rules as a way of understanding cultural artifacts such as texts and readers leads us to identify rules of formation that permitted the emergence of Matthew's parables text and the Gospel as a whole. One avenue toward such a description is an identification of those rules governing rabbinic textual interpretation and practice. Thus we would situate the Parables Discourse as serious play upon text and tradition and our reading as more than an idiosyncratic, abysmal reading in deconstructionist terms. Reconstruction of the system of rules underlying Rabbinic and early Jewish Christian textual practice should enable us to see Matthew's text as made possible by a dynamic and dialectical understanding of the relationship between tradition and revelation and the role of commentary as extending revelation. While any full description is impossible here, some idea of the direction that such a description might take will help to explain the "forms of existence and co-existence" of text and tradition in Matthew's text.

The concepts of revelation and tradition in Rabbinic thought are decisive for understanding Matthew's text and reader history. If Gershom Scholem is correct, by the end of the second century of the common era a dramatic shift had taken place in the Rabbinic understanding of revelation. Understood initially to comprise "the concrete communication of positive, substantive and expressible content" (Scholem: 289), a content expressed in Torah, revelation by the end of this period was understood to comprise "everything that will ever be legitimately offered to interpret its meaning" (Scholem: 289). This included not only Torah in written and oral forms but commentary upon Torah in both written and oral forms. This shift signals the birth of tradition. Revelation (as Torah) and tradition (as commentary upon Torah) are soon viewed in a complementary and dynamic relationship. Revelation calls for tradition to unfold and disclose the significance of the Holy One in history in order to make "effective the revelatory word in every concrete state and relationship entered into by a society" (284). In the process tradition acquires authority all its own, thereby challenging the notion of a single, self-evident and univocal expression of revelation.

The way is thus opened for the emergence and continuing growth of revelation as tradition and the attribution of religious authority to new interpretations of Torah. Just as revelation expands to make room for tradition, so too Torah as *written* text makes room for oral expression: Torah is Torah whether written or oral in form, ancient or modern in origin. Like written Torah, Torah in its oral expression assumes a position of revelatory prominence as a word which seeks to illumine, interpret or otherwise expand the meaning of Torah. Consequently, Mishnah *continues* the revelatory Word as part of a tradition that "turns the Revelation" as Talmud says, "Turn it [revelation] and twist it again, for everything is in it" (287). Furthermore, commentary, like oral Torah that precedes it, enters the tradition and becomes a means by which revelation continues, unfolds and addresses readers in new historical situations./3/

If, on the one hand, in Rabbinic thought tradition, which includes oral Torah and subsequent commentary upon Torah, is understood to be part of an on-going unfolding process of revelation, the inner logic of this thought, on the other hand, demands the "patently absurd position" that revelation *already* includes within itself as sacred tradition *all* subsequent interpretation: hence "Revelation comprises everything that will ever be legitimately offered to interpret its meaning" (289). This enables the view that all later interpretation, even that which postdates and conflicts with previously writen Torah, was given to Moses at Mt. Sinai. So Rabbi Joshua ben Levi: "Torah, Mishnah, Talmud and Aggadah—indeed even the comments some bright student will one day make to his teacher—were already given to Moses on Mount Sinai" (289).

Operating beneath this "fiction" is a view of truth that sees it as "given once and for all, and it is laid down with precision. Fundamentally, truth merely needs to be transmitted" . . . "everything that can come to be known has already been deposited in a timeless substratum . . ." (289). From this it is clear that in contrast to Hellenistic practice, Rabbinic practice does not conceive of revelation in *cyclical categories but in development, historical and textual* forms, as commentary, as new interpretation, as intertextuality, a productivity and interconnection of texts and interpretations arising within different historical moments.

As revelation's embodiment, tradition in its many textual forms is a productivity that demands a hearing. In this sense tradition is nothing short of a textual praxis on the part of the hearer/scribe. But a hearing can be either of two sorts. On the one hand, the hearer/scribe can function as a mere receptacle of preserved tradition (i.e., of past texts and interpretations), one who does not augment the tradition in any way with his own questions and experiences. Tradition for this sort of hearer is petrified, closed. On the other hand, the hearer/scribe can press the tradition *in and through his questioning* to make "Torah concrete at the point where he stands . . . Applicable *hic at nunc*, fashioning his specific form of concretization in such a manner that it may be transmitted" (sic) (297). Because tradition is active, individual hearing, it is always interpretation in response to some previous interpretation; it "perceives, receives, and unfolds that which lives in the Word." Thus "it is the force within which contradiction and tensions are not destructive but rather stimulating and creative" (298). By nature idiosyncratic and conflictual, tradition performs its revelatory function not through monologic, monovalent texts but *dialectically* in the oftentimes conflictual expansion and development of the tradition through the power of new commentary and interpretation.

Thus, within the historical development of Rabbinic Judaism two major tensions emerge that affect the understanding of revelation, tradition and interpretation that have a profound effect upon textual production and reading practice. First, the notion that revelation is "consistently unified and self-enclosed" gives way to a view in which it becomes "diversified, multifold and full of contradictions." The content of, indeed the very notion of, revelation is in process of development. The second tension is in the conflict between texts which constitute the tradition in the form of commentary. The varied possibilities for interpreting Torah and giving expression to the truth about the Word are all contained within the tradition, namely Torah itself. Witness, for instance, the interpretative debates between the schools of Hillel and Shammai. Even where Hillel interpretation comes to be considered decisive, the contradictory Shammai commentary is nevertheless preserved with great care. Tradition is a dialectical unity of conflictual, if not contradictory, interpretations.

To summarize certain elements of the discursive understandings regulating the reading of Matthew's text for a first-century reader, we can identify the following constraints:

> (1) *Revelation* as giving rise to tradition; tradition is an essential outgrowth of and complement to revelation. Tradition is the process by which revelation, codified in the form of Torah, is experienced in ever-different textual forms in ever-different historical contexts.
>
> (2) *Tradition* as both a *process* and *productivity* that generates response on the part of the hearer/scribe of Torah. Tradition demands new interpretation, questioning and expression to meet new situations. Like revelation, tradition is unfolding and never complete.
>
> (3) *Commentary* as the textual expression of tradition and the "legitimate form through which truth is approached" (289). Tradition lives in the multiplicity of texts and in the production of hearers/scribes of Torah who are thereby inserted within the developing flow of the tradition itself—the labyrinth of texts and practices—and through interpretation/commentary unfold the truth of the Word. In this way the recipient of the tradition forms and is formed by tradition in the disclosure of revelation.
>
> (4) Finally, as textual interpretation, tradition is intertextuality of a *dialectical* sort. Containing within itself mutually exclusive interpretations, tradition makes a place for both the orthodox and the heretical, Hillel and Shammai, dialogues in conflict. Were it otherwise tradition would become a dead letter, a monologue, stasis.

What stands out in Matthew's narrative midrash upon Jesus' Kingdom speaking as seen in the use of the Scribe parable is that Matthew essentially does Jesus one better: Matthew does what Jesus does and then something more, something different. Whereas Jesus speaks about God as King in parabolic ways that are unusual and disorienting (as extraordinary growth, baking bread, purchasing merchandise, fishing seas), Matthew incorporates those texts, interprets them by grafting them onto Matthew's own allegories and scripture and fashions all into a narrative that puts the tradition into "proper" perspective (Matthew's perspective, of course). In Matthew's case this peculiarly Matthean perspective emerges at a time that demanded the development of a textual competence on the part of the readers/hearers of his Gospel, to make them Kingdom speakers and Kingdom hearers for their own day, a day rich with interpretative conflict with pharisaic counterparts. If Matthew's effort in chapter 13 (and the Gospel as a whole) is any indication, to be a scribe trained in the Kingdom of Heaven is not simply a matter of miming Jesus, though following his atraditional interpretative strategy (i.e., using parabolic form and Kingdom of God content) has now become traditional and as such an authoritative way. Following Jesus' lead is not necessarily a rekindling of apocalyptic expectation or prescription of millenarian ethics but an affirmation of one's place within the larger tradition of which Jesus himself is a part and a playing of the interpretative, intertextual game competently and persuasively. Interpretation is in this sense an intertextual game, a serious game that follows rules which enable one to say many things. Textual production is an effort to win, to exert interpretative power and control by entering into the tradition's dialogues, engaging in arguments, using its images and literary texts in order to bring from out of the tradition the older elements of the tradition so that the tradition can come alive in a new way and address the present believing community in a way that counts. It is an effort to become that kind of hearer who presses the tradition's texts in and through her questioning, who makes "Torah concrete at the point where she stands."

From the point of view of intertext and discourse, Matthew's Parables Discourse is more than a mimetic historical description, or an imaginative reconstruction of the way Jesus was as speaker for God's Kingdom, or a play of semiosis for its own sake. Matthew 13 is a manual for scribal or interpretative self-development, a working template of how to be a competent scribe oneself; it is a text that leads to the production of the reader by showing narratively the way Jesus spoke and the way Matthew the narrator speaks. "If you have ears to hear then listen."

But Matthew's text indicates that it is possible to say more. Here we encounter the gaps. The reader of this text is transformed into a reader who by her very reading and practice becomes a living interpretant of Jesus' parabolic tradition, the prophetic tradition preceding him, and Yahweh's own word. As such she enters as a part of the tradition as participant in revelation's continuing expression. However, she cannot interpret exactly as either Jesus or Matthew did. Becoming a scribe/hearer of the Kingdom of Heaven necessarily means finding one's own way of saying it and being it through dialogue with predecessors, and that portends interpretation, a way characterized by conflict, reversal, undermining, challenging, contesting, and the like.

Finally, what is the point of all this parabolic effort? Certainly the play of dialectic itself can give a rush of excitement; certainly the interplay of texts yields some measure of uncanny satisfaction in its own right. But for Matthew's text and reader in its historical context intertextuality and discourse keep the tradition alive in the effort to unfold God's revelation. To read the text is to interpret the tradition and to participate in the revealing action of God in the world.

NOTES

/1/ Derrida's "Living On. *Border Lines*" is an essay in two parts with both "essays" running continuously on the top and bottom of the same pages. "Living On" refers to the top half, "*Border Lines*" to the bottom.

/2/ Said contrasts Derrida and Foucault on just this score: "Whereas Derrida's theory of textuality brings criticism to bear upon a signifier freed from any obligation to a transcendental subject, Foucault's theories move criticism from a consideration of the signifier to a description of the signifier's *place*, a place rarely innocent, dimensionless, or without the alternative authority of discursive discipline. In other words, Foucault is concerned with describing the force by which the signifier *occupies* a place . . ." (709).

/3/ In a text that sounds very much like the Scribe parable in Matt 13:50, Scholem remarks: "Out of the religious tradition they bring something entirely new, something that itself commands religious dignity; *commentary*. Revelation needs commentary in order to be rightly understood and applied" (287).

WORKS CONSULTED

Derrida, Jacques
   1979   "Living On, *Border Lines*." Pp. 75–176 in *Deconstruction and Criticism*. Ed. Geoffrey Hartman. New York: Seabury.

Foucault, Michel
   1979   *The Order of Things: An Archeology of the Human Sciences*. New York: Pantheon.
   1972   *The Archeology of Knowledge*. Trans. Sheridan Smith. New York: Harper & Row.
   1977   *Language, Counter-Memory, Practice: Selected Essays and Interviews*. Trans. Donald Bouchard and Sherry Simon. Ed. Donald Bouchard. Ithaca, NY: Cornell University.

Leitch, Vincent
   1983   *Deconstructive Criticism: An Advanced Introduction*. New York: Columbia University.

Riddel, Joseph
   1979   "From Heidegger to Derrida to Chance: Doubling and Poetic Language." Pp. 231–52 in *Martin Heidegger and the Question of Literature*. Ed. William Spanos. Bloomington, IN: Indiana University.

Said, Edward
   1971   "The Problem of Textuality: Two Exemplary Positions." *Critical Inquiry* 4: 673–714.

Scholem, Gershom
   1971   "Revelation and Tradition as Religious Categories in Judaism." Pp. 282–303 in *The Messianic Idea in Judaism and Other Essays upon Jewish Spirituality*. New York: Schocken.

Wenham, David
   1974   "The Structure of Mt XIII." *NTS* 25: 509–17.

III
READING SECULAR TEXTS

HENRY VAUGHAN:
THE READER IN CANTICLE-LAND

Georgia B. Christopher
Emory University

ABSTRACT

The reader of *Silex Scintillans* must shed any New Critical presupposition that Henry Vaughan is a metaphysical poet or that he will demonstrate Stanley Fish's view that reading poetry is a drama of verbal syntax. Rather, Vaughan's poetry relies heavily upon the semantic component in language to present randomly occurring numinous moments, which owe their power to the coincidence of two or more privileged semantic fields: nature, Herbert's *The Temple*, and Holy Scripture.

The reader of Henry Vaughan's poetry rarely comes to it with a virgin mind, for it can be assumed that he will possess at least a crypto-piety and that he will come to *Silex Scintillans* (1655) after reading the other metaphysical poets, notably John Donne and George Herbert. From this experience, if not from the old New Criticism and the poetry it spawned, the reader will most likely have internalized Donnean poetic values. The reader, however, will find this Donnean esthetic inapplicable, yet he will need to have read Herbert on a prior occasion, in order to perceive the full allusive dimension of *Silex Scintillans*. Vaughan claimed to be one of Herbert's "converts" (391), and so at its very genesis his poetry is implicated in the circuit of reader-response. Herbert is important, not so much as a mentor imperfectly emulated, than as an index to scale of Vaughan's daring metaphorical leaps. To read Vaughan, then, is to engage his immediate poetic forebears in a paradoxical way.

Readers who come to Henry Vaughan for the first time look in vain for the witty analogical reasoning and well-crafted monologues of Donne and Herbert. They find instead weak associative structures of the sort that has led some commentators to conclude that Vaughan cannot think at all

(Bennett: 72). The Donnean esthetic celebrated by T. S. Eliot in 1924 has continued to dominate the reading of all the metaphysical poets, including Vaughan, and Stanley Fish's early work in reader response criticism has done little to dislodge the privileged position that the "rhetorical" ingredients of poetry hold in the criticism of early seventeenth century poets.

Fish, for example, chose "The Holdfast" by George Herbert—a poem that does not contain a single image—to demonstrate how the reader is required to negotiate verbal syntax like an obstacle course (1970:475-95), how he must follow its twists and turns, variously finding his expectations confirmed or disappointed. Fish shows that Herbert's poem, "The Holdfast," draws the reader through a series of assertions, each of which is immediately denied. To put the matter briefly, Herbert's speaker first boasts of his "strict" observance, then of his "trust" in God alone, and finally of his confession "that nothing is our own."/1/ By the end of the poem, Herbert's speaker discovers that he has even one less thing to claim—"But to have nought is ours, not to confesse/That we have nought" (8-9). The structure (and purport) of the poem thus hangs upon a series of syntactical markers—"but," "yet," "then"—and moves toward silence because at the end of the poem the speaker has nothing left to claim before God.

It would be difficult to overestimate the distance between such a rhetorical poem dealing with a theological point and Vaughan's poems which, at their best, create a sense of present and momentary grace. If one looks for such minutely-crafted rhetorical drama in *Silex Scintillans*, one is bound to be disappointed, because the esthetic inherent in Fish's practice, if not his theory, fails to take account of the sensuous, "mystical," or uncanny in poetry. By definition such moments are removed from probability and hence from the realm of literary foreshadowing or rhetorical expectation.

The success of *Silex Scintillans* depends upon another kind of verbal play, one derived, not from syntax, but from the semantic component of language. Vaughan's poetry is famous for its luminous patches, single lines, and gilded half-lines that occur at unpredictable moments throughout long stretches of undistinguished verse. What typically distinguishes these golden lines is a vocabulary that is concrete and sensuously evocative. Vaughan's best effects—and they are often spectacular—derive from the play of semantic fields—the sudden shift from one field to another, or the sudden coincidence of disparate fields. The rhetoric of Ben Jonson's verse epistles, which is blandly discursive (Pettet: 191), provides the neutral field against which three privileged semantic—and very concrete—fields play. Though one hesitates to argue that pedestrian or merely competent verse is functional, Vaughan's grand effects depend upon the reader's recognition that on occasion competent verse is being superseded by brilliant poetry.

The privileged semantic fields which thus interrupt Jonsonian rhetoric are pastoral nature, George Herbert's devotional verse, and the text of Holy Scripture. Of the three, it is the vocabulary of the greenworld that sets Vaughan most apart from Donne and Herbert. One can, of course, find images from Nature in poems by Herbert, but when he mentions a "busie orenge-tree" it is not the mysterious vegetative presence of the tree that he invokes but the concept of productivity ("Employment II"). Neither Donne nor Herbert can manage to create the visual appeal of a line like, "The unthrift Sun shot vital gold/A thousand pieces."/2/ Nor do they take much interest in the natural world as such.

Vaughan, however, characteristically takes up the stance of someone immediately *perceiving* the natural world:

> ... heark! In what Rings,
> And *Hymning Circulations* the quick world
> Awakes, and sings.
> ("The Morning-watch," 9–12)

As in secular pastorals, the state of perceived nature expresses the state of the poet's heart./3/ So the dawning world expresses his praise and exaltation in "The Morning-watch." Nature provides him with both the locus of his devotions ("I walked the other day [to spend my hour] Into a field/where I had seen .../A gallant flower") and an object of meditation. But above all, the greenworld—with its birdsong, vocal springs, wells, groves, stars, storms, and sunrises—furnishes him with a vocabulary that is concrete, sensuous, and highly charged. As Cassirer observes, concrete, sensuous, and highly charged. As Cassirer observes, concrete language invokes the sacred versus the profane, while abstract language treats the theoretical versus the practical (2:338). If the spirit clings, not to the abstractions of rhetoric but to bodies, then the living bodies of birds and plants become the prime bearer of the numinous in *Silex Scintillans*. In "The Retreate," Vaughan longs for his childhood when both his heart and his perception were pure:

> When on some *gilded Cloud*, or *flowre*
> My gazing soul would dwell an houre,
> And in those weaker glories spy
> Some shadows of eternity. (11–14)

We shall return later to the way in which Vaughan's poetry suggests the mystery of a natural object so as to convey intimations of ultimate being.

The second—and the most problematic—semantic field upon which Vaughan's poetry draws is that of Herbert's devotional volume *The Temple*. The recognition of Vaughan's Herbertian vocabulary is of prime importance in the experience of reading Vaughan, for one immediately becomes aware of the enormous number of borrowings therefrom: some dozen titles, countless images, and an even greater number of phrases and tag-lines. As often as not, the borrowing loses its "rhetorical" flavor, once it is in Vaughan's hands. Herbert's poem "The Water-course," for example, is a drily emblematic poem in which the reader is advised to turn his tears into the right channel, that is, towards his own sin. In Vaughan's "The Water-fall," however, this image becomes an emblem of the soul's return to its source, but only after the poem's persona has paused in meditation before the water-fall as natural object and has evoked its sensuous presence. The result of Vaughan's "presentational" strategy is that he manages to suggest something numinous about the very being of the waterfall, which he apostrophizes thus:

> With what deep murmurs through times silent stealth
> Doth thy transparent, cool and watry wealth
>   Here flowing fall,
>   And chide, and call, . . .
>   ("The Water-fall," 1-4)

The recognition that the borrowings from Herbert (who himself took much from Donne) invariably appear shorn of their rhetorical ambience introduces a major variable into any reading of Henry Vaughan. These blatant debts may prove to be a hermeneutic stumbling block if the reader is disappointed that Herbert's particular brand of wit does not accompany them or if he is disappointed that Herbert's careful crafting of the total poem is missing. On the other hand, a reader may discover that Vaughan has taken the Herbertian component and given it a radically new pertinence. He may percieve a brilliant shift of reference that shocks much like the punch line of a joke when it is genuinely surprising and yet uncannily apt. In a very important sense, Herbert's poetry becomes the ground for much of Vaughan's metaphorizing.

A case in point is Herbert's "Even-song," a poem whose child-like persona begins by enumerating how little return his "play" has brought to his Father that day, but the poem ends with the affirmation: "Yet still thou goest on,/And now with darknesse closest wearie eyes,/Saying to man, *It doth suffice*" (17-19). The poem concludes with one of Herbert's characteristic images from the store of common household implements:

> Thus in thy ebony box
> Thou dost inclose us, till the day
> Put our amendment in our way,
> And give new wheels to our disorder'd clocks. (21-24)

Night is thus imaged as an "ebony box," a cabinet of safe confinement like a Tudor bed—or the ebony case of a watch that its owner winds every night and replaces in its case upon retiring. The poem ends with explicit rhetoric: "Not one poore minute scapes thy breast,/... And in this love, more then in bed, I rest" (30, 32). This poem seems to have been the point of departure for Vaughan's "The Evening-Watch," for in it he treats the theme of God's Providence and similarly introduces the image of the clock. The field of reference, however, has shifted alarmingly. It appears that Herbert's "ebony box" suggested a coffin to Vaughan, who presents two child-like speakers conversing in a cozy grave: "Farewell!" the soul says to the body, "I goe to sleep; but when/ The day-star springs, I'll wake agen..../How many hours dos't think 'till day?" (1-2; 10). What had been a homely image of diurnal Providence in Herbert's poem now becomes a rather grand symbol of eschatological provenance:

> Ah! go; th' art weak, and sleepie. Heav'n
> Is a plain watch, and without figures winds
> All ages up; who drew this Circle even
>   He fils it; Days, and hours are *Blinds*.
> Yet, this take with thee; The last gasp of time
> Is thy first breath, and means *eternal Prime*. (11-16)

While the referent of Herbert's clock is a single man, the referent of Vaughan's clock is all of history. To recognize the radical new pertinence that Vaughan has given Herbert's image is to perceive its appropriation as a bold metaphorical leap, which very often in Vaughan happens to be a leap of cosmic proportions. The epiphanic force of such referential shifts is quite beyond the reach of Herbert's quiet cerebral wit. If Vaughan were not so patently Christian, one would be tempted to say that the distance between Herbert's metaphors and those of Vaughan is just the distance between fancy and imagination. Vaughan, of course, is no Wordsworthian (Garner), yet such poems as "The Dawning" and "The Constellation" place Vaughan's esthetic on the borders of the visionary.

Though Vaughan responded very passionately to Herbert's poetry ("The Match"/4/ is a direct reply to the challenge laid down in Herbert's "Obedience") and though he claims that Herbert's poetry "diverted him from [the] foul and overflowing *stream*" of secular love poetry to the composition of devotional verse (391), it appears that Vaughan was not inspired by the same Herbert that mid-twentieth century critics have been reading. If the reader turns first to Vaughan's 1655 Preface to *Silex Scintillans*, which stands to his devotional verse as a kind of *Poetics*, Vaughan's Herbertian borrowings need not be a hermeneutic stumbling block. The reader will discover that Vaughan himself read *The Temple*—not as a "Metaphysical" poet a la Eliot—but as a "Prophetick poet." In his preface he links our gentle Herbert, the rational private man, with the visionaries. Like Saint John the Divine, who wrote *The Apocalypse* on the Island of Patmos, and *Hierotheus*, a (mythical) first-century Bishop of Athens whom Dionysius the pseudo-Areopagite mentions as a poet (Hutchinson, 392n), Vaughan's Herbert is a holy seer who had a *door . . . opened to him in heaven* (392). This identification is all the more striking because the conventional type of the divine poet was David.

There are good historical reasons, moreover, why Vaughan identifies with the exiled Saint who wrote the Book of Revelation instead of the prosperous King of Israel. Vaughan was writing his poems during the Interregnum, a time when the Puritans had killed the King and disestablished the Anglican Church. Vaughan's own brother had been ejected from his living in Breconshire and his church had been shut up. Whereas Herbert could celebrate his church in the image of a comfortable matron ("The British Church"), Vaughan depicts her as a ravished damsel whose beloved is far away among the Hills of Myrrh ("The Brittish Church" [*sic*]). Unlike Herbert's settled world that is bounded by liturgy and the church calendar, Vaughan's universe is chaotic and is bereft of familiar authority. Without King and Church, his world lacks all transcendent, validating structures; hence meaning is deferred till the end of time. Until then, as Vaughan indicates in his Preface, all that one can hope for is fitful intimations of transcendent meaning—sparks from the flint as both the author's emblem (386a) and his Latin title suggest. Vaughan's position is that of a quietist; he strains for "sanctity" because it "will *procure* for us (so easily communicable is that *loving spirit*) some small *prelibation* of those heavenly *refreshments*, which descend but seldom" to men of indifferent *holyness* (392).

In such a benighted world, it is not surprising that one of Vaughan's persistent themes is longing for the Second Coming. Nor is it surprising that typically his poems, like his world, have no settled order, so that the intermittent "golden" moments in his devotional volume appear as "prelibations of heavenly refreshment." These moments carry a touch of mystery and usually occur when one of Vaughan's privileged semantic fields (from nature, from Herbert, or from Scripture) interrupts a passage of competent but uninspired rhetoric. In "Rules *and* Lessons," for instance, two stanzas of pious advice ("Never sleep the Sun up; prayer shou'd/Dawn with the day . . ." [7-8] and "Serve God before the world" [19]) are suddenly transfused by a visionary touch—"Note the *hush*/And *whispers* among [the creatures]. There's not a *Spring,*/Or *Leaf* . . . doth know *I AM*" (13-16). Even in such a patently pedagogical poem, the act of perception is instinct with the numinous. Sometimes, as in "Regeneration," Vaughan presents a direct vision—"The aire was all in spice/And every bush/A garland wore" (45-47). Sometimes he only likens an access of "heavenly refreshment" to a suddenly remembered perception:

> midst all storms I feel a Ray of thee;
> So have I known some beauteous *Paisage* rise
> In suddain flowres and arbours to my Eies,
> And in the depth and dead of winter bring
> To my cold Thoughts a lively sense of spring.
> ("Mount of Olives II," 17-21)

To be sure, Herbert also notes fluctuation in his perception of grace, but he always treats it in conceptual terms: "thy diviner world of grace/ Thou suddenly dost raise and race,/And ev'ry day a new Creator art" ("The Temper II," 6-8). Vaughan's genius is that he substitutes a presentational strategy for discursive terms. To the principle that a change in perception indicates a change in consciousness, Vaughan adds the principle that a change in language indicates a change in consciousness.

This brings us to the third privileged semantic field that Vaughan draws upon for numinous moments—that of Scripture. Scraps of biblical language, or even recognizable paraphrases, are made to carry enormous authority in *Silex Scintillans*. As one might expect from a seventeenth century poet, Vaughan uses Scripture in a variety of ways, sometimes as a proof text giving final closure to a poem like "The Mutiny" and sometimes as the text for an entire meditation as in "And do they so?"/5/ The great epiphanic moments in *Silex Scintillans*, however, come when a recognizable bit of Scripture seems to erupt from the midst of a line whose rhetoric is transparently Jonsonian. For example, "Abel's Blood," a poem that deplores the brutality of the Puritans and the carnage of the Civil War in Britain, declares that the country bathes "not in a shallow flood,/But in a deep, wide sea of blood." It is

> A sea, whose lowd waves cannot sleep,
> But *Deep* still calleth unto *deep*:
> Whose urgent *sound* like unto that
> *Of many waters*, beateth at
> The everlasting doors above, . . . (15-19)

Here a stray line from Psalm 47:2—"*Deep* still calleth unto *deep*"—comes as a myserious divine incursion because, while it does not call up any particular passage of Scripture, it is still recognizably biblical. The phrase is given new pertinence when linked with further biblical allusion, that is, with mention of "souls [who] behind the altar move,/And with one strong, incessant cry/Inquire *How long*? . . ./Almighty Judge!" (20-24). The cry of the saints and martyrs for apocalypse thus joins with the Psalmic call of the Deep and gathers an uncanny force, as if a divine voice were speaking up within the poem and overriding the voice of the human poet. In this, Vaughan's poems replicate his experience with Holy Writ, for he confides that the Bible "would'st convey/A *sudden and most searhing ray*/Into my soul" ("To the Holy Bible" 19-21; my italics).

A strong sense of divine presence also occurs in Vaughan's poems that include quotation from a divine voice. Toward the close of "Regeneration" the speaker hears a rushing wind, though, curiously, no leaves are stirring. Suddenly a mysterious, disembodied voice whispers the cryptic message:

> *Where I Please.*

Audaciously, Vaughan is *quoting* the Holy Spirit, the above line being a version of John 3:8, in which Jesus describes the Spirit as a "wind that bloweth where it listeth." Vaughan has simply changed the pronouns to make the Holy Spirit speak in first person. This mysterious utterance has a radical effect upon the speaker, who answers, not with a mental genuflection, but with a full *metanoia*. He replies:

> *On me one breath,*
> *And let me die before my death!* (81–82)

This poem stands at the beginning of *Silex Scintillans* and so establishes the spiritual authority of all the subsequent occasions when a voice suddenly comes to Vaughan as it does in such poems as "The Search" and "The World."

The Spirit in "Regeneration," it is important to note, speaks from a garden setting, for there emerges from within the larger semantic field of Scripture a super-privileged vocabulary of epiphany. Joy, Vaughan claims exultantly, is an "Eastern traffique" that deals in

> . . . boundless Empyrean themes,
> Mountains of spice, Day-stars and light,
> Green trees of life, and living streams.
> ("The Queer," 6–8)

The items in this list have deep resonance in literary history and carry peculiar ontological weight, because "Living streams," "green trees of life," and "Day-stars" are all literally apocalyptic images, both in regard to origin and meaning;/6/ they derive respectively from Revelation 7:17, 2:7, and 22:16. Vaughan regularly conflates these images with related ones from the Canticles, a book that has long provided terms for embodying heart's desire in Western poetry (Giamatti). Because Protestants and Catholics took the Canticles to be an allegory of Christ and his bride the church (or alternatively, the human soul), its imagery melds nicely with that from the Book of Revelation, which also hails a divine marriage, the bridal supper of the Lamb. Merely to mention the hills of Myrrh or a land where "A fresh immortal *green* . . . dwells" is not only to conjure up the ultimate greenworld but to anticipate an eschatological spring ("The Agreement," 11–12).

This epiphanic vocabulary, then, is one of such richness and extreme compression that verbal syntax is almost beside the point, occasionally being omitted altogether. It provides a shorthand by which the poet may quickly evoke an entire transcendent realm. He need mention only a single image in order to evoke Canticle-land (as I shall henceforth refer to Vaughan's eternity), and this is the case whether he conceives of it vertically as a land beyond the stars or whether he treats it horizontally as a kingdom to come on the temporal horizon. Once this metonymy has been established, it can also be employed to suggest how the heart is adjacent to heaven. It can be employed to denote the Kingdom within as well as that to come. Each of the following lines, for example, brings Canticle-land momentarily into the consciousness of the speaker:

"everlasting spicey mountains"
("Fair and yong light! . . . ," 50)
* * * * * *
[A] place
Which all the year sees the Suns face.
("The Seed growing secretly," 11)
* * * * * *
There is beyond the Stars an hil of myrrh
("The Sap," 11-12)

It turns out that Vaughan's best poetry depends, not on verbal syntax, but upon what one might call cosmic syntax, for he is wont to take the reader at a flash from one temporal or spatial realm to another, usually without benefit of transition. No doubt because of the civil chaos during which he was writing, Vaughan very seldom considers the world around him. On the rare occasions when he does refer to contemporary society, he employs grotesque images from Scripture that constitute signs of the Last Days—"Owls and satyrs" haunt the land, or a plague of flies surrounds a national leader./7/ Usually, however, the poet dismisses his social world as undifferentiated shadow—a realm of "masques and shadows," of mists and Egyptian darkness. Despite a few satiric thrusts at Puritans for treating the Eucharist like "kitchen food," Vaughan is not really interested in dissecting the darkness of his time. He simply wants to get beyond it. Typical is the refrain: "O that I were winged and free . . ./Where freed souls dwell by living fountains/On everlasting, spicy mountains!" ("Fair and yong light! . . ." [47–52]).

Only two avenues of escape seem open to him. One is eschatological removal; hence longing for death and cries for the Second Coming recur in *Silex Scintillans*. The other is cultivation of the inner garden by solitary devotion. What the Eucharist had been in Herbert's poetry, Canticle-land becomes in Vaughan's. Significantly, his poem entitled "The Feast" yearns for eschatologcial nourishment and concludes by quoting Revelation 19:9: *Blessed are they, which are called unto the marriage Supper of the Lamb!* Because Vaughan cannot resort each day to the comforts of divine service, he looks instead to a final feast—or to what "prelibations" he can derive from private prayer and devotions.

Vaughan's oft-anthologized poem "Peace" demonstrates the poet's obsession with a glorious elsewhere. It also demonstrates what one might call his Gnostic tendencies, in that the land of desire is juxtaposed to a dark and barren present, with little or no attention to the means of getting from one realm to another. The "one born in a manger" is far removed in another country beyond the stars where he commands "his beauteous files," keeping all "above noise or danger." Despite an allusion to the Incarnation, Christ in this poem (and typically throughout *Silex Scintillans*) is less a mediator between heaven and earth than a *deus absconditas*. In sum, all that the poet can do about transportation thither is to restate his yearning: "If thou canst get but thither . . ." (13).

Vaughan's alternative to sheer yearning is to cultivate his interior garden and to discover there what glints and gleams of Canticle-land he can. It is in such poems as "The Relapse" that the full ontological weight of Vaughan's epiphanic vocabulary becomes clear. To receive grace is to "challenge here"

>   The brightest day;
> Sweet, downie thoughts; soft *Lilly*-shades;
>   Calm streams;
>   Joyes full, and true;
> Fresh, spicie mornings; and eternal beams. (23–27)

One reason why a first reader finds the poetry of *Silex Scintillans* "mystical" is that the imagery of Canticle-land crops up at moments of devotional exhaltation, thereby setting up what seems to be a dynamic correspondence between the inner garden and the heavenly one, as if *cor ad cor loquitur*. "Unprofitableness," for example, celebrates an unexpected visitation of grace ("How rich, O Lord! how fresh thy visits are!") as a sensory appropriation of Canticle-land: "[I] once more/Breath all perfumes, and spice;/I smell a dew like *Myrrh* . . ." (9–11).

Herbert, we remember, turns Paradise into a *conceptual* metaphor for Providence: Paradise is being a tree planted among the orderly rows of a garden whose keeper regularly prunes away the branches (and the rimes) to make the poet bear more fruit. Vaughan takes Herbert's *topos* of Christian man as a plant and treats it in a *kinetic* rather than a conceptual way. He can remember that he once "felt through all [his] fleshly dresse/Bright *shootes* of everlastingnesse" ("The Retreate," 19–20). He can recommend morning prayer because then one "shall feel/That God is true, as herbs unseen/Put on their youth and green" ("The Starre," 30–32). Furthermore, in a poem like "The Morning-watch" he can demonstrate how to lose oneself in prayer and praise. At dawn he celebrates the new world fresh with dew and exults, "O how it *Blouds,*/And *Spirits* all my Earth!" (8-9). By mid-poem it becomes difficult to distinguish the "Hymning Circulations" of the morning world from the poet's own pulse. The reader feels this radical lessening of the distance between Herbert's tenor (an access of grace) and vehicle (the greenworld) as a startling poetic intensification.

From the "gilded" lines discussed so far, one can scarcely gain any sense of how different these lines are from the bulk of Vaughan's poetry, nor any sense of the suddenness with which they appear, for it is their very randomness that makes them seem like numinous visitations. It will be necessary now to follow one poem throughout in order to demonstrate *in situ*, as it were, how Vaughan deploys semantic fields according to what I have called his cosmic syntax.

"The World" is perhaps Vaughan's most celebrated poem and one that deploys contrasting semantic fields in a spectacular way. It begins with Vaughan's familiar stance of observing the natural world, which in this case is the night sky. The first lines have all the simplicity of Herbert's child-like speaker:

> I saw Eternity the other night
> Like a great *Ring* of pure and endless light,
>   All calm, as it was bright. (1-3)

As the speaker's gaze turns earthward, it becomes apparent that he is relating a vision without the mediating frame of a dream:

> And round beneath it, Time in hours, days, years
>   Driv'n by the spheres
> Like a vast shadow mov'd, in which the world
>   And all her train were hurl'd. (4-7)

From these cosmic heights, the speaker descends to give us a closer look at this world, isolating in turn several emblematic figures. First, "The doting Lover," complete with lute and verses, gazes his time away at a Chaucerian flower. Then, with deft satiric touches, Vaughan points out a Statesman on a treadmill, who, "Like a thick midnight-fog mov'd there so slow/He did nor stay, nor go" (17-18). Quickly the scene turns surreal: While "Clouds of crying witnesses .../Pursued [the statesman] with one shout," a sinister Mole digs away beneath the whole scene "lest his ways be found." The Mole turns monster-like as he clutches his prey, feeding on "Churches and altars" (27). Again just as quickly, the scene is filled with palpable signs that the End of the World is near: a plague of gnats and flies appears (28), and "It rain'd . . . bloud and tears" (29). In fairly undistinguished lines, the reader is thus treated to a parade of figures that are alternately banal and terrifying.

The parade of figures keeps coming, but trails off anticlimactically with mention of familiar types of Sin. A Miser "on a heap of rust" is mentioned perfunctorily, then followed by equally perfunctory mention of the Epicure who "plac'd heav'n in sense." The final figures in Vaughan's cautionary parade are "the weaker sort [whom] triviall wares Inslave" (42). The poem here seems to be losing its visionary force to the routine rhetoric of the Deadly Sins.

At stanza 4, however, the poem takes a sudden thematic and stylistic turn as the speaker proclaims:

> Yet some, who all this while did weep and sing,
> And sing, and weep, soar'd up into the *Ring*,
>   But most would use no wing. (46–48)

As is usual with Vaughan, the poem focuses upon escape from an intolerable world to a bright realm above. Characteristic also is Vaughan's failure to make clear how some souls manage to rise to the world of light. We learn only that "most would use no wing" (48). The poem seems to be ending predictably with a denunciation of those who remain fixed in this world ("O fools . . . thus to prefer dark night/Before true light . . ."). If Vaughan had stopped here, we would have a fairly dull variant of a medieval dream vision. Instead, the homily with which the poem has been winding down is suddenly interrupted by an unidentified voice:

> One whisper'd thus,
> *This Ring the Bride-groome did for none provide*
> *But for his bride.* (59–60)

The final line comes as a lightning stroke connecting an apocalyptic allusion to Scripture (the coming of the Bridegroom in Matthew 25:1-13) with the sensuous perception of the night sky noted at the beginning of the poem. The new eternal referent given to *Ring* entails the same unexpected collision of semantic fields that one finds in a joke, but here induces a *frisson* of awe rather than laughter. The poem, in fact, is structurally identical to a joke, but the laughter that a joke elicits has disruptive and anarchic force, while this "punch line" from the divine Voice comes with an authority to command an awed silence—and to suppress the analytic categories adopted by the poem's human persona in describing his world.

The final line of "The World" draws together in an instant all three semantic fields that create a sense of the numinous in *Silex Scintillans*: the perceived world of nature, the "literary" world of Scripture—and the poetic universe of George Herbert's *The Temple*. In the end Vaughan seems to be answering a poem by Herbert complaining of the sorry reward that he had derived from his life of faith, until then mainly one of tears. In exasperation Herbert had cried, "I did expect a ring" (8).

"The World" offers Vaughan's rebuttal to this complaint, for he asserts that the man of faith does after all get a "ring," though it is one defined in grand eschatological (and sensuous poetic) terms. To read Vaughan, then, is to be continually surprised by grand syllepses or puns that startle our literary expectations, reveal the inadequacy of mundane rhetoric, and correct it all in an instant—almost as if (to use Vaughan's words) a door had been opened in heaven.

NOTES

/1/ "The Holdfast," in *The Works of George Herbert*, ed. F. E. Hutchinson (Oxford: Clarendon Press, 1964), p. 143, lines 9-10. All references to George Herbert's poetry will be from this edition. Henceforth only line numbers will be given in parentheses in the text.

/2/ "The Regeneration," in *The Works of Henry Vaughan*, ed. L. C. Martin (Oxford: Clarendon Press, 1957), p. 398, lines 41-42. All references to Vaughan's poetry will be from this edition. Henceforth only line numbers will be given in parentheses in the text.

/3/ See my essay, "In Arcadia, Calvin. . . : A Study of Nature in Henry Vaughan," *Studies in Philology* 70 (1970), for a discussion of the way in which *Silex Scintillans* is indebted to the structural paradigms of the pastoral songs that were published between 1590 and 1630 in such collections as *England's Helicon* (1600, 1614).

/4/ In "Obedience," lines 37-43, Herbert calls his poem a "poore paper," a deed by which he passes his heart and all he has to God. He invites the reader who would do likewise to "set his hand/And heart unto this Deed" and to "thrust his heart/Into these lines." Vaughan answers in "The Match": "Here I joyn hands, and thrust my stubborn heart/Into thy *Deed* . . ." (lines 7-8).

/5/ For discussions of how Catholics and Protestants used Scripture as an object of meditation, see respectively Martz, *The Poetry of Meditation* and Lewalski, *Protestant Poetics and the Seventeenth-Century Religious Lyric*.

/6/ For another account of Vaughan's eschatological focus, see Calhoun's chapter "An Interregnum Poetics," in *Vaughan*, pp. 58-80, in which he finds Vaughan seizing upon a Rosicrucian notion of transmutation in the face of the terror and civil disorder. For an excellent reading of the apocalyptic reference of Vaughan's poem, "The Night," see Post, *Henry Vaughan: The Unfolding Vision*, pp. 186-211.

/7/ The satyrs seem to be a reference to Isaiah 13:21. See "The Bird," lines 27-30: "The Turtle then in Palm-trees mourns,/While Owls and Satyrs howl;/The pleasant Land to brimstone turns/And all her streams grow foul." For an apparent reference to Cromwell, see "The darksome States-man" in "The World," line 16.

WORKS CONSULTED

Bennett, Joan
    1966   *Five Metaphysical Poets.* Cambridge: University.

Calhoun, Thomas O.
    1981   *Henry Vaughan: The Achievement of Henry Vaughan.* Newark: University of Delaware.

Cassirer, Ernst
    1957   *The Philosophy of Symbolic Forms.* Trans. Ralph Manheim. 3 vols. New Haven: Yale University.

Christopher, Georgia B.
    1970   "In Arcadia, Calvain. . . : A Study of Nature in Henry Vaughan." *Studies in Philology* 70: 408–26.

Fish, Stanley
    1970   "Letting Go: The Reader in Herbert's Poetry." *ELH* 37: 495–516.
    1974   "Catechizing the Reader: Herbert's Socratean Rhetoric." In *The Rhetoric of Renaissance Poetry: From Wyatt to Milton.* Ed. Thomas O. Sloan and Raymond B. Waddington. Berkeley: University of California, pp. 174–88.

Garner, Ross
    1959   *Henry Vaughan: The Experience and the Tradition.* Chicago: University of Chicago.

Giamatti, A. Bartlett
    1966   *The Earthly Paradise and the Renaissance Epic.* Princeton: Princeton University.

Herbert, George
    1964   *The Works of George Herbert.* Ed. F. E. Hutchinson. Oxford: Clarendon.

Lewalski, Barbara K.
    1979   *Protestant Poetics and the Seventeenth-Century Religious Lyric.* Princeton: Princeton University.

Martz, Louis L.
    1954   *The Poetry of Meditation.* New Haven: Yale University.
    1964   *The Paradise Within: Studies in Vaughan, Traherne, and Milton.* New Haven: Yale University.

Pettet, E. C.
    1960   *Of Paradise and Light: A Study of Vaughan's 'Silex Scintillans.'* Cambridge, MA: Harvard University.

Post, Jonathan F. S.
    1982   *Henry Vaughan: The Unfolding Vision.* Princeton: Princeton University.

Vaughan, Henry
    1957   *The Works of Henry Vaughan.* Ed. L. C. Martin. Oxford: Clarendon.

THE STORY OF READING AND/IN POPE'S *ESSAY ON MAN* AND THE *MORAL ESSAYS*

G. Douglas Atkins
University of Kansas

ABSTRACT

As is obvious and well known, Pope's *Essay on Man* and the *Moral Essays* represent and defend the Great Chain of Being and the order it connotes. Of no less importance is the way these poems employ reading as a principal metaphor for the systematic exploration of man, his actions, and the "universe." For Pope, reading the (text of the) world and human character is like reading literary texts, and though he maintains that readers should direct their efforts toward a sure grasp of meanings created by the author, controlled by him, and apparent to a "proper" reading, Pope also recognizes the complications inherent in the structural situation that defines reading. Indeed, just as he grants the important role readers play in determining textual meaning and significance, so Pope admits the dependency of God on man in His continuing work of creation. As represented especially in *An Epistle to Bathurst*, the sense of dependency revealed in Providence problematizes the valorization of Order, itself dependent on the assumption of identity, which in turn is rooted in belief in clear distinctions and absolute differences. Text and reader, it turns out, exist in a situation marked by what Jacques Derrida calls *différance*. Rather than absolute, the difference between readers and (whatever kind of) texts is, as Jonathan Culler claims, a "variable concept" and an "essential structural feature" of the situation that they in fact comprise. Confronting a literary or worldly text involves one with two "absolute perspectives" both of which are essential for the narrative in which each claims priority. Existing not only as a story of reading but also as a story of story, Pope's "moral" poems tell how readers alone or texts alone constitute a partial story in need of a supplement.

Introduction

If not for its triumphant heroic couplets, Pope's *Essay on Man* is probably best known for its presentation and defense of the Great Chain of Being and the order it connotes. "ORDER is Heav'n's first law," Pope proclaims (4.49), and even if human beings, proud, aspiring, and rebellious, find it difficult to accept, "Whatever IS, is RIGHT" (1.294)./1/ The latter view, a consequence of belief in the Great Chain and its order, rests on the assumption of identity, itself linked to a system of clear distinctions and absolute differences. In the essay that follows, I want to examine some of Pope's most fundamental beliefs concerning order, difference, and human response to worldly as well as literary texts. My focus will be not only *An Essay on Man* but also its companion-poems, the so-called *Moral Essays*.

Reading the Text of the World: Quests of Difference

I begin with a representative passage in *An Essay on Man*. The following couplets, from the fourth epistle, summarize in succinct and eloquent fashion Pope's position throughout the eight epistles that constitute these poems:

> ORDER is Heav'n's first law; and this confest,
> Some are, and must be, greater than the rest,
> More rich, more wise; but who infers from hence
> That such are happier, shocks all common sense.
> Heav'n to Mankind impartial we confess,
> If all are equal in their Happiness:
> But mutual wants this Happiness increase,
> All Nature's diff'rence keeps all Nature's peace.
> Condition, circumstance is not the thing;
> Bliss is the same in subject or in king,
> In who obtain defence, or who defend,
> In him who is, or him who finds a friend:
> Heav'n breaths thro' ev'ry member of the whole
> One common blessing, as one common soul.
> But Fortune's gifts if each alike possest,
> And each were equal, must not all contest?
> If then to all Men Happiness was meant,
> God in Externals could not place Content. (4.49–66)

A great many of Pope's major themes are on display here: the impartiality of Providence, whose concern is for the whole; the connection between this easily misunderstood impartiality and "our bliss," which, in fact, is dependent on the former; the necessity of difference if social and political order is to exist; the argument that what matters most to human beings is not external differences (for example, in fortune, condition, or circumstance) but the happiness that is purely an internal matter. Beyond the differences, transcending them, is identity, creating "One common blessing, as one common soul," ensuring that "Bliss is the same in subject or in king." The chain of differences thus ends in, and is impossible apart from, an identity ("I am who I am") that keeps things clear, straight, and distinct. That in-different origin, or *logos*, uses external and certainly real differences to maintain order, an order that could not exist without such differences.

In a variety of ways, in fact, *An Essay on Man*, like other Pope poems, focuses on differences. Built on difference, the Great Chain of Being "links th' immense design,/Joins heav'n and earth, and mortal and divine" (4.333–34), each link being distinct and therefore joined to both that above and that below it. And even if "thin partitions Sense from Thought divide," and even if entities long to cross over and mingle, they can "never pass th' insuperable line" (1.226–28) that ensures that a thing is itself and not also something else. Indeed, Pope declares, the collapse of difference would bring about total destruction: "Where, one step broken, the great scale's destroy'd:/From Nature's chain whatever link you strike,/Tenth or ten thousandth, breaks the chain alike" (1:244–46).

Difference and distinct identity stubbornly prevail; and even though difference sometimes barely appears, the distinction between entities being obscure, it is, Pope insists, a serious mistake to suppose "th' insuperable line" has ever been transgressed:

> Tho' each by turns the other's bound invade,
> As, in some well-wrought picture, light and shade,
> And oft so mix, the diff'rence is too nice
> Where ends the Virtue, or begins the Vice.
>   Fools! who from hence into the notion fall,
> That Vice or Virtue there is none at all.
> If white and black blend, soften, and unite
> A thousand ways, is there no black or white?
> Ask your own heart, and nothing is so plain;
> 'Tis to mistake them, costs the time and pain. (2:207–16)

Pope's points concerning order and difference recall *Oedipus* and Shakespeare's *Troilus and Cressida*, particularly as these have been recently (and brilliantly) interpreted by René Girard. Sophocles depicts, according to Girard, "a crisis of distinctions—that is, a crisis affecting the cultural order. This cultural order is nothing more than a regulated system of distinctions in which the differences among individuals are used to establish their 'identity' and their mutual relationships" (1977:49). In *Troilus*, as well, "culture is defined as a system of differences, of *degrees*, Shakespeare says, held together by Degree with a capital D" (1972:34). Not such differences but the loss of them leads to violence and chaos—a point that Pope evidently shares with Sophocles and Shakespeare. According to Girard, collapse of difference is catastrophic. Indeed, he writes, "Any change, however slight, in the hierarchical classification of living creatures risks undermining the whole . . . structure" (1977:39; see also 282).

But surely one must consider the degree of difference maintained, as well as the maintenance of degree and difference. Is there more than one kind of difference, one might wonder. Girard denies it: "Because there is no real difference between the various modes of differentiation, there is in consequence no difference between the manner in which things fail to differ" (1977:56). In order to consider such issues, I propose here to focus on one specific distinction, one fundamental to all questions of difference: that between the created order and the necessary human response to it, a difference (I contend) that is an allegory of reading as well as one that (obviously) involves the relationship of Creator and creation.

For Pope, of course, the very occasion of such an effort as his—to "vindicate the ways of God and Man" (*An Essay on Man*, 1.16)—is man's relentless attempt to blur the distinction between himself and God. Thus he lashes those who would attempt to topple God and take His place:

> Go, wiser thou! and in thy scale of sense
> Weigh thy Opinion against Providence;
> Call Imperfection what thou fancy'st such,
> Say, here he gives too little, there too much;
> Destroy all creatures for thy sport or gust,
> Yet cry, If Man's unhappy, God's unjust;
> If Man alone ingross not Heav'n's high care,
> Alone made perfect here, immortal there:
> Snatch from his hand the balance and the rod,
> Re-judge his justice, be the GOD of GOD!
> In Pride, in reas'ning Pride, our error lies;
> All quit their sphere, and rush into the skies.
> Pride still is aiming at the blest abodes,
> Men would be Angels, Angels would be Gods.
> Aspiring to be Gods, if Angels fell,
> Aspiring to be Angels, Men rebel;
> And who but wishes to invert the laws
> Of ORDER, sins against th' Eternal Cause. (1.113–22)

From one perspective, at least, we humans are like actors in a great cosmic drama written, directed, and given us by God. Making use of the theatrical metaphor that figures prominently in *An Essay on Man*, as well as later in *The Dunciad* (Williams), Pope claims that all comes down to this: "Act well your part, there all the honour lies" (4.194). We are thus to play the part assigned us, the goal being the proper execution of that role, what the "great directing MIND of ALL ordains" (1.266). In this area, as in so many others, "to reason right is to submit" (1.164).

From another perspective, the human situation is like that of readers faced with a written text. This is hardly surprising in view of Jacques Derrida's compelling arguments concerning the ubiquity of textuality: according to Derrida, everything is a text, the "world," society, human relations no less than literary texts, "writing" being a global term to describe the structure of difference marked by the "trace." Even if one does not subscribe to Derrida's arguments concerning writing, it is easy enough to see that, as I have argued elsewhere, reading serves as a principal metaphor for the wide-ranging exploration of man, his actions, and "universe" throughout *An Essay on Man* and the *Moral Essays* (Atkins, forthcoming). *An Epistle to Cobham*, in fact, focuses on the difficult effort to *read* human actions, character, and motivation, and in *An Essay on Man* reading is, of course, exactly what Pope indicates that he and his friend Bolingbroke will perform as they explore the "Garden, tempting with forbidden fruit," "Eye Nature's walks, shoot Folly as it flies,/And catch the Manners living as they rise" (1.8, 13-14). The controversial notion of the "ruling passion," introduced in the theodicy and developed in the *Moral Essays*, provides the key to a "proper" reading of human character and actions, being in fact, according to Pope, "*the only certain way to avoid misconstruction.*" What "unravels all" (*Cobham*, l. 178), the "ruling passion" functions in men and women like a controlling theme in a literary text, around which all other elements gravitate. Like such a theme, it is analogous to "th' informing Soul" that Pope describes in *An Essay on Criticism*, which "With Spirits feeds, with Vigour fills the whole,/Each Motion guides, and ev'ry Nerve sustains;/*It self unseen*, but in th' *Effects*, remains" (ll. 76–79)./2/

Whether or not we accept Derrida's notions of writing and textuality, we can, I think, agree that reading literary texts is like reading the (text of the) world. In responding to poems as to the world, the aim, Pope maintains, is to "*read* each Work . . ./With the same Spirit that its Author *writ*" (*An Essay on Criticism*, ll. 233–34). Like his friend Swift, in other words, Pope would have us submit to the authority of the creator. Though "a mighty maze," the world is "not without a plan," Pope writes, opening *An Essay on Man* (1.6), and the reader's efforts should be directed toward discerning the intentions of the supreme Author-ity.

Reading Literary Texts:
Stories of Reading

To say no more than the merely obvious, reading of whatever kind of material involves a certain relationship between reader and created text. For Pope, as we have seen, the reader should seek to share the space of the author, somewhat as the Hack in *A Tale of a Tub* advises the diligent reader to put "himself into the circumstances and postures of life, that the writer was in upon every important passage as it flowed from his pen," this being a sure method for introducing the desired "parity and strict correspondence of ideas between the reader and the author" (Swift: 265). The object is certainly to achieve a "fit" between reading and text. If such a "fit" is attained, then the reader has little to do, the text in no way depending on him or her, who—after all—is clearly subordinated, even effaced before it. In this way, differences are strictly maintained—and with them Pope's vaunted sense of Order.

So that we may firmly grasp the issues involved in reading, I turn to some contemporary discussions, where questions of reader-text relations are among the most urgent being contested. I begin with a recent essay that assumes a position much like Pope's: "The Ethics of Reading," by J. Hillis Miller. What is surprising is that this conventional—and evidently objectivist—statement comes from an advocate of deconstruction, the *bête noir* of recent theory and one often accused—albeit falsely—of subordinating texts to the willfulness of readers. I must quote at length from Miller's important essay. Miller claims that both "conservative" and deconstructive readings

> are necessitated by the words of the texts they treat. This means that reading is always an epistemological necessity before it is a matter of ethical choice or evaluation. More radically, it means that the ethics of reading is subject to a categorical imperative which is linguistic rather than transcendent or a matter of subjective will. Epistemology must take precedence over ethics in reading. One cannot make ethical judgments, perform ethical actions . . . without first subjecting oneself to the words on the page, but once that has happened, the ethical operation will already necessarily have taken place. . . . A reading is true as an acute angle is true to its model, or as one voice or word is true to another voice or word. The ethics of reading is not some act of the human will to interpretation which extracts moral themes from a work, or uses it to reaffirm what the reader already knows, or imposes a meaning freely in some process of reader response or perspectivist criticism, seeing the text in a certain way. The ethics of reading is the power of the words of the text over the mind and words of the reader. This is an irresistible coercion which shapes what the reader or teacher says about the text, even when what he says is most reductive or evasive. . . . The ethics of reading is the moral necessity to submit in one way or another, whatever one says, to the truth of this linguistic imperative. (40–41)

Elegant, carefully reasoned, and forceful, this statement requires careful attention. First of all, as is apparent in the echoes of Nietzsche and of Miller's own earlier, pre-deconstructive studies such as *Poets of Reality* (see Atkins, 1983a), he is interested in somehow transcending the power of the human will and of humanistic egotism, which reportedly leads to "the nothingness of consciousness when consciousness becomes the foundation of everything" (1965:3). Thus aware of Miller's continuing interests, I cannot but hear in his crisp sentences and carefully chosen words certain religious overtones, reminding me at least of the way New Criticism both reflects a sense of the text as possessing a quality of "aseity" like that of the godhead and requires of the critic the kind of self-effacement before the text figured in Christ's paradigmatic sacrifice (Scott: 131, Gunn: 55). There can be no doubt that Miller recognizes the broad dimensions of the critical questions raised, which he rather neatly resolves by insisting on the reader's "ethical" submission to the authority of the text. "Subject[ing] oneself to the words on the page" precedes, and effectively eliminates, questions of the reader's subjectivity, will, and desire. Like Pope, evidently, Miller believes that "to reason right is to submit." And like him too, Miller valorizes the created order (of words).

Despite the obvious similarities, however, there is no perfect "fit" between Pope and Miller. A major difference appears in their respective positions on the study of words *qua* words. Declining to discuss meaning, Miller carefully and deliberately focuses on *the thing itself*, "the words on the page," to which the reader must "submit." With meaning bracketed, it is the words themselves that exercise "the power" "over the mind and words of the reader." This is, I think, similar to the position that Pope satirizes in the mock-notes of *Sober Advice from Horace* (see Atkins, 1979) and throughout the fourth book of *The Dunciad*: for example in the headmaster Busby's boast that "Words we teach alone" (l. 150) and in the critic Bentley's pronouncement that "on Words is still our whole debate,/Disputes of *Me* or *Te*, of *aut* or *at*/To sound or sink in *cano*, O or A,/Or give up Cicero to C or K" (ll. 219-22). Though deliberately exaggerated, Pope's point is clear: to focus narrowly on words as words is to sacrifice important questions to more technical, merely material ones, and it is also implicitly to assume that words somehow do not require interpretation. The latter is as much a factual error as the former is a moral one, for words, hardly less than meanings, are, as Pope claims, subject to definite misunderstanding. By themselves, of course, apart from semantic and syntactic value, they may be of little interest or importance.

Even if we cannot finally accept Hillis Miller's account of the reader-text relationship, we will do well to stay a while with the linguistic focus he insists on. That focus provides a strong foundation for understanding words *and* meanings. Derrida has shown, conclusively I think, not only that language—and therefore meaning—is a matter of difference but also that "without a retention in the minimal unit of temporal experience, without a trace retaining the other as other in the same, no difference would do its work and no meaning would appear" (1976:62). With specific reference to Derrida's notion of supplementarity (the French word *supplément* means both an addition to and a substitution for), Barbara Johnson maintains that Derrida has effected "nothing less than a revolution in the very logic of meaning" (xiii). He has done so by showing that neither our belief in identities or equivalences nor our assumptions concerning absolute differences will withstand scrutiny. "Instead of 'A is opposed to B,'" according to Johnson, "we have 'B is both added to A and replaces A.' A and B are no longer opposed, nor are they equivalent. Indeed, they are no longer even equivalent to themselves. They are their own differance from themselves" (xiii).

In this story of *differance* told by deconstruction, as I have argued elsewhere (Atkins, 1983a), differences *within* mitigate differences *between*, allowing relations to exist. It appears a more complicated story than that told by René Girard, for example. Is it also more complicated than Pope's, which understands distinct difference as the key to Order? I think we should not be too quick to answer. To help us toward a clear understanding of the question, if not an answer, I propose to extend our consideration of reading.

I turn first to Jonathan Culler's recent book *On Deconstruction*. Adapting certain of Derrida's insights, Culler depicts readers and texts as always being involved in a "story of reading." He forcefully confronts the polarized claims, widely bruited about, that meaning lies "in" texts (as conservatives tend to argue) and that it resides "in" readers (as devotees of one or more varieties of so-called reader-response criticism maintain). Arguing as well against any compromise or middle-ground position, with "the reader partly in control and the text partly in control," Culler insists that such distinctions as we habitually make between texts and readers are no more than "variable and ungrounded concepts" (77). What he means, becomes clear, I think, in the following passage, which follows a deconstruction of some prominent reader-oriented discussions:

> The reemergence of the text's control, in stories that sought to recount just the opposite, is a powerful illustration of the constraints discursive structures impose on theories that claim to master or describe them. Theories of reading stories and descriptions of reading stories seem themselves to be governed by aspects of story. But there is another structural necessity at work in the switches back and forth between the reader's dominance and the text's dominance. A study of reading would not permit one to decide between these alternatives, for the situation can be

theorized from either perspective, and there are reasons why it must be theorized from both perspectives.

Culler uses the example of the joke to elucidate "the curious situation of reading." As he explains,

> The listener is essential to the joke, for unless the listener laughs, the joke is not a joke. Here, as reader-response criticism would have it, the reader plays a decisive role in determining the structure and meaning of the utterance. As Samuel Weber writes, explicating Freud's theory of *Witz*, "The third person, as listener, decides whether or not the joke is successful—i.e., whether it is a joke or not—... And yet this decisive action of the third person lies beyond all volition—one cannot will to laugh—and outside of consciousness, insofar as one never knows, at the moment of laughter, what one is laughing at." ... The listener does not control the outburst of laughter: the text provokes it (the joke, one says, *made me* laugh). But on the other hand, the unpredictable response determines the nature of the text that is supposed to have produced it. No compromise formulation, with the reader partly in control and the text partly in control, would accurately describe this situation, which is captured, rather, by juxtaposition of two absolute perspectives. The shift back and forth in stories of reading between readers' decisive actions and readers' automatic responses is not a mistake that could be corrected but an essential structural feature of the situation. (72-73)

No one, I believe, has better described the reading situation and the complicated relationship between readers and texts, and Culler's notion of the story of reading is one to which we can profitably attend.

Perhaps *because*, as I have claimed elsewhere, reader and text are caught in an unavoidable and endlessly oscillating battle of wills in which neither dominates nor acts as master to the slave-other, we try to settle the issue in favor of one party to the dispute (Atkins, 1983a). We want, it seems clear, a clear-cut decision, with definite and distinct differences drawn between what a text "itself" does and what readers do in the act of reading. Common sense may suggest that no such absolute difference is possible (even if desirable), but our vain wish remains strong and undaunted. That wish recalls Pope's quest for difference in *An Essay on Man*, the *Moral Essays*, and elsewhere.

Reading Differences

As it happens, the story of reading that Culler so well describes appears in—and is told by—Pope's "ethical" poems. This is done in at least two ways: the poems not only exist as a story moving between two "absolute perspectives," but they also depict allegorically the relationship of readers and texts as an oscillating struggle for dominance./3/ Thus even while valorizing difference ("All Nature's diff'rence keeps all Nature's peace"), Pope also knows, and says, that differences are neither clear-cut nor absolute.

Indeed, though he argues, as we saw earlier, that readers should direct their efforts toward a sure grasp of meanings created by the author, controlled by him, and apparent to a "proper" reading, Pope also writes honestly of the complications inherent in the structural situation that defines reading. These complications stem mainly, he admits, from the reader's humanity and subjectivity; that is, the reader's variability and partiality, his self-interest, desires, and even whims affect and problematize the reading done, voiding the possibility of the equivalence Hillis Miller postulates. The observer affects the observation made, no matter what is being observed. Thus implicated in the reading, he is unable to get outside to a neutral or objective position. As Pope writes in *An Epistle to Cobham*:

> Men may be read, as well as Books too much.
> To Observations which ourselves we make,
> We grow more partial for th' observer's sake;
> To written Wisdom, as another's, less:
> Maxims are drawn from Notions, these from Guess. (ll. 10-14)

Regardless of our desires and expectations, as well as our valiant efforts, an exact "fit" is never achieved between the reading and the text read, the reader being the undeniable—and unpredictable—factor in the story of reading:

> ... the diff'rence is as great between
> The optics seeing, as the objects seen.
> All Manners take a tincture from our own,
> Or come discolour'd thro' our Passions shown.
> Or Fancy's beam enlarges, multiplies,
> Contracts, inverts, and gives ten thousand dyes. (ll. 23-28)

Not only is no equivalence possible between reader and text, but there is also no "fit" *within* each reader, who differs from "himself" hardly less than he does from the texts he takes up. Pope thus clearly states what Derrida later finds to be paradigmatic in all texts. This situation of internal difference characterizes texts as well as readers; Pope's own texts tell this story, declaring *both* that readers are interimplicated with texts *and* that they are not merely neutral observers and passive recipients./4/ This internal division eliminates any hope of achieving the identity or union with what is read that Pope also (vainly) wishes for. He writes in *Cobham*:

> There's some Peculiar in each leaf and grain,
> Some unmark'd fibre, or some varying vein:
> Shall only Man be taken in the gross?
> Grant but as many sorts of Mind as Moss.
>   That each from other differs, first confess;
> Next, that he varies from himself no less:
> Add Nature's, Custom's, Reason's, Passion's strife,
> And all Opinion's colours cast on life. (ll. 15-22)

Obviously Pope believes in the existence of a single, univocal self (an "identity," from which one varies) just as he does in an objectively present text (which a reading may approach though it never coincides with it). But he also clearly recognizes the important role readers play in determining textual meaning and significance, a role that he exploits in such poems as *An Essay on Criticism* and the *Imitations of Horace*./5/

Reader Response and Responsibility: "That Dangerous Supplement"

No less clearly, Pope recognizes the dependency of God on man in His continuing work of creation. Man must not only "submit" to the order everywhere apparent to right reason, but he must also act in accord and concert with it. This latter necessity becomes a particularly important point since God's ways toward men are impartial: though not uncaring, God is, for Pope, essentially in-different toward individuals. Declining to grant our selfish and vain wishes for differential treatment, God places the responsibility on us for the creation of just and humane personal, social, and political relationships.

Pope's focus thus becomes man. Accordingly, he declares in the famous opening couplet of the second epistle of his theodicy: ". . . presume not God to scan;/The proper study of Mankind is Man." That study teaches the necessity of charity as well as the existence of a "chain of Love/Combining all below and all above" (*An Essay on Man*, 3.7-8). Pope exhorts us, therefore,

> . . . to make thy neighbour's blessing thine.
> Is this too little for the boundless heart?
> Extend it, let thy enemies have part:
> Grasp the whole worlds of Reason, Life, and Sense,
> In one close system of Benevolence:
> Happier as kinder, in whate'er degree,
> And height of Bliss but height of Charity. (4.354-60)

As exemplified in the estimable John Kyrle, the "Man of Ross" lauded in *An Epistle to Bathurst*, our responsibility is to "ease, or emulate, the care of Heav'n,/Whose measure full o'erflows on human race;/Mend Fortune's fault, and justify her grace" (ll. 230-32).

Such human responsibility raises important questions. Certainly, the relationship between God and man in the ongoing work of creation and justice is complicated, not unlike that of readers and literary texts, for the sense of dependency revealed in Providence problematizes the valorization of Order. In a recent essay, Murray Krieger has noted, albeit in somewhat different terms, the problem I am getting at in Pope's dual emphases:

> Pope's *Essay on Man* . . . seeks to use the epistles after the first to modify that epistle, which seeks utterly to reduce our confusing reality to the clarity of a perfect, if unresponsive, art world ("All Nature is but Art, unknown to thee"). What follows casts back intimations about the vanity of that confident human projection of cosmos which fills the first epistle. In the earliest lines of the second epistle there is an abrupt shift to the fragile human perspective against which the confident projection of Epistle One can no longer stand so confidently. (81)

Whether or not the difference between the first and the remaining epistles is as great as Krieger maintains, there is, alongside the emphasis on the created order, a powerful focus on human actions, a focus that never quite obliterates that on Order. What we have reflected here recalls the two "absolute perspectives" of reader and text that Culler finds in every story of reading. Pope's own writing thus constitutes, and tells, a story, a story of story, in fact.

The far-reaching implications of Pope's emphasis on human agency and responsibility emerge most clearly in *Bathurst*'s portrait of the "Man of Ross," who becomes, as it were, coeval with Providence, doing much more, that is, than simply assisting in its work./6/ Pope first describes his compassionate and caring friend as God-like: he hangs "with woods yon mountain's sultry brow" and bids "the waters flow" from "the dry rock" (ll. 253–54). Next he depicts him as an *imitatio Christi*, as he "divides the weekly bread," blesses the old and the orphaned, and "Prescribes, attends, the med'cine makes, and gives" (ll. 263–70). Pope concludes the portrait with an account of Kyrle as peacemaker, deciding differences (ll. 271–74). In several ways, then, the "Man of Ross" emulates, represents, and supplements the work of Providence.

As a supplement of "the care of Heav'n," John Kyrle *adds to* that effort. But as Derrida has shown, and as Barbara Johnson explains in a passage I quoted earlier, a strange logic operates in supplementarity. Derrida describes that logic as "dangerous," because a supplement is a *substitution for* as well as an addition to. Both these meanings appear in the portrait of Kyrle, and though Pope wants to keep distinct the different, indeed conflicting meanings of supplementarity here and elsewhere in *Bathurst*, just as he does other differences, "the shadow presence of the other meaning is always there to undermine the distinction" (Johnson: xiii). Pope's third *Moral Essay* thus carries a double message: both a declaration concerning Kyrle as simply an addition to the work of Providence and a conflicting description of him./7/ Bodying forth the strange logic of the supplement, Kyrle not only emulates and assists the efforts of Providence, but he may also rival it and even take its place. Indeed, by means of that logic according to which, by Pope's reckoning in *Bathurst* and elsewhere, good is educed from ill, Kyrle may undermine his own good efforts and what he represents: since Providence makes use of individual and collective differences, directing them in ways we fallible and limited human beings cannot begin to understand, in fact turning our actions in ways contrary to our willful and wayward intentions, attempts such as Kyrle's to "ease, or emulate" its work may countermine what they were designed to bring about. Perhaps, though, Providence is judicious and selective in its own deconstructive efforts, tampering with our evil actions so as to produce good in spite of us but gratefully accepting our good ones.

Whether or not Providence deconstructs our good actions as it does our evil, it apparently *requires* the labors of such direct supplementers as John Kyrle. If it does, then it is hardly perfect, complete, or self-sufficient. But as Pope presents Kyrle, *he* is all of these, doing everything himself, for example prescribing, making, and dispensing medicine. Pope even hints that this *imitatio Christi* is as well a spiritual healer (e.g., he "attends"). Kyrle appears, in short, to replace Providence. His efforts imply in Providence what Derrida calls "the anterior default of a presence" (145). Needing the "supply" made available by persons like the "Man of Ross," Providence *lacks*, a void becoming apparent. Because Providence requires human help just as we humans ostensibly require its care and sustenance, it needs to be supplemented.

In the same way that Providence requires persons to carry out its work, texts (and the authors who wrote them) need readers. In Geoffrey Hartman's apt phrasing, if "certain works have become authoritative, it is because they at once sustain, and are sustained by, the readers they find" (170). For Hartman, in fact, readers and texts exist in a symbiotic relationship, books taking their strength from the strength they give. It seems that the effectiveness of Providence, like that of books, "is measured by our response, or not at all" (Hartman: 177).

In any case, the unsettling work of "that dangerous supplement" disrupts and undermines such differences as Pope (and others) habitually draw between readers and texts, worldly as well as literary. Instead of differences assumed, sought, and frequently arrested as oppositions, there are relations: relations that always already exist and that form a narrative and tell a story of the inadequacy of any one "party" in each set of differences. Does the concept "reader" have any meaning apart from that of "text," and vice versa? And is the distinction between reading and writing only a variable one? May it also be that "the distinction between author and reader is one of the false distinctions" that a certain reading may make evident? (de Man: 17).

However that may be, the reading of books is like the reading of the world, not least of all in that the difference between readers and (whatever kind of) text is, as Jonathan Culler claims, a "variable concept" and an "essential structural feature" of the situation that they in fact comprise. Confronting a literary or worldly text involves one with two "absolute perspectives," both of which are essential for the narrative in which each claims priority. What these stories have to tell us is, in part, that readers alone or texts alone constitute a partial story in need of a supplement. Pope's *Essay on Man* and *Moral Essays* tell this story on more than one "level," being divided within and distributed between two "absolute perspectives." These poems exist, therefore, not only as a story of reading but also as a story of story./8/

NOTES

/1/ Numbers in parentheses refer to line numbers in Pope's poems and, where appropriate, epistle number.

/2/ An important parallel passage occurs in *An Essay on Man*, 1.267–80.

/3/ My position in the following pages reflects the influence of de Man even where it differs from him.

/4/ An analogous situation occurs in *An Essay on Criticism*, where Pope presents language as the outside of an inside that is thought and declares that "true *Expression*, like th' unchanging Sun,/*Clears*, and *improves* whate'er it shines upon,/It *gilds* all Objects, but it *alters* none" (ll. 315–17). But even these lines *describe* a situation in which language "comes" inside to *alter* thought. "The *treach'rous Colours* the fair Art betray" (l. 492).

/5/ I treat elsewhere the various ways in which Pope brings his readers into these poems, requiring their active participation (Atkins, forthcoming).

/6/ The following paragraphs draw on my essay on *Bathurst* (Atkins, 1983b).

/7/ I use Derrida's well-known distinction between authorial declaration and textual description, the latter of which inscribes "a *systematic* 'other message' behind or through what is being [declared]" (Johnson: xiii). A responsible criticism (what I call reader-responsibility) attends to both declaration and description.

/8/ I wish to acknowledge the support of the University of Kansas General Research Fund, which made possible work on this essay.

WORKS CONSULTED

Atkins, G. Douglas
- 1979 — "Strategy and Purpose in Pope's *Sober Advice from Horace.*" *Papers on Language and Literature* 15:159–74.
- 1983a — *Reading Deconstruction/Deconstructive Reading.* Lexington: University Press of Kentucky.
- 1983b — "'Who Shall Decide?': The Economy of Truth in Pope's *Epistle to Bathurst.*" *The Eighteenth Century: Theory and Interpretation* 24:65–78.
- forthcoming — *Quests of Difference: Reading Pope's Poems.* Lexington: University Press of Kentucky, 1986.

Culler, Jonathan
- 1982 — *On Deconstruction: Theory and Criticism after Structuralism.* Ithaca: Cornell University Press.

de Man, Paul
- 1979 — *Allegories of Reading: Figural Language in Rousseau, Nietzsche, Rilke, and Proust.* New Haven: Yale University Press.

Derrida, Jacques
- 1976 — *Of Grammatology.* Trans. Gayatri Chakravorty Spivak. Baltimore: Johns Hopkins University Press [*De la Grammatologie.* Paris: Minuit, 1967].

Girard, René
- 1973 — "Lévi-Strauss, Frye, Derrida and Shakespearean Criticism." *Diacritics* 3:34–38.
- 1977 — *Violence and the Sacred.* Trans. Patrick Gregory. Baltimore: Johns Hopkins University Press [*La Violence et le sacré.* Paris: Grasset, 1972].

Gunn, Giles
- 1982 — "Literature and Religion." Pp. 47–66 in *Interrelations of Literature.* Ed. Jean-Pierre Barricelli and Joseph Gibaldi. New York: Modern Language Association.

Hartman, Geoffrey
- 1980 — *Criticism in the Wilderness: The Study of Literature Today.* New Haven: Yale University Press.

Johnson, Barbara
- 1981 — Translator's Introduction. Pp. vii-xxxiii. in *Dissemination.* By Jacques Derrida. Ed. Barbara Johnson. Chicago: University of Chicago Press.

Krieger, Murray
- 1980 — "'Trying Experiments upon Our Sensibility': The Art of Dogma and Doubt in Eighteenth-Century Literature." Pp. 70–91 in his *Poetic Presence and Illusion: Essays in Critical History and Theory.* Baltimore: Johns Hopkins University Press.

Miller, J. Hillis
1965   *Poets of Reality: Six Twentieth-Century Writers.* Cambridge: Belknap Press of Harvard University Press.
1981   "The Ethics of Reading: Vast Gaps and Parting Hours." Pp. 19–41 in *American Criticism in the Poststructuralist Age.* Ed. Ira Konigsberg. Ann Arbor: Michigan Studies in the Humanities.

Pope, Alexander
1939–69   The Twickenham Edition of *The Poems of Alexander Pope.* Gen. ed. John Butt. 11 vols. London: Methuen and New Haven: Yale University Press.

Scott, Nathan A., Jr.
1969   "Criticism and Theology—The Terms of the Engagement." Pp. 113–44 in his *Negative Capability: Studies in the New Literature and the Religious Situation.* New Haven: Yale University Press.

Swift, Jonathan
1960   *A Tale of a Tub.* Pp. 241–353 in *"Gulliver's Travels" and Other Writings.* Ed. Louis A. Landa. Boston: Houghton Mifflin.

Williams, Aubrey
1955   *Pope's "Dunciad": A Study of Its Meaning.* Baton Rouge: Louisiana State University Press.

"BUT THE DRAUGHT OF A DRAUGHT": READING THE WONDER OF ISHMAEL'S TELLING

David Scott Arnold
University of North Carolina/Chapel Hill

ABSTRACT

This essay shall focus on Ishmael's telling of his story, *Moby-Dick*, of his marvelous, awesome dramatization of what Paul Brodtkorb describes as "the metaphysical isolation of otherness." My argument takes seriously the fact that Ishmael is the teller of the story told, and it is forever mindful that this particular teller is "the Ishmael," as R. W. B. Lewis says, "who tells the story after the whole of it has been completed." The ironic nature of such self-knowing narration works on the reader in such a way as to provoke the reader's participation in the matter(s) of meaning. Indeed, it is precisely this narrative entanglement with the voiced interests and questionings of the wondering Ishmael that brings into play the horizon of the reader's understanding in his voyage "into the incertitude of the void." Much attention is directed to the perceptive attitude of wonder because it is a psychological disposition crucial to Ishmael's consciousness and to the significance of those "orchestrations of consciousness" he offers so powerfully to the reader.

I

But something in [Ishmael] is compelled, like an ancient mariner, to tell the whole long story over and over again, to those who will listen. Each telling is a new attempt to fill the emptiness left by his experience of Ahab and the whale, to fill it with meaning.
—Paul Brodtkorb (82)

Ishmael does not become a captain; instead, he becomes a fabulator.
—Bainard Cowan (178)

> No tale can ever be told in its entirety.
>
> —Wolfgang Iser (280)

The proscribed ways to understand *Moby-Dick* are legion. This essay intends to look into Ishmael's imagination of wonder. In my effort "to track the antlered thoughts" set before us by Ishmael's narrative, I have hardly wished to impose an absolute interpretation upon what I judge must remain as Melville's ambiguities, in order to have them rigidly "dragooned into a pattern" (Harvey: 111). I have attempted to call attention to sundry ways that otherness has been dramatized by Ishmael's varying point of view, and I have made an effort not to brook the distinction between Ishmael as actor in events narrated ("So strongly and metaphysically did I conceive of my situation then...," he writes in "The Monkey Rope") and Ishmael "now," as teller, when he has brought all the experienced events of the whaling tale within the compass of language, when he has submitted life to the forms of art, to set the story free in the literary universe, where we readers venture to experience our own manner of "metaphysical voyaging." I hold fast to a remark offered by Paul Brodtkorb: *Moby-Dick* "seeks to create . . . a literary world of which the reader must become a part before its final reality comes into being" (148).

It is now common knowledge—for we have before us a classic—that there is much of the quest for truth in *Moby-Dick*, a forward thrust which holds out implications for the teller and for the reader. For both, this quest is experienced as a journey into something "other," and even if that otherness is metaphysically experienced as an irreducible ambiguity or as a void, it may offer forth the experience of self-transcendence. For the reader, it is a telling that on an initial level exposes the modern sensibility vividly—one might almost say viscerally—to the roiled tribulations of the emerging awareness of self as it is discovered in relation to the otherness of the cosmos. This is a crucial point I wish to address in this essay: Ishmael's quest for truth allows for imagining possibilities of otherness which the contemporary reader rarely confronts in a literary text, in significant measure because the strategy of the telling figures forth both the magnitude of the external, vast universe and the seeming insignificance of the solitary self. This self (referred to by Ahab in one of his less-enraged moments as "though but a point at best") is realized initially as the lone survivor of yet within the tale told, and consequentially, after the telling, as the reader, other than Ishmael, who is compelled self-consciously to work through the ambiguities of the story.

Ishmael's canny telling ultimately functions, as Richard Brodhead rightly notes, to release us readers "even from his own heterodox and relativistic outlook, freeing us to make what sense we can of an abiding mystery. He ceases to guide us so that we can share in his own central experience, the experience of active, self-conscious seeking in the face of a world that challenges us to read it if we can" (162). And so I shall focus on Ishmael as teller, to study the vehicle of Ishmael's complex perceptions. Hardly a disinterested narrator, Ishmael is rather one given to many moods of inquiry who, "tormented with an everlasting itch for things remote," inductively experiences much that comes strangely his way. It is his encounter with otherness that leads to his exploration of metaphysical problems and ambiguous solutions.

Before offering discussions of Ishmael and his wondering sensibility, and of the thematic of metaphysical otherness, I first wish to offer one last comment on the impact felt by the reader of the ambiguities of the narrative itself, as if a reading of *Moby-Dick* has just been performed. What might be said of this "most audacious" (Chase: 100) text, when the reader comes to recognize that it is "so literary, so *written* a book" (Chase: 102)? For one thing, the reader's entanglement with the text has been a constant wrestling with several kinds of indirection and rhetorical force, elements consistently refusing to be domesticated and always resisting full comprehension. Indeed, as I shall show, there are many moments throughout the book when the reader is lured into assuming that the unfamiliar has become familiarized; moments, say, when the whale in all its particulars is felt to have been thoroughly considered, moments when the reader is seduced into feeling that the work has become fully possessed by his consciousness. The strategy of the narrative, however, makes it increasingly difficult for the reader to gain detachment from the event of reading itself, usually because the effects wrought by the shifting forms of the narrative provide an intended ambiguity. It is an ambiguity that hinders the reader from categorizing or subverting the text into any preordained pattern, that prevents one from trying to make it fit into any specified form, from thinking of it in any one narrow way. Thus, at the very least, this crafted dimension of ambiguity works on us readers in such a way that we encounter, during our moments of reading, what A. N. Kaul describes as a "largeness of meaning" (258). The reader is left with a sense that any hope for secured meaning will be undermined. This hope for certitude is ambushed, and the gap between limited point of view (be it Ishmael's or the reader's) and the reality behind it remains permanent. This is the insight shared by Ishmael "to anyone who will listen."

II

> Is it that by its indefiniteness it shadows forth the heartless voids and immensities of the universe, and thus stabs us from behind with the thought of annihilation, when beholding the white depths of the milky way? Or is it, that as an essence whiteness is

> not so much a color as the visible absence of color, and at the same time the concrete of all colors; is it for these reasons that there is such a dumb blankness, full of meaning, in a wide landscape of snows—a colorless, all-color of atheism from which we shrink? And when we consider that other theory of the natural philosophers, that all other earthly hues—every stately or lovely emblazoning—the sweet tinges of sunset skies and woods; yea, and the gilded velvets of butterflies, and the butterfly cheeks of young girls; all these are but subtle deceits, not actually inherent in substances, but only laid on from without; so that all deified nature absolutely paints like the harlot, whose allurements cover nothing but the charnelhouse within; and when we proceed further, and consider that the mystical cosmetic which produces every one of her hues, the great principle of light, for ever remains white or colorless in itself, and if operating without medium upon matter, would touch all objects, even tulips and roses, with its own blank tinge—pondering all this, the palsied universe lies before us a leper; and like willful travelers in Lapland, who refuse to wear colored and coloring glasses upon their eyes, so the wretched infidel gazes himself blind at the monumental white shroud that wraps all the prospect around him. And of all these things the Albino Whale was the symbol. Wonder ye then at the fiery hunt?
> —"The Whiteness of the Whale," Chapter 42 of *Moby-Dick*

> The imaginative capacity for wonder—whether it takes the primitive form of awed and passive astonishment before the unexpected, or the more sophisticated form of active, imaginative penetration into modes of being other than our own—requires a special openness to the unanticipated, a certain susceptibility to surprise, and most of us can no longer allow ourselves to be so vulnerable.
> —Giles Gunn (179)

Giles Gunn has suggested that if we take the Emersonian distinction between the "Me" and the "not-Me" as the executive principle responsible for the work's formal coherence, we would note the problem of otherness emerging at those self-transcending moments of consciousness when the self comes into "contact with all that lies outside the self" (177). I suggest that these moments are given thematic point by taking note of ways that wonder functions in the text, and that the fullest portion of *Moby-Dick*'s meaning emerges when we note the responses such otherness elicits from Ishmael, Ahab, and the reader.

One's identity emerges from the dialogical interaction between the self and all that it experiences in the context of otherness. "We seem largely to become aware of otherness," writes Wesley Kort, "by encountering limiters" (36).

This situation has been addressed theologically and formulated phenomenologically, and it may be given thematic immediacy by way of a discussion of wonder as a mode of perception. A central claim of this essay is that the signature of wonder is everywhere present in Ishmael's narrative and that, because of its irony, such wonder functions significantly in the reader's realization of the text.

One's life may be drawn taut between moments of darksome anguish and an almost inebriating, and surely celebrative, sense of wonderment for the gift of life. Expressed theologically, one's existence may be polarized between self-transcending moments colored by suspicions of an unmitigated Void and by those offering a sense of the unconditioned Ground of Being. To characterize ours as a secular world is in part to suggest that the winds of meaning no longer waft confidently, no longer inform that one is at home in the cosmos. It takes little effort to hear the unsettling tone behind Hannah Arendt's description of ours as an age "where man, wherever he goes, encounters only himself" (Kermode: 38). To take note of this sense of impoverished meaning in our lives is in part to acknowledge, in Frank Kermode's words, "the growing difficulty of access to the paradigms" (166). The best that we can hope for, we may be told, is some apprehension of a limit situation from which we might shore up a condition imagined to be nothing more initially than the sundered remnants of a once-enjoyed contact with Being-Itself. And so the legacy left us by the moderns may be an abiding sense of deep anguish.

Although modern man may view himself as lodged in a one-dimensional world characterized by silence and meaninglessness, and although he may understand himself as adhering to symbols of non-transcendence accordingly, his existence bespeaks an unwillingness to settle for a world stripped down to raw immanence. Just so, we frequently find it argued by widely read theologians that the secular spirit seemingly ignores significant and real areas of experience. Langdon Gilkey says accordingly:

> In . . . areas of our ordinary experience, something strange enters, something not quite accounted for by the relativistic symbolic forms of our secular mood. A nonsecular dimension in our experience appears in the lived character of secular life, despite the fact that the forms of our modern self-understanding have no capacity for dealing with it. It has the character of ultimacy, or finality, of the unconditioned which transcends, undergirds, and even threatens our experience of the ordinary passage of things and our dealings with the entities in that passage. It is, therefore, sacred as well as ultimate, the region where value as well as existence is grounded. It is *also* because of an awareness of this dimension that our common life participates in such overwhelming negatives, that it can

become demonic, filled with terrible conflict and cruelty, a life teetering always on the edge either of fanaticism or else of meaninglessness and despair (253).

Now it is such awareness that is quite what Ishmael discovers, and the accomplished telling he offers of this experience may help us to understand why readers continue to feel *Moby-Dick* to be a notably relevant literary event. Yet to explore such latent elements of the dimension of ultimacy does not presuppose that one shall find God. These searchings of the transcendent might reveal a yawning, abysmal Void, and leave one with an abiding sense of despair. But the point being made here is that some dimensions of that which resides beyond the self will be experienced, and it may be given some form in language. Such a point relates, in several ways, to Ishmael's disinherited sensibility. Again and again, as an exile he confronts himself with the meaning of his quest for possibilities of transcending truth, possibilities of metaphysical meaning in a world of shattered significance, a world seemingly devoid of symbolized centeredness on land, a world where nothing ultimately coheres.

Just as one may feel a "felt tone of anxiety" at having confronted the deep emptiness of a "heartless void," so too one might also discover an opening up of the positive creativeness of this ultimate, transcending dimension of human experience. Ishmael offers a rich image of such a discovery in one of his most extraordinary chapters, "The Grand Armada," when the *Pequod* enters "that enchanted calm" of inner "concentric circles" of whales, "eight or ten in each, swiftly going round and round," and he beholds the following:

> But far beneath this wondrous world upon the surface, another and still stranger world met our eyes as we gazed over the side. For, suspended in those watery vaults, floated the forms of the nursing mothers of the whales, and those that by their enormous girth seemed shortly to become mothers. The lake, as I have hinted, was to a considerable depth exceedingly transparent; and as human infants while suckling will calmly and fixedly gaze away from the breast as if leading two different lives at the time; and while yet drawing moral nourishment, be still spiritually feasting, upon some unearthly reminiscence;—even so did the young of these whales seem looking up towards us, but not at us, as if we were but a bit of Gulf-weed in their new-born sight. . . . And thus, though surrounded by circle upon circle of consternations and affrights, did these inscrutable creatures at the centre freely and fearlessly indulge in all peaceful concernments; yea, serenely revelled in dalliance and delight.

Thus entranced, Ishmael reflects on his response: "But even so, amid the tornadoed Atlantic of my being, do I myself still for ever centrally disport in mute calm; and while ponderous planets of unwaning woe revolve around me, deep down and deep inland there I still bathe me in eternal mildness of joy."

Even in the angularities of life one might begin to sense with wonder and awe the sheer givenness of being itself; however tacitly, one might yet hold out a sense that, in Gunn's description, the "'traces,' the 'residues,' the 'Presence' is there" (223). Gilkey summarily states: "Every level of our life is related to its ultimate ground; and so each level feels both the wonder, beauty, meaning, and joy of existence as it comes to us from transcendence, and the terror and emptiness of an ultimate Void" (315).

Wonder and terror—there you have it: two juxtaposing yet powerfully felt experiences of depth that provide for an ontological dimension to the otherness encountered by the self. From what has been suggested thus far, it might be assumed that this framework of ultimacy appears directly in the awareness of dread, of an unconditioned Void, and subsequently—indirectly—in rapture, in the joyful wonder that somehow is experienced despite the world's contingency and relativity.

Yet the reader's expectations are jarred at just this level of reading: wonder most often functions in precisely the opposite manner in *Moby-Dick*. Ishmael experiences wonder in just about everything that presents itself throughout the voyage of the *Pequod*, to be sure. It is surely his unquenching activity for wondering that allows him to enter the metaphysical dimensions of his quest. As the world Ishmael encounters becomes more and more symbolically imbued, corresponding coruscations of wonder abound. But such wonder often never follows; rather, it precedes and is finally conjoined with horror. Alas! What appears full of wonder is suspicioned to radiate from the depths of a "palsied universe" full of "subtle deceits" and meaninglessness. It is the "graceful flexion of the motions" (chap. 86, "The Tail") of this gripping metaphysical realization that provides *Moby-Dick* with much of its power. Let us turn now to an exploration of Ishmael's wondrous telling: a discussion of Ishmael's character, of what he seeks, of his metaphysical sensibility, and of his world, a universe lying beyond the self where otherness bodies forth horror, perhaps more than wonder, as supremely reigning, where the self beholds what Daniel Hoffman describes as the "ever-present possibility of cosmic nothingness" (273).

III

> It was a sight full of quick wonder and awe! The vast swells of the omnipotent sea; the surging, hollow roar they made, as they rolled along the eight gunwales, like gigantic bowls in a boundless bowling-green; the brief suspended agony of the boat, as it would

> tip for an instant on the knife-like edge of the sharper waves, that almost seemed threatening to cut it in two . . . all these with the cries of the headsmen and harpooneers, and the shuddering gasps of the oarsmen, with the wondrous sight of the ivory Pequod bearing down upon her boats with outstretched sails, like a wild hen after her screaming brood;—all this was thrilling.
> —"The First Lowering," Chapter 48 of *Moby-Dick*

> Ishmael must have an audience that will give a particular kind of credence to his marvelous illusions, an audience retrained in the difficult balance of wonder and skepticism.
> —Warwick Wadlington (97)

As noted above, *Moby-Dick* freely makes use of conventional religious themes, but there is a certain and unsettling consciousness telling the story and devising a "careful disorderliness" as the "true method" adequate to this "enterprise" (chap. 82, "The Honor and Glory of Whaling"). Somewhere behind the screen of theme sounds a voice that never allows the reader to rest too much assured about any stated meaning, and this is the voice of Ishmael. Ishmael is the voice and consciousness of *Moby-Dick*. Ishmael's own horizon of understanding provides the frame in which the story is constructed. More than this, the reader is invited into the story, into a world calling for his participation by stimulating his need for interpretation. Ishmael draws the reader first-hand into a telling of his reading of a metaphysical journey suffered "some years ago," a telling provisioned by his lone survival of the events narrated:

> Call me Ishmael. Some years ago—never mind how long precisely—having little or no money in my purse, and nothing particular to interest me on shore, I thought I would sail about a little and see the watery part of the world. It is a way I have of driving off the spleen, and regulating the circulation. Whenever I find myself growing grim about the mouth; whenever it is a damp, drizzly November in my soul; whenever I find myself involuntarily pausing before coffin warehouses, and bringing up the rear of every funeral I meet; and especially whenever my hypos get such an upper hand of me, that it requires a strong moral principle to prevent me from deliberately stepping into the street, and methodically knocking people's hats off—then, I account it high time to get to sea as soon as possible. (chap. 1, "Loomings")

From this famous passage, the first paragraph of the novel's first chapter, the reader is invoked to note that Ishmael is to be the narrator. Both the book and the quest for Moby Dick begin from his point of view. We ought not slight this necessary fact for, as Edgar Dryden reminds us, "The world is as it is seen. Point of view is at once a literary technique and a metaphysical principle" (7). Further, Ishmael's rendering of his tale functions to involve the reader as accomplice, as co-creator, and such involvement implicates the reader with the very first utterance in this first of 135 chapters: the reader is enjoined to "call" this teller "Ishmael." We shall be led, because of this involvement in our reading, to an earned apprehension of the plural significances and ciphered ambiguities of the universe. What the reader discovers through his experience of *Moby-Dick* is a recovery of the significance of the individual act of apprehension. And yet such implicative gaps urging the creative participation of the reader vary in intensity, and may be felt to diminish considerably as Ahab assumes the center of the dramatic stage.

At least through the first quarter of the novel, Ishmael remains the protagonist. With "a damp, drizzly November in my soul" (what one critic has called Ishmael's "original disobedience" [Hoffman: 260]), it is immediately apparent that Ishmael is not at fullest harmony with either himself or the land. The illimitable sea appeals strongly to his nature: "meditation and water are wedded forever." What he sees in water is an image of the "ungraspable phantom of life; and this is the key to it all." In the same chapter, Ishmael offers a presentiment of Moby Dick, again using the word "phantom": "[T]he whaling voyage was welcome; the great flood-gates of the wonder-world swung open, and in the wild conceits that swayed me to my purpose, two and two there floated into my inmost soul, endless processions of the whale, and, mid most of them all, one grand hooded phantom, like a snow hill in the air." Thus begins a metaphysical quest into the "wonder-world" for "the key to it all."

Dissatisfied with life on land or no, we realize that Ishmael's malaise is of a kind that nonetheless allows him to be quite alive to his surroundings. This is so even before he sets sail on the *Pequod*. In Chapter 3, "The Spouter Inn," while exploring the room in which he will sleep until the onset of the voyage, Ishmael relates: "But what is this on the chest? I took it up, and held it close to the light, and felt it, and smelt it, and tried every way possible to arrive at some satisfactory conclusion concerning it." After putting down the jacket, Ishmael meditates about his strange roommate, Queequeg: "I sat down on the side of the bed and commenced thinking about this head-peddling harpooneer, and his door mat. After thinking some time on the bed-side, I got up and took off my monkey jacket, and then stood in the middle of the room thinking. I then took off my coat, and thought a little more in my shirt sleeves."

It is, then, readily apparent that Ishmael is a most inquisitive fellow. Prefigured by the "sub-sub librarian," he is a problem solver, naturally given to thinking and reflecting. If something is unclear, all observations focus entirely on the problem until it is puzzled out. We read, for example, "my sensations were strange. Let me try to explain them." Just as characteristic is his way of engaging his reader with a volley of questions: "Why is almost every robust healthy boy with a robust healthy soul in him, at some time or other crazy to go to sea? Why upon your first voyage as a passenger, did you yourself feel such a mystical vibration, when first told that you and your ship were now out of sight of land?" Thus, this Ishmael has a philosophical bent, but it must be noted that all his ruminations stem from the concreteness of that to which he is present. This feature of Ishmael's personality is characteristic of an attitude of appropriating reality evident in much nineteenth century American literature, an attitude explored in great detail in Tony Tanner's fascinating study, *The Reign of Wonder: Naivety and Reality in American Literature*.

Tanner points out that the myth of wonder provided a "key strategy" for American writers. One who wonders has the ability to see with "the naive vision, the innocent eye" the world in all its concrete particularities: "You can 'wonder *at*'—and you can also 'wonder *about*.' As well as the attitude of awed and reverent openness, there is the habit of speculation: the word connotes both, and clearly one activity can easily give way to the other. There is a small but significant shift from a passive to an active mode, the idea of uninterrupted sensory reception giving way to the energized imagination which adds and provides out of its own stirring abundance" (309).

It would be helpful to dwell a bit longer on this "wondering attitude," for it points directly to the nature of Ishmael's mind, as well as to the genius of Melville's technique. Ishmael, especially in the first chapters, must solicit his reader's attention to an understanding of his method of interpretation of reality, "else all these chapters might be for naught." The meanings of the world are generated through acts of wondering, of "looking." Ishmael "aims to tantalize," writes A. Robert Lee. "Ishmael's itch surely becomes the reader's. Who would not be called to forbidden seas, barbary, things remote? [The] reader's physical appetite is aroused; as is his imaginative need for beyondness, for journeying across watery space" (114).

And so Ishmael brings with him onto the *Pequod* a sensibility of radical openness to experience. Tanner views this disposition as characteristic of the American "paratactical vision," whereby a sense of wonderment or awe receives a sense of things without prejudgment. American writers, he argues, were searching for a new vision that would allow literature to give form to and evoke the new feelings experienced on a new, un-European continent. This childlike, innocent eye was intended to render concrete details with "dazzling freshness and vivid clarity, richly appreciative of the wonder of creation and not at all prompted to embark on any disruptive intellectual inquiry" (8-9). Thus the "tremendous hunger to discover a new access to reality, a new habit of wonder." One therefore finds stress placed on the vernacular as opposed to highly refined speech, in order that words might exude a unique, and hopefully adequate, wisdom which could be seen to grasp a "palpable, proximate reality." Just so, the veritable concrete realities of Ishmael's world can render fresh appprehensions of the radical depth and mysteriousness of experience by way of his imagination.

Now, before settling down to dealing with the "symbolic meanings" inherent in the white whale, the *Pequod*, or Ahab, the reader must admit the crucial fact that Moby Dick is not a concept but a real whale, one of the species which is described historically in page after page of often erudite, sometimes fanciful cetology; that Ahab, in like manner, is the captain of the *Pequod*, that he has been badly maimed by Moby Dick, and so forth. Ishmael realizes that "dissect him how I may, I but go skin deep," as he wonders about the whale. Maurice Friedman describes what he views as Ishmael's frustration: "Indeed, in all his laborous cetology, with its detailed accounts not only of the kinds and habits of whales and whaling but also of the various processes of butchery after the whale is killed and the many uses to which parts of the whale are put, only serves to underscore his final bafflement in his attempt to understand the Leviathan" (146). Not quite: I would redress Friedman's characterization by suggesting that Ishmael intends such an effect brought about by such "detailed accounts." We should be mindful that Ishmael exposes the reader to entire chapters that, unto themselves offer a vision of reality where the whale is nothing more than "a meat pie, nearly on hundred feet long" (chap. 65, "The Whale as a Dish"), presentations fully grounded in solid, physical, tactile reality, wherein the natural order of things does not "give off sparks far beyond themselves" (TeSelle: 178). At these moments, the world is solid-seeming, the world is physical and ordinary and everyday, a "world whose hard surface seems to be all that there is" (Brodhead: 145).

But of course the reader is seized by other presentations, where he experiences, together with Ishmael, how concrete images, placed in a rich atmosphere, add on to one another, and grow to the point whereby meaning transcends mere "factuality" and enters the realm of the symbolic. This is one manner in which, as Charles Feidelson suggests, "*Moby-Dick* is a developing meaning" (183). Ishmael's sensibility is expressed in a manner directly functional to his thematic intentions by way of his capability for experiencing an astonishing range of emotions. All experience, we learn, is multiple for Ishmael: reality can never be reduced to something more primary than "two and two." Nothing on this voyage will be discovered to exist without its opposite. Life is depicted, at its most equipollent, as "calms crossed by storms, a storm for every calm."

I have emphasized above that although the self may experience the concreteness of the world with a wondering disposition, it does not necessarily follow that celebration of life is forthcoming. Ishmael realizes this lack of assurance all too soon. And yet, this much must be allowed: it is through the experience of wonder that Ishmael's metaphysic is presented to the reader. This experience manifests itself by way of two characteristics: the transcending awareness of an ultimate Void (the absence or disappearance of God) and the Faustian possibility of affirming an ultimate truth precisely by way of a quest for such truth. I now turn to a further discussion of Ishmael's quest.

IV

I wonder, Flask, whether the world is anchored anywhere.
—Stubb, in *Moby-Dick*

Chapter 23, "The Lee Shore," presents a clear expression of the sea as that toward which one journeys to seek the "highest truth." Although he is speaking of Bulkington, Ishmael in this chapter works his way toward revealing his strong discontent with the land and his existential need to "be" at sea:

> When on that shivering winter's night, the *Pequod* thrust her vindictive bows into the cold malicious waves, who should I see standing at her helm but Bulkington! I looked with sympathetic awe and fearfulness upon the man, who in mid-winter just landed from a four year's dangerous voyage, could so unrestingly push off again for still another tempestuous term. The land seemed scorching to his feet. Wonderfullest things are ever the unmentionable; deep memories yield no epitaphs; this six-inch chapter is the stoneless grave of ship, that miserably drives along the leeward land. The port would fain give succor; the port is pitiful; in the port is safety, comfort, hearthstone, supper, warm blankets, friends, all that's kind to our mortalities. But in that gale, the port, the land, is that ship's direst jeopardy; she must fly all hospitality; one touch of land, though it but graze the keel, would make her shudder through and through. With all her might she crowds all sail off shore; in so doing, fights 'gainst the vey winds that would blow her homeward; seeks all the lashed sea's landlessness again; for refuge's sake forlornly rushing into peril; her only friend her bitterest foe!
>
> But as in landlessness alone resides the highest truth, shoreless, indefinite as God—so, better is it to perish in that howling infinite, than be ingloriously dashed upon the lee, even if that were safety! For worm-like, then, oh! who would craven crawl to land! Terrors of the terrible! is all this agony so vain? Take heart, take heart, Bulkington! Bear thee grimly, demigod! Up from the spray of thy ocean-perishing—straight up, leaps thy apotheosis!

In the souls of both Bulkington and Ishmael is the awareness that the truth sought is not finite, but infinite in the sense of being absolute, and to this metaphysical awareness Ishmael is driven beyond himself in his quest for an answer to the riddle of the univerise. The paradox is evident: as long as we stand on the shore we cannot behold the phantom, but we risk destruction once we voyage out into "that howling infinite." We have here a truth "which can be verified only through participation—the truth that discovers the limits of reality through going out to encounter them" (Friedman: 55).

Ishmael, readily identifying himself as one of "us hunters of whales," knows that truth can be sought only by "going a-whaling yourself"—only by placing oneself in the imbroglio of "landlessness." Like Bulkington, Ishmael's world can only be "a ship on the passage out." The most ultimate of realities to Ishmael, as he thrusts himself into that "howling infinite" sea, is the *experience* of encountering a whale. He is compelled to return again and again to the religious quest felt most fully only in the theater that yields the "interlinked terrors and wonders of God." He has set himself on a search for the ultimate truth with a driving attempt to comprehend the mystery of existence, to "grasp the ungraspable phantom of life," to read the pattern of the loom.

Ishmael is often able to limn the dimensions of what he is coming up against during this metaphysical voyage. The reader senses such awareness, for example, in his portraitures of two shipmates, Starbuck and Flask. First, Starbuck, the indomitably Christian chief mate of the *Pequod* who, one suspects, somehow senses the twilight of the Christian God:

> Uncommonly conscientious for a seaman, and endued with a deep natural reverence, the wild watery loneliness of his life did therefore strongly incline him to superstition, but to that sort of superstition, which in some organizations seems rather to spring, somehow, from intelligence than from ignorance. Outward portents and inward presentiments were his ... But it was not in reasonable nature that a man so organized, and with such terrible experiences and remembrances as he had; it was not in nature that these things should fail in latently engendering an element in him, which, under suitable circumstances, would break out from its confinement, and burn all his courage up. And brave as he might be, it was that sort of bravery chiefly, visible in some intrepid men, which, while generally abiding firm in the conflict with seas, or winds, or the world, yet cannot withstand those more terrific, because more spiritual terrors, which sometimes menace you from the concentrating brow of an enraged and mighty man. (chap. 26, "Knights and Squires")

The reader witnesses here that Ishmael is aware not only of the "ordinary irrational," but of a deeper dimension, one imbued with the spiritual horrors that one as open to the ructions of life as Ishmael must confront in his struggle for meaning informed by such experience.

We note Ishmael's manifest sensibility again in another passage, this one where it is bodied forth in his disparaging comments regarding Flask. Such details as here offered derive precisely from the fact that whales, for Flask, are merely things to be killed:

> A short, stout, ruddy young fellow, very pubnacious concerning whales, who somehow seemed to think that the great Leviathans had personally and hereditarily affronted him; and therefore it was a sort of point of honor with him, to destroy them whenever encountered. So utterly lost was he to all sense of reverence for the many marvels of their majestic bulk and mystic ways; and so dead to anything like an apprehension of any possible danger from encountering them; that in his poor opinion, the wondrous whale was but a species of magnified mouse, or at least water-rat, requiring only a little circumvention and some small application of time and trouble in order to kill and boil. [Thus, he had an] ignorant, unconscious fearlessness.... (chap. 27, "Knights and Squires")

It is evident to the reader that Ishmael is fully present to a growing aura about whales. To him they dawn upon his consciousness as marvelous, mystical, dangerous, and wondrous—all qualities of the transcendent, qualities finally concretely focussed on the Leviathan, "this ante-mosaic, unsourced existence" symbolizing for Ishmael the problem of universal reality.

V

> Ahab reduces Moby Dick to an analogy of his mad idea of nature, making inscrutable blankness a mask of universal malice. Ishmael, though suspecting a fearful contingency, suspects nature to be at base a hollow sham, hiding absolutely nothing.
> —John Seelye (64)

> The sailor Ishmael, who feels the strong pull of this "quenchless feud," is countered by the retrospective narrator, who can see through Ahab's maneuvers as "more or less paltry and base." [As] a character Ahab still exerts his enchantment on Ishmael, and only a heroic effort can capture his nearly ineffable nature.... What *shall be* grand—the task for author Ishmael thus parallels the one for sailor Ishmael: to read, and to write, Ahab.
> —Bainard Cowan (97-98)

Both Ishmael and Ahab are driven to know the truth. Both are exiles, therefore, from the land. And yet only Ishmael can work through to an acceptance of such an identity and live without being a solipsistic rebel like Ahab. Ishmael's is a "saving skepticism" (Seelye: 4). Ahab, that moral tyrant, I would argue, has fixed the significance of those things he would know, for all that comes within his purview secured with determinate meaning. For Ahab, there lies the certain rigid pattern of his destiny: "This whole act's immutably decreed. . . . I am the Fates' lieutenant," he memorably declares. Ahab finally does not submit to transformation. Contrariwise, Ishmael, rejecting determined closure, is flexive, fluidly willing to be open to the process of perceiving experience this way, and then that, and then both, refusing to unify what essentially cannot be joined.

Submitting fully to Promethean desires, Ahab is possessed with such blinding, disproportioned vengeance against Moby Dick that all possibility for dialogue with existence is lost. He personalizes everything that could possibly be evil. As Richard Chase remarks: "In Ahab the reason and the aesthetic sense pull apart. He has his humanities, as we are told. [But] gradually his intellect is drawn apart from whatever might nourish, harmonize, and symbolize it, and in its isolation, it grows willful, obsessive, and finally suicidal. Except for the narcissism that makes a mad allegorist of Ahab, he is blind to all the imaginative versions of reality that his own mind or that of others may offer him" (91-92). As Ahab, reflecting his obdurate mind, says of himself: "I'm demoniac, I am madness maddened!" And he remains that way, unrepentant to the last (with one dramatic exception), as Moby Dick pulls him down. This motif of narcissism has been evident in most critical considerations of Ahab. The following statement by Friedman, for example, nicely points to the essential difference between Ishmael and Ahab, particularly with respect to the capacity Ishmael has for bringing a sense of self to the confrontation of the surrounding evil: "Ishmael's narcissism lies not in contemplating his own mirrored image but the image of life and the world, and if he is as likely to drown as Narcissus, it is not from reaching for himself but for 'the undeliverable, nameless perils' of the great whale" (68).

Enigmatic though Ahab surely is, he just as certainly as a figure of large and tragic proportions. As Ishmael recedes as a figure in the action, Ahab, this "maimed, maddened, predestinated old man" (Hoffman: 240) assumes greater dramatic focus, until there is no release from his annihilative quest for the white whale: "In his fiery eyes of scorn and triumph, you then saw Ahab in all his fatal pride." Hounded by his confrontation with the "personified impersonal," Ahab is driven to defy all that otherness perceived to be over against the self. Writes Brodhead: "Ahab is obsessively conscious of inhuman supernatural powers. Ordinary reality simply evaporates before his boiling mind as he projects himself out of it to engage in cosmic contests" (146). Such projection is marvelously rendered in one of *Moby-Dick*'s most famous chapters, "The Doubloon," when Ahab, peering his "bright coin," says:

> "There's something ever egotistical in mountain-tops and towers, and all other grand and lofty things; look here,—three peaks as

proud as Lucifer. The firm tower, that is Ahab; the volcano, that is Ahab; the courageous, the undaunted, and victorious fowl, that, too, is Ahab; all are Ahab; and this round gold is but the image of the rounder globe, which, like a magician's glass, to each and every man in turn but mirrors back his own mysterious self. . . ."

Yet there is a moment, near the end, when this self-bound vision opens to admit the reality of another self, a tragic, final glimpse when he finds himself able, as Bowen remarks, to forget his anger and answer love with love: "the Prometheus in him was not wholly yielded to the fiercer Enceladus" (135). Before he finally crosses the deck, thus ultimately choosing to side with Fedallah, Ahab admits to Starbuck feelings betraying the closest he will ever get to values of the heart. He says, in "The Symphony": "Close! stand close to me, Starbuck; let me look into a human eye; it is better than to gaze into sea or sky; better than to gaze upon God. By the green land; by the bright hearthstone! this is the magic glass, man. . . ." But this deeply affecting vision is only momentary; it is Ishmael's identity that survives, for, unlike Ahab, he has achieved some sense of equipoise with ambiguity. "Buoyed up by that coffin," the potentiality for meaning is generated by Ishmael's desire to narrate. Ending the chapter, "The Castaway," Ishmael writes: "And in the sequel of the narrative, it will then be seen what like abandonment befell myself."

VI

Ishmael's narrative strategy, as he understands, is grounded in a supreme fiction. He tells the story of his life in the form of interesting adventures, although he is aware that experience is composed of gratuitous events and disconnected sensations without significance or direction. This disturbing truth, which makes an orderly life impossible, usually remains hidden behind the many forms which man imposes on his world, since he convinces himself that they are inherent in the nature of experience.
—Edgar Dryden (83)

Ishmael survives it and resumes his ongoing orphan's life with his questions unanswered. In writing Ahab's book he similarly tests to the utmost the possibility of creating a final fiction, of committing himself to one narrative mode and its determinate vision of reality, but in the end he must return to write a book that includes this as one fiction among many, a book that is more faithful to the uncertainty and variety of "this strangely mixed affair we call life."
—Richard Brodhead (161-62)

Ishmael's is a troubled self, "with the problem of the universe revolving in me." His quest is to seek a resolution to this cosmological dilemma, but what he discovers time and again during "this deeply vexed odyssey" (Lewis: 130) is a profound legerdemain of metaphysical proportions. For what Ishmael comes to realize, after contemplation of Moby Dick's whiteness, is a horror that stuns one's imagination: "Though in many of its aspects this visible world seems formed in love, the invisible spheres were formed in fright." This is a crucial statement embodying Ishmael's developing sense of reality. What he suspects at this stage is an atheistical void behind appearances. Yet he *does* work through to a conditioned balance as he forgoes any static resolution to his epistemological quest. Implications of this more flexible resolution for Ishmael and the reader shall take us to the conclusion of this essay.

The central problem, certainly, deals with appearance and reality. A sea that appears to be wondrous is realized to be only an ersatz balm covering the depths of reality wherein horror resides. As his mind drifts through images of whiteness, Ishmael finds no example of wonder that does not rest on a transcendent horror. Anything eliciting wonder because of something seemingly good only announces the deeper realization that it shall be ultimately terrible. And this is so whether or no that ultimate manifests itself as absolute and infinite, malicious and hostile, or cold, silent and different. In the following passages from Chapter 42, "The Whiteness of the Whale," we see Ishmael's awareness that experiences of wonder inform the perceiver of, and finally link with, the deepest of transcendent horrors:

> [Y]et for all these accumulated associations, with whatever is sweet, and honorable, and sublime, there yet lurks an elusive something in the innermost idea of this hue, which strikes more of panic to the soul than that redness which affrights in blood.
>
> This elusive quality it is, which causes the thought of whiteness, when divorced from more kindly associations, and coupled with any object terrible itself, to heighten that terror to the furthest bounds. Witness the white bear of the poles, and the white shark of the tropics; what but their smooth, flaky whiteness makes them the transcendent horrors they are? That ghastly whiteness it is which imparts such an abhorrent mildness, even more loathsome than terrific, to the dumb gloating of their aspect. So that not the fierce-fanged tiger in his heraldic coat can so stagger courage as the white-shrouded bear or shark.
>
> Bethink thee of the albatross whence come those clouds of spiritual wonderment and pale dread, in which that white phantom sails in all imaginations? Not Coleridge first threw that spell; but God's great, unflattering laureate, Nature.

The "wondrous sight of the ivory *Pequod*" is seen two pages later when "the thick mists were dimly parted by a huge, vague form." Any glance at the emerald calm and beauty of the sea now brings with it the perception that sharks with a "wondrous voracity" lurk beneath the surface.

Quite early in the novel, Ishmael allows: "Not knowing what is good, I am quick to perceive a horror, and could still be social with it." Friedman rightly notes that "at the heart of horror is wonder, and horror and wonder are wedded, as nowhere else, in *Moby-Dick*. . . . The ultimate terror, to [Ishmael], is the indifference of an absolute the excludes man. Now indefiniteness is not a characteristic of truth but an irrational force that threatens us with annihilation" (68–69).

Considering the scope and intent of *The Reign of Wonder*, one might be initially surprised to discover that Tanner mentions Melville only briefly. The absence of a chapter on Melville is significant, though not because of Tanner's negligence. Rightly understood, the vision of reality experienced by Ishmael is exactly contrary to the "myth" of wonder being explored by Tanner. Nonetheless, at one moment he does suggest a central issue of this essay, and he does so in such a way that it makes Ishmael's vision of reality all the more prescient as a tacit awareness of the twentieth century reader: "What all these writers stress in their various ways is the radical importance of a true way of seeing; the generous, open, even naive undulled and reverent eye—as opposed to the self-interested squinting and peering of the greedy utilitarian social eye, and the cold myopia of the scientific, analytic eye. Their ideal is an eye of passive wonder. . . . But as the wonderer has become more and more alienated, the things miraculously revealed to him are not always such as will leave him "stupid with wonder": sometimes he is stupified wih nausea, sometimes paralyzed with horror" (355–56). The "portrait here of innocence and naivety unprepared for the deeper enigmas and shocks of the human condition" is most fully rendered, I believe, when wonder is felt to connote radical insecurity, isolation, and the disappearance of God; when wonder no longer heralds a transcendent "Good" but rather suggests an unmitigated evil lurking beneath the appearance of good. Such expectations of wonder work ironically on the conventional understanding of the reader to thrust him back into a world of reality where the "innocent eye" of the passively wondering child becomes, in William James's famous line, "the buzzing, booming chaos which is the child's world," which, *at the level of reading*, is Ishmael's world. But if such irony implicates the reader, it may be his experience, too.

To seek out reality one must go to sea, where one may find the whale. However, to come up against this living reality, this Moby Dick, is quite possibly to find the gaping maw of death. In "The Chase—First Day," Ahab makes this discovery:

> But suddenly as he peered down and down into its depths, he profoundly saw a white living spot no bigger than a white weasel,

with wonderful celerity uprising, and magnifying as it rose, till it turned, and then there were plainly revealed two long crooked rows of white, glistening teeth, floating up from the undiscoverable bottom. It was Moby Dick's open mouth and scrolled jaw; his vast, shadowed bulk still half blending with the blue of the sea. The glittering mouth yawned beneath the boat like an open-doored marble tomb. . . .

Thus we realize this paradox, or ultimate dilemma: both land and sea become hostile to human existence. Ishmael says in "Brit": "For all this appalling ocean surrounds the verdant land, so in the soul of man there lies one insular Tahiti, full of peace and joy, but encompassed by all the horrors of the half-known life. God keep thee! Push not off from that isle, thou canst never return!"

To shelter oneself from "the tough nature of reality" (as R. W. B. Lewis is wont to put it) is to slight oneself from the full truth. Yet the wondrous world yields a truth perhaps so diabolical that one cannot possibly bear it. Pip, to summon a striking example, goes mad "when carried down alive to wondrous depths." Reflecting on Pip's near drowning, Ishmael writes: "But the awful lonesomeness is intolerable. The intense concentration of self in the middle of such a heartless immensity, my God! who can tell it?" Nearly one hundred pages later, he seems to answer his question: "For whatever is truly wondrous and fearful in man, never yet was put into words or books." Man will never tell of a truly felt "heartless immensity" because such a truth is too awesomely inhuman.

For many, this outlook emerges as the tragedy of the modern predicament: numbed by the crisis of modernity, there may be little to assist the self in rebounding from shock after disabusing shock, so few touchstones to inform, to balance the self's sensibility. Mirroring this critical spirit of the 1960s, we find Nathan Scott writing:

> The tragic protagonist is overborne by a sense of shipwreck, a sense of radical fissure or rift in the realm of ultimate reality. [T]he tragic story is, then, a story of man besieged by hazard and adversity, and of man standing at last amidst shipwreck and defeat: on some forsaken heath or ash-heap the tragic man comes finally to see himself as outmatched and overborne by the terrible, voiceless Mystery of the world. The tragic vision is, in short, an unpalliated vision of shock and crisis, and of man in the extremest possible situation where all guarantees of meaning and security in his pilgrimage on earth have disappeared. (123, 131)

Throughout this pessimistic metaphysic presented by Melville is an Ishmael who somehow maintains some semblance of centrality, no matter how much wondrous horror he feels to the depths of his soul. We hear Ishmael cry out: "So man's insanity is heaven's sense; and wandering from all mortal reason, man comes at last to that celestial thought, which, to reason, is absurd and frantic; and weal or woe, feels then uncompromised, indifferent as his God." And yet, Ishmael is never completely overwhelmed by the wonders of the terrible reality he confronts. Melville does not submit to nihilism, for *the self survives the voyage to tell of the ambiguities of the quest for certainty.* Not allowing to be swallowed by a madness such as Ahab's, Ishmael's sensibility cannot rest, for his quest for truth is of a kind that cannot be closed, a "story that cannot achieve a completion or significance beyond what he himself has discovered in his experience" (Brodhead: 161).

Ishmael's account presses for a sense of observed coexistence with the dual aspects of nature. His confrontations with otherness, he learns, body forth a plural world of both/and rather than either/or. Such experiences can be startling, fearfully strange (recall the tombstones of Father Mapple's chapel, or the apparition of the "spirit-spout," or "The Jeroboam's Story"), terribly alienating (think of the cosmic voids betokened by "the whiteness of the whale"), astonishingly numinous and peacefully secure, or utterly beguiling and mysterious (such as when Ishmael is gripped in moments he calls "significant darkness"). Because of such experiences, the reader participates in "Ishmael's insistence on the relativity of perception" (Seelye: 6), and so hears Ishmael's voice revealing "a Catskill eagle in some souls that can alike dive down onto the blackest gorges, and soar out of them again and become invisible in the sunny spaces" (chap. 96, "The Try-Works").

The underlying unity of *Moby-Dick* is the responsive sensibility of Ishmael. In light of this essay's argument, we may assent to Bert Bender's admission that "*Moby-Dick* is founded in Ishmael's capacity for wonder" (354), but we would have to add that *Moby-Dick* is realized by the reader's participation in the tale told. Ishmael's telling directs the reader to the possibility of a like capacity for wonder. Restless Ishmael has moored his view of the cosmos in an ever-emergent pattern, and it is because of the reader's share in the shuttle of meaning that we are justified in asserting that Ishmael's "loom is still a-weaving" (Hoffman: 237). Having experienced the otherness of his quest, Ishmael realizes his experience in the form of a narrative. Ishmael's solitary survival at the end of the tale, Marius Bewley rightly suggests, "is the validation of his vision" (205).

Rather than seeing a confrontation with the whale as the generative source of all meaning, Ishmael's telling secures for the reader the experience of meaning in the strategies of the narrative itself. Once the reader sees the tale as Ishmael's survival after the told quest for final meanings, he may better appreciate the degree to which he has been ironically implicated throughout the course of the reading. To hold that Ishmael's narrative is retrospective, to distinguish the Ishmael of the action and the later Ishmael of the telling, is to be caught, as a reader, by the levels of the telling.

The recognition of this entanglement offers the reader the experience of his own horizon of understanding in the act of interpreting what is beyond (other than) himself. The process of reading is part of the meaning; Ishmael offers his narrative to the reader in just this way, though this is not apparent until the reader has completed *Moby-Dick* and has begun it a second time, after the *telos* of the telling has been revealed in the "Epilogue." Indeed, at one point in his writing, Ishmael looks up and out at the reader to ask: "And what are you, reader, but a Loose-Fish and a Fast-Fish, too?" Ishmael's problems are felt meaningfully to be our problems in reading. The reader's realization that Ishmael is aware of such difficulties for the reader heightens the significance of irony for such self-knowing narration. The telling of *Moby-Dick* is offered by Ishmael as one awesome, grand strategy of self-transcendence, a telling that functions in such a way for us readers as to reveal our participation in "but a draught of a draught" of a literary universe where one reading can never suffice.

WORKS CONSULTED

Bender, Bert
    1978   "*Moby-Dick*: an American Lyrical Novel." *Studies in the Novel* 10: 346–56.

Bewley, Marius
    1963   *The Eccentric Design: Form in the Classic American Novel.* New York: Columbia University.

Brodhead, Richard H.
    1976   *Hawthorne, Melville and the Novel.* Chicago: University of Chicago.

Brodtkorb, Paul
    1965   *Ishmael's White World: A Phenomenological Reading of "Moby-Dick."* New Haven: Yale University.

Bowen, Merlin
    1960   *The Long Encounter: Self and Experience in the Writings of Herman Melville.* Chicago: University of Chicago.

Chase, Richard
    1957   *The American Novel and Its Tradition.* Garden City, New York: Doubleday Anchor.

Cowan, Bainard
    1982   *Exiled Waters: "Moby-Dick" and the Crisis of Allegory.* Baton Rouge and London: Louisiana State University.

Dryden, Edgar A.
1968   *Melville's Thematics of Form: The Great Art of Telling the Truth.* Baltimore: Johns Hopkins University.

Feidelson, Charles
1953   *Symbolism and American Literature.* Chicago: University of Chicago.

Friedman, Maurice
1970   *Problematic Rebel: Melville, Dostoievsky, Kafka, Camus.* Chicago: University of Chicago.

Gilkey, Langdon
1969   *Naming the Whirlwind: The Renewal of God-Language.* New York: Bobbs-Merrill.

Gunn, Giles B.
1979   *The Interpretation of Otherness: Literature, Religion and the American Imagination.* New York: Oxford University.

Harvey, W. J.
1965   *Character and the Novel.* Ithaca, NY: Cornell University.

Hoffman, Daniel
1965   *Form and Fable in American Fiction.* New York: Oxford University.

Iser, Wolfgang
1974   *The Implied Reader.* Baltimore: Johns Hopkins University.

Kaul, A. N.
1963   *The American Vision: Actual and Ideal Society in Nineteenth-Century America.* New Haven: Yale University.

Kermode, Frank
1967   *The Sense of an Ending: Studies in the Theory of Fiction.* New York: Oxford University.

Kort, Wesley A.
1975   *Narrative Elements and Religious Meaning.* Philadelphia: Fortress.

Lee, A. Robert
1978   "*Moby-Dick*: The Tale and the Telling." Pp. 86–127 in *New Perspectives on Melville*, edited by Faith Pullin. Kent, OH: The Kent State University.

Melville, Herman
1967   *Moby-Dick.* Norton Critical Edition. Edited by Harrison Hayford and Hershel Parker. New York: W. W. Norton.

Scott, Nathan A., Jr.
1966   *The Broken Center: Studies in the Theological Horizon of Modern Literature.* New Haven: Yale University.

Seelye, John
1970   *Melville: The Ironic Diagram.* Evanston: Northwestern University.

Tanner, Tony
    1965   *The Reign of Wonder: Naivety and Reality in American Literature*. New York: Harper & Row.

TeSelle, Sallie
    1966   *Literature and the Christian Life*. New Haven: Yale University.

Wadlington, Warwick
    1975   *The Confidence Game in American Literature*. Princeton: Princeton University.

BRECHT AND THE BIBLE: A COUNTERSACRAMENTAL READING

Petermichael von Bawey
American College in Paris

ABSTRACT

Critics have wished to engage Brecht's art in the service of political theology and theological anthropology (for example), but persist in misreading his methodology based on an emergent Marxist orientation. His early use of biblical material suggests how he will employ other traditional *Kulturgut* as "gestural content" to examine the great spiritual systems. Thus in the early play *Baal*, Brecht still in a pre-Marxist stage creates a primitive materialist protagonist who understands that art is a market commodity and gains social significance for its exchange value. The songplay *Mahogony* dramatizes the alienating power of money via the Marxist argument regarding the lack of a natural relationship between producer, product, and user; and in *St. Joan of the Stockyards* Brecht reworks the material of classical German humanism and Christian values to show how these are appropriated by capitalism. Joan Dark not only fails in her mission to mediate between employers and workers but is at last cynically "canonized" by the meat monopolist so that he can consolidate his power.

The critics who take Brecht's gestural content at face value and miss its coded nature interpret him as espousing humanistic values, but his dialectical method intends the opposite: it wishes to engage society in an openended fashion with an ongoing critique of itself.

Theological Misreadings

The works of the German dramatist Bertolt Brecht have for some time now attracted interest in theological circles. As is well known, Brecht was familiar with the Old and New Testaments, and many of his works of drama, poetry, and fiction contain biblical phrases, images, or story elements. His first experience with drama, when he was fifteen, is an eight-page piece entitled *The Bible*. Already in the 1950s Brecht's religious beliefs were investigated by Peter Michelsen; and biblical images in his plays were studied by Thomas O. Brandt. But, as Reinhold Grimm advanced, biblical themes in Brecht's works are estranged or distanced (*verfremdet*) to allow the recipient to see a familiar situation in a new, different light. Hans Mayer recognized this in Brecht's parodistic use of the Bible. Although he observed that there is more than blasphemy or ideological criticism in Brecht's work, he did not explore this aspect.

More recent theological critics tend to agree. While their evaluations of Brecht's use of the Bible widely differ, they concur that the works of the commonly recognized Marxist are important for contemporary religious debates. Hans Pabst finds that Brecht used the Bible against the church, and with his works criticized the church's support of the established order to the neglect of the lower class (168). Pabst refuses to deal with the question of Brecht's atheism because atheism is a metaphysical concern and not a political one. Brecht, according to Pabst, rejected religious sacrifice, prayer, solace, inwardness, and acceptance of God insofar as they are ideologies and prevent change in modern social conditions (262). But Pabst also finds in Brecht's demand for social change an affinity to the demands and works of Jesus Christ, "whose life stands for the many" (212). Brecht uses the Bible, therefore, as an interpretive model that can criticize contemporary social relations (212). The problem that Brecht identified for criticism is also the concern of a "political theology" that has as its goal the practice of Christianity in this world. Thus "political theology joins Brecht in the criticism of misrule . . ." (263).

In contrast to Pabst's focus on Brecht's criticism of church hierarchy—a political question—Peter Goergen's book focuses on Brecht's interest of what man does in society—a socio-anthropolitical question. Goergen concludes that "Brecht's atheism is total and uncompromisable" (301), yet he hopes to enlist Brecht's works for a "theological anthropology" that takes its initiative from Brecht's imperative "to change the world" (310). Although Brecht rejected the existence of God in nature, in human production, in love, and in the social struggle for a better world (Goergen: 317), he remains an important discussion partner for a theological anthropology that seeks to learn about man's present social situation (Goergen: 20).

Whereas Pabst and Goergen privileged Brecht's political and anthropological concerns over traditional religious questions (although these are examined), they perceived Brecht's questions as ultimately of interest and a challenge to contemporary theology. Two other studies attempt to bring Brecht's thought within religious traditions. G. Ronald Murphy holds that Brecht "sees religion as man's terrified response, almost the response of the trapped animal, to his feeling being totally abandoned in the universe that gave him birth . . . and to his uncontrollable fear of the oncoming darkness of death" (10). For Murphy, the fear of abandonment and of "being good" are "the key to Brecht's nonsatiric use of the Bible" (ibid.). Brecht's "first drama," *The Bible*, is a prototype for later works where "the identification of the hero with the Passion and Death of Christ . . . is used to gain sympathy (not at all *Verfremdung*) for human weakness, human frailty" (20). Thus Murphy insists "that the 'conventional wisdom' on Brecht's atheism must be modified. The question of the mystery of God is a constant presence in Brecht's works" (90).

In another study, Eberhard Rohse concludes in his examination of the young Brecht that "the perpetuation of his early Bible reception, in constantly changing variations," is found "in practically the whole of Brecht's later poetic and dramatic productions" (Rohse: 578). Young Brecht's Bible "play" of 1913 served him as a "future-directed, critical hermeneutical model" for his later dramatic works (Rohse: 307). The consequence of this paradigm is a genealogy of figural dramatic types that portray the Passion and Death of Christ in different variations. Just as Brecht's gymnasial Bible teachers read Isaac's sacrifice as the prefiguration of Christ's sacrifice, so Brecht, from a secular point of view, gives figural meaning to his characters by using various biblical exempla, the most common being the Passion and Death of Christ with its motifs of betrayal, imprisonment, renunciation, death and burial (Rohse: 297). Hence, Brecht's figural characterization is the result of the typological historical method he acquired from his religious instructors.

These studies offer readings of Brecht's works on several different levels (political theology, theological anthropology, prototypical model, and postfigural method) that challenge Brecht's theory of modern society and art and also question Marxist as well as other interpretations of Brecht. That "the language of art means the excess of meaning that is present in the work," as Hans-Georg Gadamer holds, has certainly been demonstrated by these critics (102).

New questions, nevertheless, arise that will have to be directed to other interpretive material. How, for example, is Brecht's earlier materialism and his later Marxism, with its anthropocentric view (against *Genesis*), to be reconciled with the "mystery of God?" or, how does a postfigural method function with a dialectical one? and, what does a political theology share with dialectical materialism? Other questions can be raised, but these should suffice to launch an inquiry into Brecht's methodology and to consider three frequently quoted plays in a brief analysis of his theory and its relation to his dramatic productions.

Brecht's Methodology

In part we will primarily take old things as material.

—Brecht

The publication of the songs of Brecht's successful *The Threepenny Opera* brought censure from the theater critic Alfred Kerr. He announced that Brecht's lyrics were taken from K. L. Ammer's German translation of Francois Villon's verses. The critic, no friend of the playwright, had previously charged Brecht with plagiarism in taking verses from Rimbaud and Verlain for his *Jungle of the Cities*. The accusation was casually accepted by Brecht who admitted that 25 of the opera's 625 verses were indeed identical with those of Ammer's translation. How does one use quotations on stage, he asked, and later added that in questions of intellectual ownership he was always lax. Brecht's satirical poem, which appeared in a re-edition of Ammer's translation, encouraged the reader to take material he finds useful, for that is what Brecht had done. What to many a reader may have appeared a cheeky response to having been caught "cheating" was actually a theoretical consideration of Brecht's attempts to modernize the theater./1/

Already in 1920 Brecht advocated experimentation with the material of drama rather than with forms of language. He felt the theater did not lack material for the stage. What was missing in theatrical representation was a careful treatment of well-known works from a new point of view. His concern with existing cultural material became a methodology apparent as early as *Baal* where he used a contemporaneous drama (Johst's *Der Einsame*) for his own production.

The innovative staging of classical dramas by Leopold Jessner's "Junge Bühne" also offered Brecht many examples of how fruitful a new approach to old works can be for the theater. What interested him, however, was more than novel representation of the classics. He sought to extract what he called the material value (*Materialwert*) from existing works. Schiller's *Wallenstein* and Goethe's *Faust*, for example, possess "a not meager material value" (VII, 106)./2/ But if they are perceived as "cultural treasures" (*Kulturgut*) then they are merely museum pieces and useless for the modern stage. To counter the monumental character of traditional art, Brecht argued for a new perspective coming from outside of aesthetics.

Application of such a point of view emerged at first out of his critique of middle class values and soon developed into what he considered a scientific approach to art, coming from sociology and later from Marxism. By 1928, he had turned to a critical study of Marxism in order to develop a method for drama and theater production that would integrate social questions into analysis and the making of art: "Entire complexes of imagination in art works are to be investigated, and here the methods of Marxism are to be allied and developed" (VIII, 113). Brecht sought to transform the classical lines of inquiry into the work as an ideal artistic whole—its totality, appeal to beauty, harmony, unity, balance, and embodiment of truth—into a new line of inquiry of art's social function. In particular he singled out for criticism the standard acceptance of art's eternal value (*das ewige Schöne*) and of its intellectual ownership (*Besitzfrage der Kunst*). Both had obtained normative status beyond historical discourse and thus hindered their use as existing material. Brecht's language is particularly strong: "Ownership obsession hinders the thrust to the material value of classical works" (VII, 178). To get at the material value of traditional drama, Brecht went so far as to recommend the elevation of art to collective property. As such the modern theater could really start mining the past to dig out material and thus challenge the eternal value of historical works.

Brecht is, however, no iconoclast of traditions. He recognizes their necessity for any real innovation: "For true revolutionary continuation, tradition is necessary" (VIII, 201). The new theater needs tradition but not in re-presentational form. A classical or well-known work must not be staged, thought Brecht, "the way it really was" in the past, as L. von Ranke estimated it should be. Rather Brecht felt, in Walter Benjamin's sense of history, that it is the dramatist's "task to brush history against the grain" (257).

Transformations in the production of art include changes in its reception. Calculated in Brecht's production is the eventual response of the audience. To inform and educate the recipient, his usual empathy or sympathy for the dramatis personae must be avoided and attention directed to their actions./3/ To succeed in this Brecht gave the material he extracted from the "cultural treasures" at hand a use value (*Gebrauchswert*). This he called "gestural content." For an interview he wrote the following response in the plural form, referring to himself and his co-workers: "We have always attempted to take from those works, which we used as mines of material, only what we call the gestural content" (VII, 181). That is to say, in his use of familiar material the old content becomes a formal aspect—it is functional as gestural quotation—in a new production holding a socio-historical and critical position against its former (normative) content ". . . in the extraction of the *gestural content* of a familiar work, the intellectual postures that are to be revealed can be situated (by the producer and user) *against* the material" (VII, 223; italics in original). The actions of Brecht's characters are distanced (*entfernt*) and thus evident to the audience as the familiar material emerging as gestural content counters (brushes against the grain of) its original source (the way it really was) and thereby produces a dialectical hermeneutic that mediates between past cultural experiences, or contemporary norms of culture and the content of the dramatized reality.

Baal: The Value of Art

> What is the value of a poem: four shirts, a loaf of bread, half a milk cow?
>
> —Brecht

The opening scene of *Baal* is important for understanding the action that follows. The setting is historically familiar: the characters are in the traditional bourgeois salon where the common marriage of money and art will potentially take place. A benefactor and a critic of art are in discussion with the recently discovered genius, the new "hope" of a modern poetry, Baal. Mech, who transforms virgin Brazilian forests into European lumber, is willing to finance the publication of Baal's lyrics. Brecht's analogy here is revealing: the transformation of natural forest into commercial product is similar to the transformation of poetic work into socially accepted art. As Piller, the critic in the play, remarks, his favorable reviews of Baal's lyrics will make them acceptable to the public at large: on the one hand, the metamorphosis of forest into lumber, on the other that of "art" into "Art." At what level does one become the other? "What is the value of a poem . . . ?"/4/ asked Brecht. The analogy informs us that art obtains social substance (or even aesthetic essence) once it is recognized as having exchange value.

To the astonishment of the company, Baal appears disinterested. Rather he expresses interest in eating and drinking, and having satisfied those wants, he turns his attention to Emilie, Mech's wife, whose beauty aroused his sexual appetites. The too evident animal appetites of the artist bring censure and rejection and quickly terminate Baal's chances of becoming the new hope of poetry. The scene ends as Mech says: "I like all animals on God's earth. But with this animal one cannot do business. Come Emilie, come ladies and gentlemen" (I, 9).

The following scenes show Baal in the taverns of workers singing his lyrics, in an attic room satisfying his lusts with female visitors, in the fields fulfilling his homosexual yearnings with his friend Ekart, whom he later kills, and finally in the forest fleeing from the police and in the company of lumberjacks who are as indifferent to his existence as he is to theirs. He dies devoid of social rites and ceremony, under the sky "listening to the rain." Brecht wrote: "*Baal* was conceived with a ridiculous conception of genius and amorality to drive a weak, popular drama into the ground" (1978:207; see Johst).

As mentioned above, the material of *Baal* was inspired by Johst's successful play that Brecht thought preposterous. To the preposterous he responds with a "ridiculous conception of genius and amorality"—ridiculous understood as mocking what is commonly accepted behavior or thought. The contrasts are sharp: Johst's drama advocates a sentimental and idealistic notion of the suffering genius, whereas Brecht describes the amoral and sensuous life of the artist Baal whose actions are devoid of any transcendental interests. Whereas Johst's protagonist expresses the romantic duality of living in two worlds—the mundane, shabby reality of everyday life and the transcendental sphere of art—Brecht's Baal glories in living out sensations to the neglect of anything spiritual (to the accompaniment of Brecht's lyrics of sex, drink, and death): not mind related to spirit, as was the traditional *Bildungsgang* of the German artist that Johst tried to rejuvenate (to the accompaniment of Beethoven's music), but existence as sense and sensation in union with matter—the material of life and that of nature. That is the essence of Baal's being.

Where Johst's protagonist is obtuse to modern social conditions and laments the spiritual duality of the artist, Brecht's Baal illustrates the changed social circumstances. The significance of Baal's sensuous materialism is found in the first scene. There Baal rejects the accepted social transformation of art into commodity and with it his integration into the world of the bourgeoisie. This is not an adherence to "moral anarchism" and "self destruction" as M. Esslin would have it (173). In *Baal* Brecht clearly perceives that in his society exchange value dominates art.

Brecht did not yet have a solution to the problems of contemporary society; hence, Baal could only find a place of safety distanced from the transformation of natural forces into social products. Located in the raw and still unprocessed world of lower class taverns, of the fields, the meadows and the forest, he seeks to fulfill his essence, the unity of thought and being. Thus Brecht was able to write of Baal: "His observation was historical, had causes and consequences. What Baal did and what he said was material about him, against him; his thinking and his essence appeared identical" (VII, 218-19), a central point of materialism. To Johst's doubtful transcendence of art, Brecht posits the immanence of art in the world of nature's and humanity's physical essence. This sort of materialism brought Brecht close to Marxist thought, although seven years would pass before he studied Marx. Baal's sensuous materialism is primitive, yet socially unprocessed; it is a refuge from the market place of art. And because of it "Baal eats! Baal dances!! Baal transfigures himself!!!" as Brecht declared in the orginal title (VII, 955)./5/

Mahogonny: The Cult of Money

> Art is commodity—not to be produced without the means of production (the mechanisms). An opera can only be made for the opera.
>
> —Brecht

The material of Brecht's opera or "songplay," *Mahogonny*, comes in part from his earlier published poems (in *Hauspostille*) that describe the decadence and collapse of capitalist society. Set in a city of pleasure, a mixture of Berlin's "Golden Twenties" and of Las Vegas, the action of the opera's twenty loosely connected episodes tells the story of Paul Ackermann, a lumberjack. Similarities to *Baal* are apparent. The sensuous life is once more investigated, only the circumstances have changed considerably. In the earlier drama, sensuousness is a natural human response of social interaction; in the opera, all natural human action is alienated by the power of money. As Ronald Hayman sees it: "Life in Mahagonny is ruled by greed for money, whiskey, sex and food; the crime is to run out of money" (123). Paul Ackermann is imprisoned, tried and executed as a result of his inability to pay his bar bill.

But this is the consequence and not the cause of the problem the play deals with. For if the deadly crime in *Mahagonny* is to run out of money, the cardinal error is to let human affection influence the spending of it. Paul Ackermann's lack of money is the result of his sentimental judgment to bet on his friend Joe in an unequal boxing match with Trinitymoses. Their mutual friend Heinrich sees clearer (and survives): "Joe you're humanly close to me/But to throw away money/I lost my nerve/When I saw Trinitymoses" (I, 538). Expression of emotion or even mawkish tenderness in relation to money can be fatal. Money transforms all natural and human qualities into their opposite; it is, as the opera shows, the "alienated power of humanity," an intermediary that becomes a god.

Brecht perceives his work as taking issue with traditional opera. *Mahagonny* is entertainment just as traditional opera is culinary, as he termed it. Yet it is entertainment *about* entertainment, entertainment that is examined and questioned. In his notes: "Pleasure was at least to be the object of the investigation, even if the investigation was to be the object of pleasure. It appears here in its contemporary historical form: as commodity" (VII, 1007). Brecht's analysis of the socio-historical status of the opera follows a Marxist line of argument. The producers of the opera and their product (an opera) have no direct relations; the intermediary—the mechanism: the administration (or owner) of the opera house—has the real power over that which is produced. Consequently, the natural quality of the product (the labor of the producers) is transformed by the intermediary into that which supports its existence, i.e., the financial survival of the mechanism. Opera as commodity is the result. (Brecht formulated a similar argument in his legal suit over *The Threepenny Opera* against the film industry [VIII, 139–205].) Thus the content of *Mahagonny* is also commodity according to Brecht. But not its form. The structure is gestural: a set of social gestures informs us of the social situation of the characters. Brecht maintains: "The narrow confines did not prevent us from working in something direct, didactic and subordinating it to the gestural. The eye that directs everything to the gestural is morality. Thus a moral tableau. But subjective. What sings here are subjective moralists" (VII, 1007). Four moral exempla of eating, loving, boxing, and drinking characterize the commodity form of entertainment. In the first, Jacob the Glutton satiates himself to death. If the glutton dies by eating greedily, he does this because hunger exists, comments Brecht: "Even if not everyone dies of gluttony who has something to eat, there are many who die of hunger because the glutton dies of eating" (VII, 1008). If Paul Ackermann's and Jenny's love duet sounds "romantic," this too has its purpose: "The romantic here is also commodity" (VIII, 1008), particularly in a brothel. The inversion of natural social behavior reflects the values lost in a world of dehumanized activity.

In a provocative style, the exempla signify the transformation of natural human activity. The characters describe themselves and in doing this give us their moral standards. In these moral tableaux there are no external messages; the didactic viewpoint (*das Lehrhafte*) is found in the actions of the characters. Their behavior expresses their morality and in turn passes moral judgment upon them. In a two-term dramatic dialectic, the gestural content of *Mahagonny* speaks for and against itself.

St. Joan of the Stockyards: The Failure of Christian Love

> What is up for discussion here is the conduct of the religious human being (as far as this can be perceived), the talk of God and the efforts of man to generate faith.
> —Brecht

Brecht's method of reworking old material is perhaps nowhere more fully realized than in this play. The gestural content is the *Kulturgut* of the classical age of German humanism, the poetry of Hölderlin and Goethe, and Schiller's *Maid of Orleans* (1801), a drama that paid homage to Jeanne d'Arc in response to Voltaire's scathing parody, *La Pucelle* (1755, 1762). The German audience familiar with the works of their greatest poets would naturally draw comparisons, what Brecht intended in this examination of "the great spiritual systems" (VII, 1017).

Schiller's Joan of Arc fights not only the English but also struggles with her dual (Kantian) essence: she desires love (*die Naturkraft* or nature's force) yet must heed the higher demand of moral and spiritual striving (*das Sittengesetz* or the categorical imperative) if she is to save her nation. This Kantian dualism is supported by Schiller's threefold scheme of the drama's emplotted action that follows his philosophy of history: (1) Joan's natural and unreflective consciousness (the naive); (2) her deeds for a better world (consciousness in historical conflict); and (3) her harmony (ideal society) (see Santermeister: 20–46 and 180–82). The individual's *Bildungsgang* thus parallels liberation from historical oppression, a philosophical ideal central to Schiller and to German humanism.

This classical ideal is visible in Brecht's drama but in antagonistic form. Joan Dark of the Black Straw Hats seeks to meet her spiritual obligations by aiding the poor. This ideal leads her to the stockyards, where she encounters the workers, and to the stock exchange, where she meets Mauler and his cohort, who appear to control the meat industry. Brecht sketches stark contrasts of the class below, the victims of economic injustice, and the one above, the manipulators of economic conditions. Driven by sympathy for society's oppressed and a sense of Justice, Joan mediates between the two worlds only to "be useful to neither and perish" (I, 725) as Synder, the captain of the Black Straw Hats, predicts.

In response to Schiller's idealistic philosophy of history, Brecht posits a materialistic one taken from Marx's analysis of the industrial cycle of capitalist economy. Following Marx's five phases closely, Brecht emplotted the action of his episodes as (1) end of prosperity (episodes 1 to 2); (2) overproduction (episodes 3 to 8); (3) crisis (episodes 9 a to J); (4) stagnation (episodes 10 to 11); and (5) moderate activity (episode 12)./6/ Marx, describing the "historical process," holds, as does Brecht in this play, that the economic phases determine the "condition of existence" (1975:I, 453, 763). Joan, aware only of the human misery she seeks to combat, does not know that she is in the midst of a class struggle. She appeals to rich Mauler with the hope that "one just man must be among them" (1975:III, 251). But her belief in human goodness blinds her to the intrigues of Mauler to control the meat industry. Thus the Kantian ethic of Schiller's age and her Christian love function as impediments, and only serve further social exploitation. Mauler's behavior demonstrates how easily Joan's moral striving can be appropriated for economic manipulation. Brecht's argument: the humanistic ideal of harmony—where individual moral imperative joins social obligation—and Christian love have fallen in the hands of perverters. The travesty embodies a Marxist critique: the classical heritage and Christian service have become the ideology of the ruling class. Joan, realizing that she can only help the workers by joining their struggle, participates in a massive strike. But when told she will have to resort to violence to improve social conditions, she takes fright and fails in her assigned task. The strike collapses. But Joan cannot use force: "I could do nothing/That must be done with force and/Results in force" (I, 754). Violence would put her in a "no longer recognizable world" without "the old rules" and deprive her of "innocence" (I, 754). Joan abandons the struggle to remain true to her religious morality (Christian love) and to her (and Schiller's) spiritual ideals, with the broader result that she fails to liberate her society.

In the language of the Weimar poets, Brecht describes the triumph of "profit" over "labor" in the final scene. Meat packers and stock breeders plead for the necessity of a divided world. Their chorus in trochaic tetrameter signified the "two languages above and below"

(I, 780) that maintain the ideology of class society. Their choral is joined by the Black Straw Hats who sing: "Give riches to the rich" (I, 783), a paraphrase of Luke, 19:24-26). The rejection of her faith, however, does not prevent Mauler from claiming her for his newly formed meat monopoly. The myth of "St. Joan of the Stockyards" is born; the ritual of canonization is completed in Goethe's well-known Faust verses. In Brecht's investigation of "the great spiritual systems," the corpus of humanism and of Christian *agape* have been appropriated and equated to a language of mystification, a modern *Warensprache* (language of commodities) of German culture and of Christian efforts "to generate faith."

Dramatic Dialectic

> The dramatic experiments . . . lead to the discovery of the gestural. The gestural was for these experiments dialectical.
> —Brecht

Brecht conceived of his dramas as examinations of "the great spiritual systems" or cultural traditions. The gestural content in his plays is drawn from institutional or cultural stock. It is coded material containing messages that have often been read in a normative manner. If such a reading is less true today it is in part due to Brecht's work. Ulrich Plenzdorf's *New Sufferings of Young W.*, to name only one, is a good example of a Brechtian approach to cultural monuments. Not only the works of known poets, but the Bible too is commonly perceived as coded material that is read in a set way, regardless of the individual hermeneutic experience. Brecht drew heavily from dramatic and poetic material in circulation; in particular, he took much from the Bible. Brecht's gestural material thus contains a multilayering of meanings which allow the previous meaning (or code) to continue. This is the case of the plays I use as examples of his methodology, yet it is no less true of his other dramas where gestural content appears. In *Baal*, Brecht's sensuous materialism would lose its force without reference to sentimental idealism, just as Baal's amoral actions would appear foolish detached from the social mores and morality of the bourgeoisie.

Codes of traditional material remain in Brecht's plays. This is what has allowed the critics referred to above to read to a great extent Brecht's gestural content in the original code. Murphy sees Baal's death as ". . . a poetic identification of the dying hero with Christ" and has Brecht "insist on the unpleasant aspects of the tragedy of Christ's death" (30). In *Mahogonny* Brecht is to have formulated a "negative theology" based on "the fear of death as the origin of the problem of evil" (65). Paul Ackermann's death "becomes the ideal vehicle for Brecht's thought on the fate of the good person in this world. Still, it is Jesus Crucified and Him dead that Brecht preaches" (Murphy: 66). Pabst, in turn, finds that in *Mahagonny* Brecht uses the Bible as an "interpretive model against existing society;" hence, *Mahagonny* is Brecht's interpretation of the New Testament parable of "The rich man and Lazarus," Luke 16:19–31. Brecht describes in the opera the situation of the rich. And in *St. Joan of the Stockyards* Pabst discovers that "Joan's actions fall in with those of Jesus and meet the Bible's demand of Christians: Do not follow your own interests but do what is of use to others" (157).

The critics, therefore, place emphasis upon the original source, the cited biblical phrase, image or theme in the plays. Goergen, more perceptive than the others, is aware of Brecht's methodological approach but at the expense of Brecht's innovative use of familiar material and his message. The gestural material's function requires the original meaning to remain in the dramas. When Goergen, however, infers that "The insight of the dying Joan—that only real social change and not 'ineffective' goodness is good—that insight must have a place in theological ethics" (311), he avoids Brecht's critical demonstration of the gestural content that only force can bring about social change and not Christian goodness or love (*agape*). The same holds for Pabst, who follows the universal biblical message that Joan's actions are "of use to others," whereas Brecht curtails human efforts to the Marxist demand of class action. Joan's actions are directed to the interests of the proletariat and therefore limited to class considerations.

These by and large one-dimensional readings neglect Brecht's dialectical method./7/ Brecht is actually saying the opposite but *without* giving up the contrary. To be sure, the gestural content re-introduces the historical character of its original source, but it obtains a completely different emphasis in its reappearance. Brecht's reading of cultural material is similar to Marx's reading of history when Marx wrote: "Hegel remarks somewhere that all facts and personages of great importance in world history occur, as it were, twice. He forgot to add: the first time as tragedy, the second as farce" (1959:320). Marx's point and Brecht's as well, I think, is not that the original historical source is farcical, but the new historical situation transforms it into a farce. The socio-historical conditions that produce such a situation are criticized.

Finally, Brecht's dramas are not postfigural in construction as Rohse would have it. Frank Kermode, following Erich Auerbach's argument, points out that the figurally structured narrative "ensure[s] pleromatic conformity with clues laid down in an earlier part . . . [because] . . . the writers had a passion for fulfillment, fullness, completion, which are in Greek *pleroma*"—(see Auerbach: 15–16, 23, 48; Kermode: 106). But Brecht's method does exactly the opposite: the dramas are openended in a dialectic of question and answer which is kept going by the juxtaposition of gestural content to contemporary social situation. Examination of the past points to solutions in the present when the paradoxes of the meanings are seen: idealism and materialism (*Baal*), entertainment and human alienation (*Mahagonny*), and goodness and force (*St. Joan*). Brecht's dialectic of gestural quotations breaks the continuum of history to re-orient the recipient's awakened memories of the familiar material to a demystified consciousness of present social conditions (see Jauss, 1974a, b). If the material of the past appears as farce in its new setting it is because present social circumstances have transformed its historical content. And if the recipient finds this situation perverse or appalling Brecht offers him the choice to change the world.

NOTES

/1/ All Brecht quotations are taken from the *Gesammelte Werke*. For the Kerr affair see VIII, 99–102, and VII, 215 and 969.

/2/ Although good English translations of Brecht's works exist in the United States, they are not so readily available in Paris. To make Brecht's thoughts accessible to those who do not read German, I have translated all quotations in this essay.

/3/ Murphy misses Brecht's argument. After so much ink has been spilt over Brecht's rejection of empathy or sympathy (see VII, 125–387), Murphy still "finds" this in Brecht's dramas (Murphy: 47, 57, 64, 80, 87).

/4/ Brecht posed this question in September, 1920, over half a decade before he became familiar with Marx's argument on exchange value.

/5/ The original German title reveals more than my translation. For my "Baal eats!" Brecht has "Baal frisst!" which cannot be translated into English. In German, humans eat (essen) and animals "fressen," which Baal does. The verb "fressen" is also used to describe satiated eating.

/6/ Rülicke first brought attention to Marx's phases in Brecht's plays and Grab (introduction to Jones, trans. *St. Joan of the Stockyards*) refers to these phases, but neither one follows Marx's phases in the episodes of Brecht's plays.

/7/ For an analysis of Brecht's dialectical method, see von Bawey, 1980 and 1981.

WORKS CONSULTED

Auerbach, Erich
    Mimesis. Princeton: Princeton University.

Benjamin, Walter
  1969   *Illuminations*. Ed. Hannah Arendt. Trans. Harry Zohn. New York: Schocken.

Brandt, Thomas O.
1964 "Brecht und die Bibel." *PMLA* 79: 171-76.
1968 *Die Vieldeutigkeit Bertolt Brechts.* Heidelberg: Lothar Stiehm.

Brecht, Bertolt
1967 *Gesammelte Werke in acht Bänden,* I-VIII. Frankfurt/Main: Suhrkamp.
1978 *Tagebücher 1920-22, Autobiographische Aufzeichnungen 1920-54.* Ed. Herta Ramthun. Frankfurt/Main: Suhrkamp.

Esslin, Martin
1971 *Brecht: The Man and His Work.* Garden City, New York: Anchor.

Gadamer, Hans-Georg
1976 *Philosophical Hermeneutics.* Ed. and trans. David E. Linge. Berkeley: University of California.

Goergen, Peter
1982 *"Produktion" as Grundbegriff der Anthropologie Bertolt Brechts und seine Bedeutung für die Theologie.* Frankfurt/Main: R. G. Fischer.

Grimm, Reinhold
1962 *Bertolt Brecht: Die Struktur seines Werkes.* Nürnberg: Hans Carl.

Hayman, Ronald
1983 *Brecht: A Biography.* London: Weidenfeld and Nicholson.

Jauss, Hans Robert
1974a *Literaturgeschichte als Provokation.* Frankfurt/Main: Suhrkamp.
1974b "Literary History as a Challenge to Literary Theory." Pp. 11-41 in *New Directions in Literary History.* Ed. Ralph Cohen. Baltimore: Johns Hopkins.

Johst, Hanns
1925 *Der Einsame: Ein Menschenuntergang.* München: Albert Lang.

Jones, Frank, trans.
1969 *St. Joan of the Stockyards* by Bertolt Brecht. Introduction by Frederic Grab. Bloomington: Indiana University.

Kermode, Frank
1982 *The Genesis of Secrecy.* Cambridge: Harvard University.

Marx, Karl and Friederich Engels
1959 *Marx and Engels: Basic Writings on Politics and Philosophy.* Ed. Lewis S. Feuer. Garden City, New York: Anchor.

Marx Karl
1975 *Capital.* New York: International Publishers.

Michelsen, Peter
    1957   "Bertolt Brechts Atheismus." *Eckhart-Jahrbuch* 26: 48–56.

Murphy, G. Ronald
    1980   *Brecht and the Bible*. Chapel Hill: University of North Carolina.

Pabst, Hans
    1977   *Brecht und die Religion*. Graz: Verlag Styria.

Ritchie, J. M.
    1982   "Johst's *Schlageter* and the End of the Weimar Republic." Pp. 153–68 in *Weimar Germany: Writers and Policis*. Ed. Alan Bance. Edinburgh: Scottish Academic.

Rohse, Eberhard
    1983   *Der frühe Brecht und die Bibel*. Göttingen: Vandenhoeck & Ruprecht.

Rülicke, Käthe
    1959   "Die heilige Johanne der Schlachthöfe." *Sinn und Form* I: 429–44.

Santermeister, Gert
    1971   *Idyllik und Dramatik im Werk Friedrich Schillers*. Stuttgart: Kohlhammer.

von Bawey, Petermichael
    1980   "The Dramatic Structure of Revolutionary Language." *CLIO* 10: 21–33.
    1981   *Rhetorik der Utopie*. München: Wilhelm Fink.

IV
CONCLUSION

WHAT IS A SACRED TEXT?

Robert Detweiler
Emory University

ABSTRACT

The important although seldom addressed question of what constitutes a sacred text is discussed in the contexts of history and canonization, via a phenomenological characterizing of sacred texthood, in terms of reader involvement, and in the framework of contemporary philosophical-literary criticism. An examination of the process of the canonization of the Hebrew Bible shows the importance of power and authority in formally designating certain texts as sacred. The phenomenological examination uncovers seven traits of a sacred text; e.g., its claim to transform lives. A reader response approach reveals that believing readers of a sacred text encounter it with an aggressively "faithful" attitude. Sacred texts viewed in terms of current deconstructive practice are seen to lose their all-important "presence," but the secular texts that take their place are shown to depend just as fundamentally on logocentrism.

Authority, Privilege, Respect

The question, "what is a sacred text?" is one of those that tend to go unasked because we think we know the answer. Once asked, it turns out to be mischievous and subversive as it splinters into many sub-questions: "sacred for whom? sacred for whom when? made sacred by whom? according to what definitions of textuality?" It emerges then as a most important constellation of questions, for it causes us to inquire into the nature of our *regard* for the texts we interpret (do we believe them? believe *in* them? venerate but not believe them? treat them "disinterestedly?"), into our relationship to tradition and convention as we examine our attitudes toward sacred and secular canons, and into our relationship toward (the texts of) other cultures.

One way of addressing the questions is to cast them in the mode of inquiry that has to do with readerly attitudes and reactions. For example (and to plunge immediately into the thick of things), the readers or the community of interpreters who believe in the sacredness of the text they address will treat it differently than a non-sacred text. They will feel more constrained in their interpretation of the sacred text because it has, after all, a divine authority that commands reverence and restricts a free play of response. A sacred text ought really to mean only one thing: that which its divine author wishes it to mean. This, in turn, leads to the phenomenon of privileged interpreters—priests, shamans, prophets, preachers, ayatollahs—who assert themselves or are selected by the community of faith as enjoying a special relationship to the divinity whose scripture is to be interpreted and thus able to disclose the text's "true" meaning. Surely Martin Luther's radical doctrine of the priesthood of individual believers—and hence of the legitimacy of non-privileged, individual sacred text interpretation, however guardedly it was practiced—did a great deal to confuse issues of authority of interpretation in the western Christian tradition. It was one of the forces that exacerbated the perplexing matter of whose relationship to divinity behind the text is the closest and hence of whose exegesis is "truest." And since in most cases the interpreter's authority was established by the persuasiveness of the interpretation, and not by some extra-textual evidence, authority and interpretation become entangled in a circularity that proved nothing at all.

In contrast, the reader/scholar who deals with a traditionally sacred text without believing in it—someone else's sacred text, in other words—may or may not treat it with more respect than she would a secular text, depending probably on whether that text has a strong social-cultural standing in the interpreter's locale. One supposes that western readers from the Jewish and Christian traditions who do not practice their faiths will still treat the Torah and the Bible with more regard than they will, say, the Book of Mormon and the Koran, because it is a social-political imperative, or at least an expediency, for them to do so, and because a residual power of reverence-without-belief that a tradition can generate retains a hold on most of them.

I will organize my discussion of sacred texthood around four points of emphasis. The first one I have already been addressing in these introductory paragraphs: it is the question of what has in fact been considered a sacred text in the past. This historical inquiry leads to a more phenomenological one; namely, what are the traits of a sacred text as its readers who are believers understand them? My third consideration is more hermeneutical and returns to the matter of reader involvement. It brings up the questions of what conditions determine the sacredness of a text, and how the context determines whether a text is sacred. My fourth concern, finally, is to situate the problem of sacred texthood in the context of contemporary literary-philosophical discourse. I wish to examine here how our current situation perceived as "criticism in the wilderness," to borrow Geoffrey Hartman's resonant phrase, derives some of its bemusement from a failure to address the "presence" and function of sacred texts in modern life.

Sacred Texts and Canonization

A cynical response to my first consideration,"what has been regarded as a sacred text in the past?" would be: "Anything a particular community of believers decided to regard as a sacred text." That response would be both largely true and far too simple. A main thing wrong with it resides in the terms "community" and "decided." Communities of believers do not (or did not), for the most part, decide much of anything about their sacred texts while these are in the making. Rather, the traditional sacred texts have tended to evolve over relatively long periods of time, developing as and through the myths of the people (myths are other groups' sacred texts, or our own that we have come to disbelieve), through chronicles, laws, instructions for ritual, the language of worship itself, prophecy, moral and spiritual instruction. There seems to be no particular common critical stage at which the believers (the constitution and nature of whom obviously change over decades and centuries) become collectively self-conscious about the texts evolving in their midst and initiate a canonization process./1/ Rather, powerful segments of the community—the priests, prophets, and shamans—are always at work to establish or discredit the purported divine authority of a particular emerged text, which leads to a set of conditions under which canonization will be undertaken. The struggle among the religious leadership of a community, perhaps for generations, regarding the divine authority of various texts leads eventually to a reservoir of such texts, from which wealth some will be chosen formally as constituting the canon. The emergence of the sacred text, then, occurs not as some natural (or supernatural) process but from an interplay of tradition and religious-political design. The import of this explanation—which is no news to biblical scholars—is that not only is the canonization process an operation of arbitrary decision-making, but all along the way the texts have been manipulated in a similar arbitrary fashion. Paradoxically, a sacred text emerges through particular authoritative figures in a community of believers who work to lend a given text divine endorsement and thus render it sacred. Here again one sees a circularity in action. Texts become sacred because someone (or ones) manages to imbue them with an aura of divine authority, but conversely, their divine authority is accepted by the community because they have been persuaded that the text is "sacred."

This is a very general description of the dynamics of canonization, of how sacred texts in a particular culture become confirmed as sacred through canonization, and I wish to show the limitations and problems of such a broad depiction by reference to a study of a particular canonization process: Gerald Bruns' "Canon and Power in the Hebrew Scriptures." Bruns' careful and very perceptive treatment of just a few passages, mainly from II Kings and Jeremiah and constituting what Bruns calls canonization stories, discusses three theories of how canonization came about during the years of exile, which is to say how certain Hebrew texts were established as authoritative, and stresses the key roles of power and of writing in the process. For a text to be canonical is, for Bruns, for it to be "forceful in a given situation" (465). "The power of the text is not intrinsic to it. On the contrary, the text draws its power from the situation which belongs to a definite history and which is structured by this history to receive just this text as it will no other" (466). The process of the canonization of the written Torah, Bruns says, can be explained as the result of a power struggle between the prophets and the priestly class, or, just the opposite, as the result of a strategic cooperation between them. According to the first view, one promulgated by an older generation of biblical historians represented by Julius Wellhausen (and revived by Blenkinsopp in 1977; see Bruns: 474), the Hebrew prophets, individualistic figures standing outside of the political-religious institution and making oracular utterances which they claimed were directly from Yahweh, threatened the order of king and priest, the status quo. A way of bringing this charismatic power under the control of institutional authority was "by means of the superior forces of writing and textuality" (474). Bruns does not spell out just how this would have worked, but obviously the existence of a *scripture*, or a written fixed text claiming to be the words of Yahweh, would be a powerful and well-nigh irresistable means of countering the mere spoken words of the prophets. The steady presence of the written text, in other words, would offset the charisma of the oracle by resituating the divine power in an object that could be contemplated and manipulated instead of merely responded to. The sacred text as text, divorced from a speaker, becomes some*thing* that can be appropriated in ways that the prophet cannot and that greatly reduces the prophet's authority; he becomes at best an outsider seeking to amend—to interpret—in a radical way the sacred text.

According to a newer view among biblical scholars rehearsed by Bruns, the priests did not oppose and domesticate prophetic authority through written texts but rather appropriated the prophecies and attempted to render them comprehensible and viable for the religous community through their incorporation into scripture. Brevard Childs, a proponent of this position, explains it as the principle of actualization or *Vergegenwärtigung* (Bruns: 473), the "process by which an ancient historical text . . . derives chiefly from a need to 'update' an original tradition" (quoted by Bruns: 473). In this view the priests are alert hermeneuts who wish to give the prophetic message a meaning for their own, temporal situation. An example would be the Book of Jeremiah that Childs analyzes as comprised of three sources: "an original poetic tradition made up of sayings or oracles handed down by the prophet's disciples; a secondary prose tradition containing sermons and stories about Jeremiah . . . ; and a Deuteronomic redaction investing this prophetic material with a priestly understanding" (Bruns: 473).

A third theory of canonization that Bruns reviews is much like that of Wellhausen and Blenkinsopp and is advanced by a "radical historian," Ellis Rivkin. Rivkin argues that when the political crisis (destruction of Jerusalem and Temple followed by exile) weakened the attempt of the priests to gain control over the prophets, the "prophets such as Jeremiah and Ezekiel refused to give up their prophetic freedom" (476). Yet the period of exile was also a time of "furious scribal activity" at the end of which "suddenly, stood a monumental Torah: the Pentateuch" (476). The creation of the Pentateuch, then, brings about the end of prophetic power where the pre-exilic priests had failed. The hero or villain of this action is Ezra, who as legendary powerful priest and ruler is also a prophetic scribe, someone who writes down the words of Yahweh, instead of merely uttering them. In the apocryphal II Esdras, the story of Ezra's grand composition is given. He dictates ninety-four books of scripture to five scribes in forty days. Of these, twenty-four are designated by Yahweh for public hearing but seventy are to be kept private for the "wise men" only to read and interpret. This new "double canon," Bruns says, consisting of public and private scripture, both settles the charismatic prophetic word in a fixed sacred text and preserves a portion of that word for a privileged reading and interpretation. Sacred utterance becomes textualized and the material for a sort of "prophetic" rabbinical exegesis (Bruns: 477–78).

Canonization, the promotion and acceptance of a text as sacred and hence binding, is thus conceived by Bruns as mainly a matter of power. A text becomes sacred when a segment of the community is able to establish it as such in order to gain control and set order over the whole community. How that process works and differs in a relatively modern situation can be seen in radically concentrated form in the genesis of the *Book of Mormon*. In this situation Joseph Smith, guided by an angel, "finds" the sacred text on a hillside, is given special assistance to read the sacred language, and produces his "translation" of the text that becomes the scripture of a new religion. Here the charismatic, prophetic, and scribal roles are all concentrated in one individual (like Ezra, Smith dictated his scripture to a number of transcribers) with the difference that whereas Ezra composed by divine inspiration, Smith received the text intact and fulfilled his prophetic and scribal roles simultaneously in the act of divinely inspired translation. Further, whereas Ezra rewrites the Torah at Yahweh's command, and thus participates in the resolution of a centuries-long political-religious conflict, Smith finds a new text which he claims is sacred and in effect canonized even though it has as yet no constituency to endorse it. It remains mainly for Brigham Young as prophet and priest figure to persuade persons after the fact that Smith and his document are authentic and hence that the *Book of Mormon* should be authoritative.

In discussing the matter of canonization I have referred to three documents with varying degrees of acceptance as to their status as sacred texts: the Pentateuch, the Old Testament Apocrypha, and the *Book of Mormon*. Virtually all modern westerners would, I think, grant that the Pentateuch has attained a status as a traditional sacred text, although relatively few, probably, would confess to a belief, a personal faith, in it. Few, however, would grant sacred status to the Apocrypha, with the probable logic that they had been subjected to the tests for sacredness and failed them, and fewer still would consider the *Book of Mormon* sacred, viewing it rather as a pseudo-sacred text. What accounts for the differences? It is obvious that even among modern non-believers, not all texts are equally sacred or profane, and the reasons for this discrimination must lie in the history and status of the believing community. Thus the respect that the modern west maintains for the ancient Hebrews, and for the traditions of Judaism and Chrisitianity, compels us to respect the judgments of those traditions regarding the sacredness of the Pentateuch and the non-sacredness of the Apocrypha, whereas the relative lack of influence of Latter-day Saints causes us to be less tolerant of their claims for the *Book of Mormon*, and to view it, more likely, as a sectarian fantasy. It is entirely conceivable, however, that if the Latter-day Saints would emerge as more politically and culturally influential, we would come to view the *Book of Mormon* with something of the same regard we give to the Pentateuch.

Traits of Sacred Texts

The analysis in the foregoing paragraphs suggests but does not articulate the characteristics of sacred texts. I want to turn to an informal phenomenology of sacred textuality, in order to identify common traits of traditional sacred texts without which they would not be—or would not have been—considered sacred. I find seven (an appropriate sacred number) significant features of sacred texts that distinguish them from other writing. The first and most obvious of these, as we have observed from the historical examination of canonization, is that sacred texts are considered to be divinely inspired. Sometimes the texts themselves claim such inspiration; sometimes it is made extra-textually by the community that sponsors the text. The canonization stories that Bruns cites are examples of the textual claims for divine inspiration: when Jeremiah reports on Yahweh's command "to the men of Judah and to the inhabitants of Jerusalem" (Jer. 11:1–53; Bruns: 472), and then utters those illocutionary words, he is offering textual evidence of divine inspiration. The witness of any "born-again" Christian as to how reading the Bible saved him or her is an instance of extra-textual attribution of divine inspiration.

A sacred text needs to be considered divinely inspired by the believing community because such an endorsement guarantees the text's truth, and this veracity must be declared against the truth claims of competing texts. The truth of a sacred text is not the product of logical argument but is rather apodictic, self-declarative. As such, then, it is revelatory, and that is a second trait of sacred texts: they are not only divinely inspired; they bring a message from a deity or deities in the form of a disclosure. The attitude generated by sacred texts is that divinities are hidden in mysteries not to be penetrated by human reason and are accessible only through revelation. Such unveiling can take place through epiphanies or, perhaps, indirectly through ritual and sacrament, and it can of course occur through the prophetic utterance, but its most substantial form is through the sacred text. This is what the believer can return to, repeatedly, to study, to interpret toward her redemption or ethical instruction.

The fact that the text needs "unveiling" suggests that it is somehow hidden, or secret, and indeed, a third trait of sacred texts is that many of them are encoded and need decoding. There are various reasons for veiled scripture. One is that the sacred text, like divinity itself, would be too holy, too powerful for humans to encounter and bear unmediated, so that the oblique language serves as a buffer to protect the reader from what would be the text's lethal purity. A second reason for the sacred text's encoded form is that this veiled writing represents the infinitely complex nature of the divinity which has inspired it. The gods who speak through sacred texts are as a rule fundamentally unknowable, so that the text's opacity, paradoxically, conveys the incomprehensible otherness of the gods. Its mystery both reveals and hides the mystery of its inspiring force. The third reason why sacred texts remain veiled is to prevent their misuse and abuse by irresponsible persons. There is always the danger of false shamans learning the secret formulas that will enable them to gain access to power and use it against the forces of good. The cryptic text makes it harder for this power to fall into the wrong hands.

Sacred texts viewed in this way are not just vehicles for divine communication; they contain some of the divine essence or substance or spirit that has become objectified in scripture and thus vulnerable to perversion. Something of this attitude is portrayed in the Acts of the Apostles (8:9–24), in the story of the Samaritan magician Simon who, even after being baptized as a Christian, wishes to purchase the power of the Holy Spirit from the apostles. In this instance, what might otherwise be the secret power objectified in the text is objectified in divinely ordained persons, namely the apostles.

If the text is veiled, who will uncover it? It may need a specially empowered interpreter, someone who holds the key to the text's secret. The implication is that the god/gods who inspire the text and render it enigmatic as a protection against mischief also select their hermeneuts and provide them with the gift of understanding. This is a different role from that of the prophet. The prophet does not necessarily grasp the message he proclaims. He can be merely the medium for the utterance that passes through him. But the gifted interpreter, which is to say the one who has been blessed with insight, in the act of unveiling, shapes and informs the text's message. This view persists even in the Christian heritage, which has a complicated relationship to the veiled text, in the tradition of candidates for the ministry responding to a *"calling."* A sacred voice, in other words, invites the neophyte to a *vocation* of disclosing the secrets of the sacred texts.

The complicated relationship of Christianity to secret sacred texts is reflected in the millenia-long discussion of the New Testament parables. The parables, illustrative narratives that both help to explain Jesus' teachings and to obscure them, seem to betray a first-century uneasiness with the concept of a divine language that is at once revelatory and hidden. In the Gospel of Matthew (chap. 13), when the disciples ask Jesus why he speaks to the crowds in parables, he replies, "To you it has been given to know all the secrets of the kingdom of heaven, but to them it has not been given. . . . This is why I speak to them in parables, because seeing they do not see and hearing they do not hear nor do they understand" (11–13). He follows this with a quotation from Isa 6:9–10, where Yahweh commands Isaiah (at the time of Isaiah's calling) to speak to the people of Judah and Jerusalem so that they do not heed the message, "lest they see with their eyes and hear with their ears and understand with their hearts, and turn and be healed" (Isa 6:10). Although Jesus does not give the passage the strong negative connotation that it has in Isaiah, he nevertheless suggests that there are privileged auditors, and indeed, in Mark 4:33–34 one learns that "With many such parables he spoke the word to them, as they were able to hear it; he did not speak to them without a parable, but *privately to his own disciples he explained everything*" (my italics)./2/ We observe, thus, that even the New Testament gospel, generally regarded as containing a kerygma open and accessible to all, is characterized by a sacred text that is sometimes self-consciously "difficult" and "hidden" and in need of privileged interpretation.

The phrase from Isaiah, "lest . . . they turn and be healed," hints at another trait of sacred texts: they purport to change lives. They effect such transformations indirectly or directly. Indirectly they do so by describing some extra-textual path to salvation, enlightenment, nirvana, unusual power. Generally it involves a formula to follow, a discipline to exercise, a trip to undertake, a savior figure to recognize, emulate, and obey. In these instances the text is not the instrument of transformation but the document of instruction toward change. But sometimes the sacred text is actually the instrument itself. Its very language claims a redemptive or transformational power, as if divinity indwelt the words and caused them, through articulation of them, to bring about altered states of being. Such language is incantatory or sacramental. Incantation language, which operates through a carefully expressed formulation of often secret terms, wishes to bypass or concentrate the process whereby one employs language to evoke the presence or action of the gods and to make the words themselves the efficient cause. It is related to what speech act theorists (Searle, 1971:265–68; 1979:68) call phatic acts. This is of course what magic does, and as supernatural power divorced from divinity, magic has been considered dangerous; it may release forces that are more powerful than the humans who would manipulate them.

One can observe in evangelical Christianity sacred texts functioning simultaneously as directly and indirectly life-transforming. The New Testament, especially the gospels, is held to contain the formula for redemption (consisting of, minimally, an expression of contrition for one's sins and of belief in a "personal" savior), but it also is sometimes treated as if it possesses near-magical properties: if only persons could be persuaded to read it, the very encounter with the words would change their lives.

The involvement of sacred texts in sacramental acts, on the other hand, suggests the view that certain language is sacred because it engages the believers in life-transforming *symbolic* events which bring them, the believers, into a particular enhanced relationship with the sacred powers "behind" the text. In the Christian Eucharist, for example, the words "this is my body, this is my blood," are crucial not because they tell the communicants something they do not already know, not even primarily to remind them of the awesome event of a god's sacrificial death, but precisely to effect a metaphoric transformation that confirms a human, spiritual transformation. Participants in the eucharistic celebration, even transsubstantialists, know perfectly well that the bread and wine do not magically become flesh and blood in their (or the priest's) mouth. Rather, the declarative "this is my body/blood" asks them to perform a linguistic operation and an act of the imagination that symbolize their "redeemed" condition. To accomplish the metaphoric leap necessary to comprehend "this is my body/blood," indeed to act out this metaphoric assertion in the eucharistic celebration, is to perform the symbolization that is the basis of the believer's faith. For the believer believes that the sacred language she reads, hears, and speaks is both her own "normal" language and one that participates in some divine reality, and hence one that connects her to that reality. In this sense, in fact, all sacred language is symbolic language even when it employs discursive modes, because it always presupposes a divine, usually "transcendent" reality and purports to represent that reality.

Part of the persuasive power of sacramental language, which is to say sacred texts put to work in the service of maintaining a believer's transformed condition, is that it is *enacted*; and another trait of sacred texts is that they form the basis of cult and ritual. One does not need to rvive the old argument at this point of which came first, the myth or the ritual, to declare the primacy of sacred language in religious celebration. It is hard to imagine a ritual that does not significantly involve language, even if that language is employed mainly to give instruction on how the ritual should be performed, so that sacred texts are generated both as the narrative counterparts of ritual and as "manuals" for proper ritual enactment. Nevertheless, the point to be made is that sacred texts as a rule call for a response that is more athletic than the general reaction to non-sacred writing; and that response is a call to some sort of enactment of the text. One conjectures that drama in the west originally evolved out of religious rituals, probably Dionysian mysteries, so that the performance of modern scripted plays, with their lingering aura of ritual, recalls an ancient interplay of sacred language and action. In any case, just as it is hard to imagine a ritual that does not involve sacred language, it is also hard to imagine a sacred text that does not somehow involve ritual.

A purpose of ritual, as we saw in the examination of sacrament, is to evoke a divine reality, but the sacred text itself has been understood as both an evocation of and substitute for divine presence. This reference to and replacement of divine presence is the final trait of sacred texts I wish to identify. Sacred texts, in calling attention to divinity, wish obviously to make that divinity present, and generally to make it present with an intensity not found in other texts evoking other kinds of reality. One could suppose that an ultimate goal of a sacred text would be to provoke an epiphany, a literal sacred presence, and indeed some claim to do so or have done so. At the same time, this strong desire for the god's presence evinced by the text indicates that it is not there, and hence the text becomes a substitute for it. The longed-for object is replaced by a message about that object, and in the process of that operation the message assumes some of the missing objects's numinosity. Clearly there are things going on here, in this play of presence and absence, that may be paradigmatic for the contemporary deconstructive argument regarding writing and the metaphysics of presence, and I shall return to this concern. For the moment, we can summarize the traits of a sacred text as

1. claiming or generating claims of divine inspiration;
2. revelatory of divinity;
3. somehow encoded or "hidden;"
4. requiring a privileged interpreter;
5. effecting the transformation of lives;
6. the necessary foundation of religious ritual;
7. evocative of divine presence./3/

Belief, Non-Belief, and the Reading of Sacred Texts

My discussion thus far has been dogged by the need to make generalizations, in order to state what would be the main characteristics of a majority of sacred texts. This is in many ways a questionable approach to a foolhardy endeavor. Even if I were able to name most of the world's sacred texts, the thousands of texts which some community of believers somewhere sometime deemed sacred, I might not emerge with the list of seven traits I just described. That list is obviously derived from a cursory examination of a few casually selected traditional sacred texts in the western world. But one needs to start somewhere, and this modest phenomenology can serve until corrected by an analysis of more such texts. Yet even an exhaustive study of the world's traditional sacred literature would not answer some other basic questions about sacred texts. It would not, for example, tell us very much about what expectations a reader brings to a sacred text that he would not bring to another sort of writing, or about what conditions or circumstances obtain that give some texts an aura of sacredness whether or not they belong to any canon. I pointed out earlier that a believing reader of a sacred text will be constrained in his interpretation by a fear of tampering unduly with divine property, and even a non-believing interpreter will offer a sacred text in his own tradition a certain interpretation-inhibiting sort of veneration. The reader thus expects the sacred text to delimit his freedom of interpretation, and he submits to it with varying degrees of compliance. Further, a believer will expect the sacred text to evince the seven traits I discussed, whereas the non-believer will anticipate only one of those traits, namely that the text will probably be "hidden" or "difficult"—although he will expect the text to project an awareness, which he will not accept for himself, of the other traits.

But what else? The reader of such a text, believer or not, has her expectations shaped by a double consciousness. She needs to read it in terms of both its standard and special indeterminacies, for a sacred text emits two (at least) sets of signals. One of them is the usual system or convention that any genre, or rhetorical model, posits and that we learn to interpret or "read," just as we would interpret any text. The other, however, is unique to sacred texts and consists of what we could call kerygmatic signals that the reader must constantly decipher and respond to. In reading a novel, for example, the reader recognizes (via a mental operation that Michael Polanyi would call tacit thinking) conventions of authorial involvement, narrator perspective, plotting, characterization, etc. that stimulate her into "completing" the story. She fills in, with her own imagination, the gaps left by the author's necessarily incomplete narration—a lengthier and more complicated version of what E. H. Gombrich and the Gestalt psychologists tell us we do when we "see" a human or a horse where only a stick figure is actually drawn.

But even before, or at least along with, undertaking this effort, the reader has tacitly assumed other important things. She assumes that she is indeed reading a fiction and thus brings to the task (or pleasure) of reading an attitude that Coleridge (as every earnest student of English knows) called "the willing suspension of disbelief" or what we nowadays might refer to as "quasi-pragmatic reception," "pseudo-referential reading" (Stierle: 84, 89), or a temporary surrender to fictionality. The reader of a piece of newspaper journalism, on the other hand, or of a history, or a scientific paper, or a letter to Ann Landers, or a satire by Art Buchwald, will bring correspondingly different attitudes of receptivity to these texts. In no case, I think, will he be totally open to the text, but he will no doubt always distinguish between what is "real," which is to say mainly reported from historical experience, and what is "made up," which is to say mainly a product of imaginative projection—even if contemporary writers try hard to blur the differences. We do not have a reliable lexicon of desirable or even possible readerly attitudes, no doubt because we do not have a reliable catalogue of types of writing, and it doesn't look as though we will get either, because mutations and hybrids of genres seem to be proliferating these days. The scholars of genre have their work cut out for them.

What happens when the reader encounters instead of a novel, say, a New Testament gospel? Here too she can rely on her knowledge of narrative and rhetorical conventions and "complete" the discourse. She might have problems with the parables, which are obfuscatory by design, yet by and large she would find—and make—the text comprehensible. But what about her *pre*textual attitude? The reader approaching the gospel as a text that is crucial to her religious faith will take a position of willing suspension of disbelief that is quite different from the fiction reader's attitude. It is in fact not a passive stance, not a mere suspension, but an intensified act of believing in the message of the text against the evidence outside of it in the reader's world. If not quite Tertullian's *credo quia absurdum est*, it is still heading in that direction. The faithful reader approaches the text aggressively, determined to believe it, and hence she "fills in" the indeterminacies in an attitude of acceptance, adopting a position she would not take with any other kind of text. She does so because she has been persuaded, pre- and extra-textually, by her community that this text is sacred and hence demands this response. The gaps she needs to fill, then, have to do with the space between what is conventionally credible to her, according to the evidence of physics, biology, and history, and what is not.

If the reader is no longer able to respond that way—literally—to the sacred texts of his tradition, he still approaches them with a "special" attitude, for they remain the texts of his disenchantment, and even if he himself has never undergone that disenchantment, has never been a believer who stopped believing in his culture's sacred texts, he will at least have been educated in the traditional specialness of them. The history of secularization in the west is, in one important sense, the story of readers learning to read our sacred texts in a different way—and then perhaps of how we have in some measure given up reading them at all. This is one of the things Hillis Miller told us in *The Disappearance of God*, and it is good to discuss its ramifications in this particular context, above all because we will be able to see clearly why a sacred text for modern western humankind is no longer what it once was.

The pre-textual attitude of an early nineteenth-century reader of Genesis 1–3, for example, would have strongly affected his formal "narratological" reading. Because he would have been conditioned to accept the text as a combined factual, historical, and moral account, he would not have noticed (or at least not dwelled on) the gaps that the modern "disenchanted" reader observes, and hence would not have acted to fill them in. For him, the sacred text of his culture would have grounded a still intact, unified, and coherent world view. The modern reader of Genesis 1–3, by contrast, sees the text as comprised primarily of gaps, as radically fractured and fragmented, so much so that it virtually becomes a record of twentieth-century biblical scholarship, and so that what one brings to it, in an effort to render it hermeneutically significant, is an overwhelming combination of linguistic, anthropological, historical, literary, etc. considerations that tend to overdetermine the text and make the sheer interpretive effort competitive with meaning. Whereas the faithful nineteenth-century western reader of our sacred texts viewed them mainly as the context of answers to life's problems, we see them mainly as repositories of the problems themselves, and it is not too much to say that the sense of numinosity that used to inhabit our sacred texts for believers has been replaced for non-believers or non-literal believers at least in part by a sense of the problematic.

Sacred Texts, Presence, Logocentrism, and History

To say these things is to suggest a different concept of texthood from the one that has prevailed in the past, and indeed the question of "what is a sacred text?" is encompassed these days by the question of "what is a text?" Why has the matter of texthood per se become problematic, and how does it relate to the identity of sacred texts? The two questions are crucially interrelated. Our recently recognized uncertainty derives from two things. One is the difficulty introduced by the reader response critics (among others) about where the text leaves off and the reader begins, or, what is text and what is interpretation. Whereas at one time this looked like a simple thing to determine—the text is the written document in front of you—we now tend to think that texts must be more than an organized accumulation of words on a page, that they must consist of an interaction of printed words, reader, and context. This expanded sense of textuality—which surely has its vulnerable aspects—is joined by a second and still more problematic view: the appellation "text" should not be restricted to works that have achieved some particular status of respectability, and hence the term "text" as a document for serious interpretation is accorded to journalistic pieces, letters, advertising slogans, graffiti, and restaurant menus. And beyond that, via the influence of semiotics, sign systems that do not depend on writing or on words at all come to be referred to as texts, and the term "text" thus becomes a metaphor for any system of signification.

There ought to be a correlation between this expanded definition of textuality and Derrida's critique of the metaphysics of presence. Derrida's argument that western humankind has viewed presence and meaning as interacting involved first a criticism of the assumption that meaning resides predominantly in the spoken word, because our oral utterance is closer to what we "mean," not having gone through the secondary medium of writing. But along with a demystifying of such meaningful presence in orality, Derrida (by showing how speech also functions, like writing, via difference and separation) also accuses western thought of an indulgence in a "logocentrism," not merely a "phonocentrism," that posits some ultimate absolute, some transcendental signified, some originary meaning on which all future meanings can be grounded (see Eagleton: 130–31). Once this Derridean critique is accepted, privileged texts lose their privilege. Sacred texts, claiming the greatest privilege as the writings through which divinity as the ultimate presence is made manifest, stand to lose the most in the antilogocentric reevaluation. They also emerge as the main culprits in the centuries-old process whereby the illusory metaphysics of presence has been perpetuated, since they have, obviously, purported to host the most illustrious of such presence.

If sacred presence is an illusion, one must then conclude that the authority of sacred texts is subverted: no sacred presence, no sacred text. Yet the history of secularization is also the history of scholars and poets replacing the sacred presence with some other presence, offered as or assumed to be authoritative, so that a loose "canon" of texts emerges that has *some* authority because persons or groups of influence claim preeminence for these works. The "presence" of these works is not divine, but it "carries weight," and hence we now have an aggregate of privileged texts that substitute for the old sacred texts. A crucial displacement has occurred. The old sacred texts may be among the new collection of privileged texts, but they now derive their common authority from the secular, "common" regard for them. The degree of respect that such a text commands seems to be a main trait that makes it authoritative and privileged and a substitute for the old sacred texts.

That this influence derives from an illusory sense of logocentric presence is what Derrida (whose own texts have become influential and authoritative) has argued, and thereby precipitated the crisis of interpretation that we now experience. Critics respond to this crisis by producing more texts, some of which become influential and join the very flexible "canon." At this point the concept of canon retains mainly metaphoric value, since we have no genuinely authoritative body or cohesive community to confer and accept the formal canonizing of texts in the west, and what Jameson refers to as "master narratives" (25–26) or "cultural text" (288) may be more appropriate terminology. Although to use "master narrative" this way is not quite what Jameson, borrowing from Althusser, means (master narratives for Jameson are hidden and allegorical), we can do so without inflicting serious damage on his scheme. The master narratives informing and guiding (the unconscious of) the modern west would be at least three and possibly five or six. The three clearly discernible ones are the old Judeo-Christian story, followed by the "narratives" of Marx and Freud. These three have most definitively shaped our understanding of human nature, behavior, and destiny; of community, time, and history. One might wish to add to these the "narratives" of Hegel and Nietzsche and what Lyotard has called the "great narrative" of scientific and cultural progress (for which there is no master text as such) as contributing to the central themes (or the "plot") of our lives and culture. In any case, the new master narratives (Marx and Freud) are like the old one (Judeo-Christianity) in claiming privilege and inviting to belief. That is why they are *master* narratives: they assert control over societies and individual lives via the force of their vision. Insofar as they are truly believed in, insofar as people allow their lives to be molded and directed according to the vision of these narratives, they become substitutes for the texts, and the vision, of the old sacred canon, or they merge, however subtly, with that older and now profaned vision. If presence is nevertheless absent from all of them, if this immanentized sacred derives its mana from some not-here and not-yet, this is still in substance a religious reflex—for the Marxist celebration of history and of a utopian future projects a sacred time, while the Freudian focus on the unconscious projects a sacred space./4/ Both of these are in curious ways fictions (the Marxist utopia and the Freudian unconscious can only be imaged and imagined), and in this sense too they come to constitute master *narratives*—elongated metaphors—rather than, say, argumentation.

Two books which have come to represent the secular critics' use of these three master narratives in a crypto-religious sense are Geoffrey Hartman's *Criticism in the Wilderness* and Fredric Jameson's *The Political Unconscious*. Hartman's deconstructive study functions as an updating of Matthew Arnold's program for replacing an enervated religion with great literature (i.e., with a secular canon), and Jameson's work blends Marx, Freud, and Christian typology in an effort to overcome the privatizing of interpretation that Hartman's approach reflects. Timothy Reiss in a review of the two books calls attention (198) to the religious undertone of Hartman's project: "What Hartman overlooks in this plea to the critic's subjectivity, a subjectivity whose representative and permanent human-ness sacralizes its everlasting play with meaning, is that the concept of such subjectivity, the subjectivity itself, and the meanings with which it plays are not disembodied ideas, coming to us from some Idea of Absolute Being 'out there': they are historically produced and socially created. The answer to the difficult crisis does not lie in a garden in a wilderness, but in plunging into the reality that produces that subjectivity and its forms of activity." Reiss agrees with Jameson on the need for "a recognition of the primacy of History itself" (203; Jameson: 14), but I do not see that this amounts to much more than an apotheosizing of history in a way quite similar to Hartman's apotheosizing of subjectivity. Paul Jay's demonstration that both of these texts rely on unexamined or at least unannounced theological (I would say religious) presuppositions strikes me as a more accurate and persuasive situating of them.

This is not the place to engage in further deconstruction-versus-history argument. My point is only that the present-day commentary on the crisis of interpretation involves critics (are we the secular scribal priests?) in a struggle for the authoritative texts, and that in the process we play out the ancient *agon* of dependency and freedom: making messages we attribute to the gods, then seeking through interpretation to liberate ourselves from the text's domination, only to see that interpretation become the new master. As long as we interpret (and how could we stop?), we will create sacred texts. And it is our sacred texts—in whatever guise—that compel us to interpret.

NOTES

/1/   This essay, for lack of space, does not deal with sacred texts that exist in and influence a community/culture without undergoing formal canonizing. All canons consist of texts that are in some fashion "sacred," but not all sacred texts belong to a canon.

/2/ The passage could, however, also be a late addition to Mark's gospel.

/3/ I am indebted to Robert Ensign of Emory University for pointing out that some of these traits belong primarily to texts in the process of *attaining* sacred/canonical status and some primarily to texts *maintaining* such status. For example, 1 and 2 would belong mainly to texts attaining sacred status.

/4/ Cf. Francesco Alberoni (161): "What attracts us is always the divine time of origins, situated in the past (as with religious myths), in the future (as with Marxism) or in the present (as with the experience of falling in love). This is the cultural tradition of the West."

WORKS CONSULTED

Alberoni, Francesco
1983 *Falling in Love.* Trans. Lawrence Venuti, New York: Random House.

Blenkinsopp, Joseph
1977 *Prophecy and Canon: A Contribution to the Study of Jewish Origins.* South Bend: University of Notre Dame.

Bruns, Gerald L.
1984 "Canon and Power in the Hebrew Scriptures." *Critical Inquiry* 10/3: 462–80.

Childs, Brevard S.
1979 *Introduction to the Old Testament as Scripture.* Philadelphia: Fortress.

Derrida, Jacques
1978 *Writing and Difference.* Trans. Alan Bass. Chicago: University of Chicago.
1982 "Of an Apocalyptic Tone Recently Adopted in Philosophy." Pp. 63–97 in Robert Detweiler, ed., *Derrida and Biblical Studies (Semeia* 23). Chico, CA: Scholars.

Eagleton, Terry
1983 *Literary Theory: An Introduction.* Minneapolis: University of Minnesota.

Gombrich, E. H.
1968 "Mediations on a Hobby Horse, or The Roots of Artistic Form." Pp. 209–22 in Lancelot Law Whyte, ed., *Aspects of Form.* Bloomington: Indiana University.

Hartman, Geoffrey H.
1980 *Criticism in the Wilderness: The Study of Literature Today.* New Haven: Yale University.

Jameson, Fredric
1981   *The Political Unconscious: Narrative as a Socially Symbolic Act*. Ithaca, NY: Cornell University.

Jay, Paul
1984   "The Return of the Repressed: The Theological Unconscious in Recent Critical Theory." *Critical Texts* 2/2: 10–17.

Lyotard, Jean-François
1984   *The Postmodern Condition: A Report on Knowledge*. Trans. Geoff Bennington and Brian Massumi. Minneapolis: University of Minnesota.

Miller, J. Hillis
1963   *The Disappearance of God: Five Nineteenth-Century Writers*. Cambridge, MA: Harvard University.

Reiss, Timothy J.
1983   "Critical Environments: Cultural Wilderness or Cultural History?" *Canadian Review of Comparative Literature* 9: 192–209.

Rivkin, Ellis
1971   *The Shaping of Jewish History: A Radical New Interpretation*. New York: Scribner.

Ryan, Michael
1983   *Marxism and Deconstruction: A Critical Articulation*. Baltimore: Johns Hopkins University.

Sanders, James A.
1984   *Canon and Community: A Guide to Canonical Criticism*. Philadelphia: Fortress.

Schneidau, Herbert N.
1976   *Sacred Discontent: The Bible and Western Tradition*. Baton Rouge: Louisiana State University.

Searle, John R.
1968   "Austin on Locutionary and Illocutionary Acts." *Philosophical Review* 77/4: 405–24.
1979   *Expression and Meaning: Studies in the Theory of Speech Acts*. Cambridge: Cambridge University.

Stierle, Karlheinz
1980   "The Reading of Fictional Texts." Pp. 83–105 in Susan R. Suleiman and Inge Crosman, eds., *The Reader in the Text*. Princeton: Princeton University.

www.ingramcontent.com/pod-product-compliance
Lightning Source LLC
Chambersburg PA
CBHW021808220426
43662CB00006B/229